The Appearance
of Truth

The Appearance of Truth

The Story of Elizabeth Canning and Eighteenth-Century Narrative

Judith Moore

DELAWARE

Newark: University of Delaware Press
London and Toronto: Associated University Presses

PR769
.M66
1994

Associated University Presses
440 Forsgate Drive
Cranbury, NJ 08512

Associated University Presses
25 Sicilian Avenue
London WC1A 2QH, England

Associated University Presses
P.O. Box 338, Port Credit
Mississauga, Ontario
Canada L5G 4L8

Library of Congress Cataloging-in-Publication

Moore, Judith, 1939–
    The appearance of truth : the story of Elizabeth Canning and
eighteenth-century narrative / Judith Moore.
        p.   cm.
    Includes bibliographical references and index.
    ISBN 0-87413-494-3 (alk. paper)
    1. English prose literature—18th century—History and criticism.
2. Women—England—Crimes against—History—18th century—
Historiography.   3. Trials (Perjury)—England—History—18th
century—Historiography.   4. Truthfulness and falsehood in
literature.   5. Canning, Elizabeth, 1734–1773.   6. Narration
(Rhetoric)   I. Title.
PR769.M66   1994
364.1'34—dc20   93-46260
                                                       CIP

Contents

Acknowledgments

The first stirrings of this book came in the summer of 1989 when I took part in John Richetti's NEH Seminar on Social Change in Early Modern Britain and the Rise of the Novel at the University of Pennsylvania. Professor Richetti and the other members of the seminar, particularly Mary Anne Schofield and Arlene Wilner, may scarcely remember their encouragement, but I certainly do. I am also indebted to the University of Alaska Anchorage for a full-support sabbatical in the spring of 1991 and for a travel grant from Associate Dean Robert Spurr of the UAA College of Arts and Sciences which facilitated my pursuit of the documents of the Canning case in London. The UAA Consortium Library's Inter-Library Loan Department was helpful in the period between my stay in Philadelphia, where the Special Collections of the Van Pelt Library were a valuable resource, and my sojourn in London, where I worked very productively in the British Library, the University of London Library, the Guildhall Library and the Public Record Office. At all of these institutions, I found the staffs both professional and sympathetic. Since my return to teaching I have had the opportunity to present a discussion of the Canning case orally at the UAA English Department Colloquium and have been encouraged by the response of students and colleagues. My family, Vera Crosse, Ted Herlinger, Dawson Moore, and Neith and Sean Flood, have been—as ever—wonderfully supportive.

A Note on Style and Documentation

Spelling, capitalization, and punctuation in quotations in the following chapters are as in the original documents in spite of considerable resulting inconsistency. One writer's Canning case is not another's, and these mechanical divergences serve as a constant reminder of the diversity of views. I have tried as well to reinforce the reader's awareness of the differing voices that constitute the case for us by interrupting my own text with parenthetical documentation. Notoriously, this practice may impede narrative flow, but since a part of my purpose here is to draw attention to narrative practices themselves that frustration of expectation is a part of my argument. I have certainly not tried to render my text unreadable and do not believe that I have, but in making these stylistic choices I have favored consciousness over comfort.

The Appearance
of Truth

1

Elizabeth Canning's Story

At a little after ten o'clock at night on 29 January 1753, a Monday, as the apprentice sawyer James Lord was about to fasten the street door of his mistress's premises before going to bed, the latch—"it goes with a bit of string"—lifted and a frightening figure appeared. "I did not know her at first," Lord later testified, "because she looked in such a deplorable condition" (*State Trials*, 19: 491). As he continued to stare, however, he recognized his mistress's eighteen-year-old daughter, so when Mrs. Elizabeth Canning called out from the second of her two rooms to ask who was there, he was able to reply "It was Betty," and then, in clarification, "Our Betty."

Mrs. Canning, at the sight of the daughter she had been seeking without success since 1 January, fell in a fit. James Lord had never seen his mistress faint before, but he was sure "it was far from a sham fit." On her recovery, Mrs. Canning sent the apprentice for three of the neighbors who had supported and sympathized with her during her daughter's disappearance: Mary Woodward, Mary Lyon, and Mary Myers. The three women came quickly, but the news also spread throughout the neighborhood and created such interest that on his return James Lord discovered that "So many people had come in, I was obliged to keep the door to keep people out." As Mrs. Canning herself put it, "in two minutes the house was full" (19: 485).

The younger Elizabeth Canning, always so called in the ensuing public discussion of her story but Betty or Bet to the neighborhood in which she had been brought up—Aldermanbury Postern, in the Parish of St. Giles Cripplegate—was indeed in a "deplorable condition." Described in one of her mother's advertisements for her on 6 January as "fresh-colour'd, pitted with the Small-Pox, has a high Forehead, light Eyebrows, about five Feet high, eighteen Years of Age, well-set" (*The Daily Advertiser*, 6 January 1753), Betty Canning was now "e'en almost dead, as black as the chimney-stock, black and blue. . . . She had no hat, nor cap, nor stays on; her ear was cut, and all bloody" (Lord, in *State Trials*, 19: 491). It was not surprising that Mrs. Canning's "little girl [a nine-year-old named Mary] ran screaming up to the chimney," near which James Lord had led Betty to a seat and that Mrs. Canning herself at first "thought [her daughter] was an apparition. She came in . . . almost double, and walking sideways, holding her hands before her" (Mrs. Canning, in *State Trials*, 19: 479).

Mrs. Canning and her neighbors certainly wanted to know what had reduced Betty to this condition and where she had been for the past four weeks, but they were more immediately concerned to keep her alive. Mary Myers attributed the lividity of Betty's skin to cold—it had been a snowy January—and noted that "her nails were as black as my bonnet, and her fingers stood crooked" (19: 504), and her mother "pulled off [her] own stockings and put them upon her" (19: 480). Mary Lyon, called Polly in the neighborhood, brought some wine and mulled it, "about half a tea-cup full, and about the value of a nutmeg in quantity of bread soaked in wine," but Betty "rolled it about in her mouth, and said, 'Mrs. Woodward, I cannot swallow it,' and spit it out. She spoke very faint and low" (19: 508). An apothecary, Sutherton Backler, who had known Betty Canning "some years" (19: 521), did not come until next morning, but his "man came in that night; he wiped her ear, and put a plaister to it; he gave her some drops, and then went away (Mrs. Canning, in *State Trials*, 19: 480). The next morning Mr. Backler found Betty, whose "face used to be of a remarkable red complexion," now "very wan" and her arms still "of a livid color, spotted. . . . She was so extremely low that I could scarcely hear her speak. She was in bed, with cold clammy sweats upon her" (19: 521). As Mrs. Canning observed of the stockings she had put on her daughter the night before, "you might have wrung the things about her, she was in such a sweat" (19:480).

Fifteen months later, Mrs. Woodward was asked upon oath, "Do you believe [Elizabeth Canning] was really in that bad state of health in which she appeared to be?" and she replied, "I believe she was as bad as she appeared to be; I am sensible of that" (19: 508). Everyone who saw Betty Canning on 29 January was equally convinced, and every medical practitioner who examined her agreed, both that Betty Canning had been reduced to a condition near death and that the probable causes for her state were starvation and exposure. If what was to become the public controversy over Elizabeth Canning had any factual touchstone on which all parties could agree, it ought to have been, as Henry Fielding wrote, Canning's "dreadful condition" on 29 January.

> [This part of the] Story . . . is incontestably true, as it is a Matter of public Notoriety, and known by almost every Inhabitant in the Parish where her Mother dwells. . . . This being an established Fact, a very fair Presumption follows, that she was confined some-where, and by some Person; that this Confinement was of equal Duration with her Absence; that she was almost starved to Death; that she was confined in a Place, where it was difficult to make her Escape; that, however, this Escape was possible; and that, at length, she actually made it. All these are circumstances which arise from the Nature of the Fact itself. They are what Tully calls *Evidentia Rei*, and are stronger than the positive testimony of any Witnesses. (*A Clear State*, 19–20)

In the Canning case, however, one writer's "established Fact[s]" are another's "Misrepresentations, . . . imagined Arguments, and . . . Puerility" (Hill, *Story . . . Considered*, 7). According to Dr. John Hill, whose journalistic persona as the Inspector gave him a regular public forum in which he had already identified him-self as an enemy of Fielding's, "She returned you say emaciated and black . . . [but] she was not black upon this 1st of February. A Day or two had made an amazing Change; for those who were present tell me, she was at that Time red and white like other People" (*Story . . . Considered*, 22). Earlier disagreements be-tween Hill and Fielding and the well-documented willingness of both to take sides, for whatever reasons, in public controver-sies might lead their readers to see the Canning case as almost a contrivance for the better carrying on of a personal vendetta, but other writers, presumably otherwise motivated, took equal or larger parts in the affair.[1] It was written about anonymously, pseudonymously, and by observers not otherwise literary in their ambitions, such as the painter Allan Ramsay, who employed the persona of an elderly clergyman writing to a young lord to whom he had been tutor, and by the former Lord Mayor of London, Sir Crisp Gascoyne, very much over his own signature. Signatures and interpretations, in fact, loom as large in the case as evidence and argument, with which they blend and shimmer, and there is no presenting the story of Elizabeth Canning without, as Hill's title *(The Story of Elizabeth Canning Considered. . . .)* ac-knowledges, "considering" it.

Nor has the passage of time shaken out the sort of established interpretation which is sometimes called the truth, although the case continued to be written about in the nineteenth and twentieth centuries. Samuel Johnson's premise "that what has been longest known has been most considered, and what is most considered is best understood" (*Preface*, 10), with its hopeful rationality, is unconvincing here, and the arguments on which he based it, transferred from Shakespeare to Elizabeth Canning, ring hollow: "The effects of favour and competition are at an end; the tradition of [her] friendships and [her] enmities has perished; [her case] support[s] no opinion with arguments; nor suppl[ies] any faction with invectives; [it] can neither indulge vanity nor gratify malignity" (*Preface*, 11). The Canning case, arguably unlike a Shakespearean drama in this respect although perhaps not convincingly to many late twentieth-century minds, has no such Olympian remoteness; it has continued to evoke favor and competition, friendship and enmity, and vanity and malignity, and, in fact, the later history of these phenomena are now an integral part of it. "Considering" the case of Elizabeth Canning means also considering the commentary upon it, arguing opinions, and often engaging with, if not in, invective.

Thus, writing in 1936, F. J. Harvey Darton cites "the strongest facts in the case—the only facts we can be sure of: that Elizabeth Canning had a 'guilty secret,' that she was in some way acquainted with Mother Wells's house, and that Mary Squires was also aware of that unsavoury brothel" (21). In 1989, John Treherne found that "Despite scores of witnesses, a welter of testimony and an avalanche of writings, only three certainties emerge about Elizabeth Canning's adventures in January, 1753. First, that she disappeared—somewhere between Houndsditch and Aldermanbury—on the evening of New Year's Day. Secondly, that she was starved and brutally treated until she was black in the face. Thirdly, that Mary Squires was in Dorset at the time of Elizabeth Canning's disappearance. All else is probability" (144). It will of course be obvious even to readers hitherto unfamiliar with the case that Darton's and Treherne's "facts" and "certainties" resemble each other only in number. Treherne's list is based more clearly, as will become apparent, on documentary evidence, but it is documentary evidence that is strongly contradicted by other evidence of the same character. The credibility of witnesses underlies—or fails to underlie—even sworn testimony, and has been further entangled from the very beginning of the case with the other issue Treherne names, probability. As Allan Ramsay put it in a passage Treherne also quotes: "This is not barely an enquiry concerning a pair of old stays, or the bad diet of a servant wench; nor about the life of an old gipsy . . . but it is an enquiry of a much more interesting kind: no less than *an enquiry into the nature of moral evidence*, the basis upon which all human affairs turn" (*Letter*, 49; emphasis in original).

Before looking more closely at the old stays, the servant wench's diet, Mother Wells, Mary Squires, and all the other slippery human components of the case of Elizabeth Canning—for as Ramsay observed in the parenthesis previously omitted from the passage just quoted, "no man ought to think himself too great to interest himself in the distresses of the meanest," although Ramsay and most other commentators on the case can normally muster sympathy for only a few of the "meanest" with whom the case teems—it is worth pausing upon and foregrounding the issue of probability.

It was Fielding who first named this idea that would figure so largely for other writers on the case by acknowledging what he saw as the most surprising elements in Canning's own version of what had happened to her in January 1753, and we can begin as he did with the affidavit that she swore before him in his capacity as a magistrate on the following 7 February:

MIDDLESEX] The information of Elizabeth Canning, of Aldermanbury Postern, London, spinster, taken upon oath this 7th day of February, in the year of Our Lord 1753, before Henry Fielding, Esq., one of His Majesty's Justices of the Peace for the County of Middlesex.

This Informant, upon her Oath, saith, That on Monday, the First Day of January last past, she, this Informant, went to see her Uncle and Aunt, who live at Saltpetre-Bank, near Rosemary-lane, in the County of Middlesex, and continued with them until the Evening, and saith, That upon her Return home about Half an Hour after Nine, being opposite Bethlehem-gate in Moorfields, she, this Informant, was seized by two Men (whose Names are unknown to her, this Informant) who both had brown Bob-wigs on, and drab-coloured Great-coats, one of whom held her, this Informant, whilst the other feloniously and violently, took from her one Shaving Hat, one Stuff Gown, and one Linen Apron, which she had on; and also, Half a Guinea in Gold, and Three Shillings in Silver; and then he that held her threatened to do for this Informant. And this Informant saith, That, immediately after, they, the same two Men, violently took hold of her, and dragged her up into the Gravel-walk that leads down to the said Gate, and about the Middle thereof, he, the said Man that first held her, gave her, with his Fist, a very violent Blow upon the right Temple, which threw her into a Fit, and deprived her of her

Senses (which Fits she, this Informant, said she is accustomed and subject to upon being frighted, and that they often continue for six or seven Hours). And this Informant saith, That when she came to herself, she perceived that she was carrying along by the same two Men, in a large Road-way: and saith, That in a little Time after, she was so recovered she was able to walk along; however they continued to pull her along, which still so intimidated and frighted her, that she durst not call out for Assistance, or speak to them. And this Informant saith, That, in about half an Hour after she had so recovered herself, they, the said two Men, carried her, this Informant, into a House (which, as she, this Informant, heard from some of them, was about Four o'Clock in the Morning, and which House, as she, this Informant, hath since heard and believes, is situate at Enfield-wash in the County of Middlesex, and is reputed to be a very bad and disorderly Bawdy-house, and occupied by one _____ Wells Widow,) and there this Informant saw, in the Kitchen, an old Gipsy Woman, and two young Women, whose Names were unknown to this Informant; but the Name of one of them this Informant hath since heard and believes is Virtue Hall, and saith, That the said old Gipsy Woman took hold of this Informant's Hand, and promised to give her fine Cloaths if she would go their Way (meaning, as this Informant understood, to become a Prostitute); which this Informant, refusing to do, she, the said old Gipsy Woman, took a Knife out of a Drawer, and cut the Lace of the Stays off her, this Informant, and took the said Stays away from her; and one of the said Men took off her Cap, and then the said two Men went away with it, and she, this Informant, hath never since seen any of her Things. And this Informant saith, That soon after they were gone (which she, this Informant, believes was about five in the Morning) she, the said old Gipsy Woman, forced her, this Informant, up an old Pair of Stairs, and pushed her into a back Room like a Hay-loft, without any Furniture whatsoever in the same, and there locked her, this Informant, up, threatening her, this Informant, that if she made the least Noise or Disturbance, she, the said old Gipsy Woman, would cut her Throat, and then she went away. And this Informant saith, That when it grew light, upon her looking round to see in what a dismal Place she was, she, this Informant, discovered a large black Jug, with the Neck much broken, wherein was some Water; and upon the Floor, several Pieces of Bread, near in Quantity to a quartern Loaf, and a small Parcel of Hay: and saith, That she continued in this Room or Place, from the said Tuesday Morning, the second Day of January, until about Half-an-hour after Four of the Clock in the Afternoon of Monday, the twenty-ninth Day of the same Month of January, without having or receiving any other Sustenance or Provision, than the said Bread and Water (except a small Minced-pye, which she, this Informant, had in her Pocket); or any Thing to lie on other than the said Hay, and without any

Person, or Persons, coming to her, although she often heard the name
of Mrs. and Mother Wells called upon, whom she understood was
the Mistress of the House. And this Informant saith, That on Friday,
the twenty-sixth day of January last past, she, this Informant, had
consumed all the aforesaid Bread and Water, and continued without
having any Thing to eat or drink until the Monday following, when
she, this Informant, being almost famished with Hunger, and starved
with Cold, and almost naked during the whole Time of her Confinement, about Half-an-hour after Four in the Afternoon of the said
twenty-ninth Day of January, broke out at a window of the said Room
or Place, and got to her Friends in London, about a quarter after Ten
the same Night, in a most weak, miserable Condition, being very
near starved to Death. And this Informant said, That she ever since
hath been, and now is, in a very weak and declining State and Condition of Health, and altho' all possible Care and Assistance is given
to her, yet whatever small Nutriment she, this Informant, is able to
take, the same receives no Passage through her, but what is forced
by the Apothecary's Assistance and Medicines.

The mark of
EC
Elizabeth Canning

Sworn before me,
this 7th of Feb. 1753.
H. Fielding.

(*A Clear State*, 33–38)

This was not the first or the last time that Canning was to tell
her story—a phrase in itself of considerable significant ambiguity, with its implications both of factual truth, supported by the
generic weight of the affidavit sworn and signed before a magistrate, and of fictional representation of an imaginary sequence of
events. Dr. John Hill was later to refer to Canning sneeringly as
"that famous modern story-teller" (*London Daily Advertiser and
Inspector*, 2 June 1754, quoted in *A Refutation*, 45). The various
versions of the story—including in addition to her sworn
information before Justice Fielding that given to her mother
and neighbors on 29 January and afterward, before Alderman
Thomas Chitty on 31 January, to Justice Merry Tyshemaker on
1 February, in court at the trial of Mary Squires for theft and
assault and of Susannah Wells as accessory on 21 February—
were repeatedly compared and found consistent, contrasted and
found inconsistent, and both supported and challenged in detail,
but this was the story as Fielding (or a clerk) took it down, and
the one to which he addressed himself on the question of probability.

To begin with, Canning's is "a very extraordinary narrative"

(*A Clear State*, 11). Her captors' motivations are obscure, and her own survival, lingering in captivity, and, at long last, escape and journey home are all highly improbable events. Fielding puts this case, however, in order to refute it. "He who gives a hasty Belief to what is strange and improbable, is guilty of Rashness; but he is much more absurd, who declares that he will believe no such Fact or any Evidence whatever" (19). Motiveless malignity, "which delights and feeds itself with Acts of Cruelty and Inhumanity," is a phenomenon with which "History as well as our own Experience" (14) acquaints us, and "common Experience" is also the touchstone for our prolonged endurance of "many Inconveniences of Life, while we overlook those Ways of extricating ourselves which, when they are discovered, appear to have been, from the first, extremely easy and obvious" (17). Thus Canning languished in Wells's hayloft, shocked and without appetite, until "Despair, which is a Quality that is ever-increasing as its Object increases, grew to the highest Pitch, and forced her to an attempt, which she had not before had the Courage to undertake. . . . Despair . . . is known to add no less strength to the Body than it doth to the Mind, a Truth which every Man almost may confirm by many Instances" (18).

The appeal to "common Experience" rests on the assumption of common humanity—what everyone shares, everyone must acknowledge to be true. The concept of probability thus rests on the assumption of a universal human nature. What is noteworthy, however, is that Fielding's idea of common humanity is not identical to that of other commentators on the case. Despite his well-known skepticism about Richardson's fictional Pamela, another abducted servant girl, Fielding found the flesh-and-blood Elizabeth Canning "a poor simple child" (17), "a virtuous, modest, sober, well-disposed Girl," (21), "a Child in Years, and yet more so in Understanding, with all the evident Marks of Simplicity that I ever discovered in a human Countenance" (23). The necessity of telling her story "in large Assemblies of Persons of a much higher Degree than she had ever before appeared in the Presence of: Before Noblemen, and Magistrates, and Judges, Persons who must have inspired a Girl of this kind with the highest Awe . . . without Hesitation, Confusion, Trembling, Change of Countenance or other apparent Emotion [displayed either] Impudence (or) Innocence." Since the former would have required "the highest Art," supported by "the longest Practice and Habit to bring it to such a Degree of Perfection," the latter was the more probable (23–24).

By emphasizing Canning's youth and short statue—"a little girl" (11)—Fielding in effect, however, de-emphasized her gender. That in itself, however, raised quite different probabilities to prominence for other writers. Dr. John Hill, specifically addressing Fielding, was probably the first to appeal to them in print: "Where a Girl, like this, could be; and how employed during the Time; is not difficult to imagine. Not with a Lover certainly, say you! You would be happy, Sir, if all you beg should be allowed you. Not with a Lover, Sir! Eighteen, let me remind you, is a critical Age; and what would not a Woman do, that had made an Escape, to recover her own Credit, and screen her Lover" (Story . . Considered, 24).

Allan Ramsay also resorted to a generalized idea of adolescent female sexuality to support his argument that Canning's story exceeded the limits of probability: "There are such distempers as lyings-in and miscarriages, to which young servant-maids of eighteen are very much subject; distempers that will hold them as long and reduce them as low as has been related of E. Canning, especially if attended and nursed in the manner we may easily suppose her to have been. It may not be amiss to hint, that thirteen shillings and six-pence, with the sale of a gown and pair of stays, is hardly more than sufficient to defray the expences of such an operation; even altho' no part of it was expended in a christening, a wet nurse, or a coffin" (Letter, 20).

Elizabeth Canning, in short, is for Fielding an instance of "injured Innocence" (6), for Hill a liar and a slut, and for Ramsay an infanticide: the basis for all three conclusions is probability, and probability, it is argued on all sides, must provide the final resolution to the case's contradictions. As one later legal writer, Courtney Kenny, argued, "the principal lesson of this famous trial [Canning's eventual trial for perjury, but every earlier phase of the case can be included in the same judgment] seems to me to be the importance of *a priori* considerations of credibility or incredibility as guides in forensic inquiries" ("The Mystery of Elizabeth Canning," 377).[2] Kenny eventually sides with Hill and Ramsay, and shares their reasoning:

> Was this girl, whose whole traceable career, throughout an extraordinary variety of surroundings, remains unbrokenly one of simplicity and innocence, a person who would be likely to swear away the lives of two [sic: only Squires was tried for or convicted of a capital offence] of her fellow-creatures? I will not answer my own question. For perhaps the most generally useful lesson to be drawn from the

Canning mystery, useful enough in forensic difficulties but far indeed from being limited to them, is the wisdom of a modest agnosticism in all questions that hinge upon the incalculable and insoluble mysteries of the feminine mind—mysteries in which the greatest masters of human nature are soon at fault. . . . [I]t may be suspected that even Henry Fielding, who could portray so minutely the hearts of Molly Seagrim and Miss Slipslop and Mrs. Jonathan Wild, did not quite penetrate to the innermost recesses of that of Elizabeth Canning. (130)

The positing of a "feminine mind," distinct from "human nature," is one of the most obvious features of both contemporary and subsequent comment on and analysis of the Canning case, but it is not the only assumption that goes into the constitution of the canons of probability applied to it. Class and criminality are two other constitutive ideas influencing not only the interpretation but the definition of evidence, and while such mediating categories may alter over time they never simply vanish. All versions of the story of Elizabeth Canning, including the actual events of her life, are ideologically constituted.

The account that follows, therefore, cannot be exempt from the conditions which have gone into the making of all of its predecessors. It, too, is shaped by ideological assumptions, generic conventions, and the biases that Johnson believed must lapse over time but which I believe are only in continuous re-creation as circumstances change, ever ready to select evidence and to shape interpretations.

With the introduction of the pronoun "I" in the last sentence, something of the effect of such ideological assumptions can be demonstrated. The personal pronoun is not a newcomer to discourse on the Canning case. Fielding and Hill both used it, evoking their own established personae as authors interested in the public good; Ramsay and other anonymous and pseudonymous writers used it to create similarly authoritative individual voices. It tends to disappear, however, with the establishment in the nineteenth century of a preference for apparent objectivity and in the twentieth of an academic style in which personal references were held to be incorrect. For readers trained in this latter tradition especially, the "I" in the last sentence of the previous paragraph may have been experienced as jolting.

Nevertheless, it is my intention to attempt to mingle the two styles, the academic and the personal, in my account of the Canning case and its documents. The personal style reflects my belief that no account is in actuality unbiased or objective in any simple sense, that an ideologically constructed personal point of view must constitute it, and that this bias is better avowed than concealed. It is at this perhaps paradoxical point, however, that I find the academic style useful. The purpose of avowing bias is in my view to control it. As firmly as I hold that my own opinions and judgments are influenced by my experience and beliefs, and that those experiences and beliefs are not identical to everyone else's—"universal"—but strongly affected by, among other things, gender, education, nationality, and historical moment, I also believe that the prevalence of opinion does not imply the absolute extinction of fact. Elizabeth Canning really lived, even if our only access to her is through partial representations of her life, and I am thus attempting both to examine the roles played by representation in constituting that life for various audiences, and, by analyzing and manipulating those representations, to glimpse beyond them the reality I can never fully know and to illuminate that reality for others.

2

The Crime, First Version: Assault and Theft

Elizabeth Canning and Her Family

Mrs. Elizabeth Canning was the forty-two-year-old widow of William Canning, a sawyer, who had died in 1751, leaving four children and his wife pregnant with a fifth—"the child in my arms," Johanna, to whom Mrs. Canning referred in her oldest child's perjury trial in 1754 (*State Trials*, 19: 484). The family occupied two rooms in Aldermanbury Postern, an extension of Aldermanbury running between London Wall and Fore Street, which no longer exists, as most of the sites associated with the case do not. It was a respectable neighborhood; none of its inhabitants seem to have been wealthy, but few were as poor as Mrs. Canning and her children, who managed—all but Elizabeth, the oldest by eight years, who had been living out as a maidservant since she was fifteen or sixteen—to live in the one back room in order to house the apprentice, James Lord, in the front one. After Elizabeth Canning's return to her mother's home on January 29, 1753, James Lord seldom saw her because she was at first in bed in the back room, where "it was not so proper for me to go" (19: 494), and on 6 February she was moved across the street to Mary Woodward's house in order to have a better chance of recovery (*A Refutation*, 9).

The Canning family's poverty is one of the undisputed facts in the case, although its interpretations vary. Mrs. Canning's neighbors clearly liked and respected her and were helpful and supportive when her daughter disappeared on New Year's Day, 1753, financing her advertisements for the missing girl—"I could not have advertised her, had I not had assistance, and my neighbours put me upon it" (19:484)—although they had no results. Mrs. Canning herself "went to all the agents and places where I could think of, fearing some casualty. . . . I prayed by myself, and gave up bills in the church, both at Aldermanbury

and Cripplegate, and at the meetings and Mr. Wesley's. I did not
leave a meeting or a place where I could put up a bill in" (19:
483–85). She also consulted a conjuror, again at the instigation
of "[a] great many of my neighbours; one gave me six-pence, and
another three-pence, till I got a shilling, and then I went directly"
(19: 484–85), having been recommended to an "astrologer" in
the Old Bailey by an out-of-place cook: "I was wringing my
hands and tearing about, and she advised me to go to the cunning
man. There were a crowd of people about the door, like a fair
about me" (19: 485). The cunning man alarmed Mrs. Canning so
much that her account of him is less coherent than the rest of
her testimony—"When he shut the door, and lighted the candles
up, he looked so frightful, I was glad to get out at the door again"
(19: 484)—but prosecuting counsel attempted to suggest collusion:

> Did he tell you she was in the hands of an old woman?—No, he
> did not.
> Recollect yourself.—I don't know whether he did or no: he might,
> for what I know.
> Whether he did not tell you she was in the hands of an old black
> woman?—The word "black" I don't remember. I know he frighted
> me. . . .
> Did you tell him of a dream you had?—No, I did not.
> Had you not a dream or a vision about it?—I don't know of any
> such thing.
> Or an apparition?—No, but I had wandering thoughts.
> What did you mean just now, by saying you had wandering
> thoughts?—I say, I never had rest night or day, for my thoughts were
> wandering. [distracted?]
> How came you to imagine she was confined by an old woman?—
> It never came into my thoughts that she was; I more thought she
> was murdered in Houndsditch, and thrown into some ditch there.
> (19: 484)

A later writer on the case, Hugh Childers, characterized Mrs.
Canning as a "nervous, excitable woman" (3), but this seems
unfair. Our very limited view of her is shaped by the circumstances of her daughter's disappearance and return, scarcely an
appropriate index to her everyday demeanor. Of that we only
know, in summary, that she contrived to support her family after
her husband's death and earned the respect, affection, and loyalty of her neighbors. Her own voice as recorded in the two trials
in which she was a witness strikes me as frank and truthful,

admitting circumstances that might reflect badly on her, not only her "wandering thoughts" and "tearing about" but her knowledge of a small fraud perpetrated by a group of sawyers who bilked a curious inquirer of half-a-crown by introducing him to another sawyer rather than to James Lord, whom he had paid to see, and denying knowledge at some points when she might safely have claimed it in a way that would support her daughter's case:

> Was anything mentioned of Enfield-Wash the night of your daughter's return?—I don't know when it was first mentioned. I believe it was when they all came together the next morning.
>
> . . . .
>
> Was Scarrat there when hay was mentioned?—I don't know, the house was full of people. (19: 487)

The bond between Mrs. Canning and her eldest child was still strong, although Elizabeth had been living out for two years or more at the time of her disappearance, first in the household of John Wintlebury, a neighborhood publican, proprietor of the Weavers' Arms, who had known Mrs. Canning "fourteen or fifteen years" and her daughter nearly as long (Wintlebury, in *State Trials*, 19:510), and more recently with Edward Lyon, an elderly carpenter, who had also known the family from Elizabeth's childhood (Lyon, in *State Trials*, 19: 467). Both testified to the Canning family's honesty and good character, and both praised Elizabeth's dutifulness as a servant. Wintlebury noted, "I don't believe she went out once in a quarter of a year. When she went away from me, many of the neighbors would have had her" (19: 510).

The wives of Wintlebury and Lyon were never called as witnesses, but they later swore an affidavit that there had been no interval between Elizabeth's successive employments, and that

> she was modest, reserved, and diffident, that she never had any companions come after her of either sex; that she never loitered when sent out upon business; that she very rarely asked to go out, and then only to her mother, with whom she seldom staied [overnight]; or to go to church on a Sunday evening, from whence she returned as soon as the service was over; and that she was never absent from either house, without the approbation of her master or mistress. As to the holiday on the first of January, 1753, Mrs. Lyon positively declares, that she said to her, "Betty, you shall have a holiday this

Christmas; and, as the shop will be shut up, I think you shall have it on Monday." (Appendix 44, *A Refutation*, 38)

The 1 January holiday was thus not a long meditated one, and Elizabeth spent it as she normally spent free time, with her family. She stopped in Aldermanbury Postern, where she gave her little brothers and sisters a penny apiece from the "half a guinea in gold, and three shillings in silver" Mrs. Lyon had given her for the holiday and made plans with her mother to go out "that afternoon to buy a cloak and a pair of mittens" (Mrs. Canning, in *State Trials*, 19: 482) after visiting her aunt and uncle, Alice and Thomas Colley of Saltpeter Bank (now Dock Street). Her plans were then changed by circumstances—the Colleys were able to offer her only a cold dinner and insisted that she stay for a warm supper as well (Thomas and Alice Colley, in *State Trials*, 19: 475–78). One of Elizabeth's little brothers, probably ten-year-old Benjamin rather than two-year-old Joseph, had "huffed her" before receiving the penny the other children got (Mrs. Canning, in *State Trials*, 19: 483), and some time later in the day Elizabeth bought a penny mince-pie to give to him to make up the quarrel and put it in the pocket of her petticoat (Elizabeth Canning, in *State Trials*, 19: 264).

Mr. and Mrs. Colley were questioned at the perjury trial over a year later about what Elizabeth had eaten and how heartily. Her uncle thought she had eaten dinner "as heartily as I did" but "she could not eat much" of the roast sirloin of beef on offer for supper: "She eat a small quantity of that. . . . She drank a small quantity of ten-shilling beer" (19: 476). Mrs. Colley affirmed that Elizabeth "was, in all appearances, as well as I am now" but "she eat but a very little, not very heartily; but I cannot say I minded her much" (19: 477). In spite of Elizabeth's solid form and florid complexion, she was not, in fact, in the habit of eating much. Her mother observed that "she had a very little stomach [appetite] always; that they know where she lived. . . . She drank very little, without it was a dish of tea; but not plentiful of that." Asked if she had not found her daughter's story of survival for a month on a gallon jug of water and a broken quartern (approximately four-pound) loaf "a very strange one," she replied almost combatively—and certainly revealingly—"No, I did not think it strange at all. I have known her, at home, to live upon half a roll a day, when things have gone hard with me" (19: 486).

Elizabeth Canning's health prior to her disappearance was

something apparently taken as a matter of little importance by everyone around her, and there is no evidence that she thought otherwise herself. Four years before her disappearance a garret ceiling had fallen on her head, and thereafter she had been liable to faint "when anybody speaks hastily to her, or at any surprize" (Mrs. Canning, in *State Trials*, 19: 269), but this nervous weakness had not hindered her from going into service and giving satisfaction to her employers. Dr. Daniel Cox, who examined Canning closely, wrote in her defense, and became one of her most consistent supporters from March 1753 onward, reported that Canning had not had a menstrual period for about five months prior to New Year's Day 1753: "[O]ne night being up at washing when she was out of order, she took cold and they [her "courses"] ceased, nor had returned again but since she came home: This is no uncommon case with servants who are obliged to dabble in cold water, the obstructions frequently continuing some months, and sometimes without any great complaints of illness" (*An Appeal*, 19).

Elizabeth Canning was in any case clearly not a girl given to great complaints. All the evidence suggests that she and her family accepted their lot in life unquestioningly and got on with it as best they could. If she suffered from malnutrituion, however, or from conditions we might now label abusive, they were not seen at the time as anything other than necessity, and they are certainly not evidence of any indifference to her on the part of her family or the community. When Elizabeth Canning disappeared and her mother, helped by her neighbors, advertised for information about her whereabouts, her brother Thomas Colley told her to include an offer of a reward: "It was her uncle bid me to do that, and said, he'd pay that, if he stripp'd his skin" (19: 482).

The Disappearance

Because she had stayed for the warm supper, it was around nine o'clock at night when Elizabeth Canning set out to return to Aldermanbury. It was too late to go shopping with her mother, and she intended to return to her room at Mr. Lyon's house. It was also late to be out in the streets quite safely, and the Colleys accordingly walked her about two thirds of the way home, "to Houndsditch, almost to the Blue-Ball; there we parted with her, about a quarter or very near half an hour after nine o'clock"

(Thomas Colley, in *State Trials*, 19: 268). Elizabeth continued "over Moorfields by Bedlam wall," an unsavory sounding route to us but quieter than the Houndsditch portion of her way and only ten or fifteen minutes' further walk from her destination. In Moorfields, however,

> two lusty men, both in great-coats, laid hold of me, one on each side; they said nothing to me at first, but took half a guinea in a little box out of my pocket, and 3 s. that were loose. . . . They [then] took my gown, apron, and hat, and folded them up, and put them into a great-coat pocket. I screamed out; then the man that took my gown put a handkerchief, or some such thing, to my mouth. . . . They then tied my hands behind me; after which one of them gave me a blow on the temple, and said, Damn you, you bitch, we'll do for you by and bye. I having been subject to convulsion fits these four years, this blow stunned me, and threw me directly into a fit.
>
> Are these fits attended with a struggling?—I don't know that. (*State Trials*, 19: 263)

This account, given on oath at the trial of Mary Squires and Susannah Wells, is consistent with Canning's deposition before Fielding, and, for the most part, with the earlier deposition taken on 31 January by the sitting alderman, Thomas Chitty. The latter, which I will discuss in some detail later, includes the phrase "and forced her along Bishopsgate street" (Chitty, in *State Trials*, 19: 374)—not an explicit contradiction but a reference which would later be seen as a part of the evidence undermining the credibility of Canning's whole story. For the time being, however, I want to concentrate on the story as given as much as possible in Canning's own words, and there are good grounds for doubting the adequacy of Alderman Chitty's minutes in meeting that criterion.

The story so far is in any case wholly unremarkable. Robbery with violence was a fairly common experience in the London of 1753, and the assault outside Bedlam Hospital occurred at a spot where the thieves might wait some time for prey but once prey arrived were unlikely to be observed or interrupted. What followed was rather stranger.

Elizabeth Canning, stunned, unconscious, perhaps for a while semiconscious but unresisting, first became aware of herself and her surroundings again "by a large road, where was water, with the two men that robbed me." She said nothing to the two men nor they to her, apart from such occasional remarks as "You bitch, why don't you walk faster?" (19:263).

At Canning's perjury trial in May 1754, one of the many witnesses was Robert Beals, a turnpike keeper whose post was at Stamford Hill turnpike in Tottenham Road, about three miles from Moorfields. He testified that in February 1753 he heard from his children the story of "a girl being forced away from her friends near Moorfields, to a bad house at Enfield-Wash," and that that recalled to his mind something he had seen at his turnpike gate "about the fore-end of January"—Beals refused to be definite about the date but was sure of it approximately. He also did not identify Canning, and would not swear to how the woman he had seen was dressed beyond that, in "a dark night," it was in something "lightish," and that "she had something on her head." With these limitations, he told his story:

> I was standing at the gate between ten and eleven, or near eleven at night; it was a very calm still night; I heard something of a sobbing, crying voice; it came from towards Newington, going towards Tottenham; and first I saw nobody; I stood still; it came nearer me. . . . At last I perceived there were more than one. As they came near, I saw there were two men, and a young person, seemingly by her voice. I had a large candle burning (the stile is at the end of the turnpike over the way ["about eight or ten yards" from Beals's post as keeper]). As soon as they got up to the light, I saw them more plain. One man was taller than the other. They went towards the stile; one, the foremost, began to say, Come along, you bitch, you are drunk; that was said when the candle began to shine upon them. I put myself a little farther without-side the posts, that they might see me. The woman seemed not willing to go along with them, by her crying and sobbing, but never spoke a word. The man behind made a sort of laugh, and said, Damn the bitch, how drunk she is! When they came up to the stile, the tall one got over first and the hindmost lifted her over by either one leg or both legs; she came down upright on the other side; then she hung back, and fell on her breech upon the step, and cried bitterly. I thought she would go no farther. As I thought they could see me, I expected she would have said something to me; but she did not speak a word. He before plucked her up by the hands at full length, and said, Damn you, you bitch, come along; you are drunk; the other came on the other side of her, and they went away together; he laughed, and said, Damn the bitch, how drunk she is! he that came over last jostled her along. I could see them some way after they got over the stile. One of them never let go her hand all the time I saw them.

Two questions asked by one of the attorneys representing

Canning provide some illuminating background on this ugly episode:

> Mr. Morton. Why did you not attempt to give her your assistance?—Beals. There were two men with her, and we are fearful in our business; except they ask us any questions, we never meddle with such; and I was then alone. . . .
> Mr. Morton. Is it a common thing to see a drunken woman along with two men?—Beals. I never saw one so particular as this. (19: 524–27)

Meddling in defense of apparently victimized females would in any case probably have been uncommon, as a case cited by Lincoln Faller suggests:

> In 1752, returning to the City from Holloway, Thomas Tipping witnessed a rape. "The Woman was down on her Back," he later testified in court, "her Cloaths up, her Legs open, and the Man upon her. She said, *For God's Sake Master, Help; Murder, Murder!* The Man said, *Hold your Tongue, you Bitch.*" Reluctant to intervene, Tipping continued on his way. Later, however, "reading in the Papers that a Man was taken up, and hearing the Woman had a good Character," he offered to come forward and testify. He had been "afraid," he explained, that "there was more in it than there should be, there being many Traps to draw People in, such as Stratagems of Women crying out, and the like." (151)

Fielding also had noted "the Darkness of the Night at that Season of the Year, and when it was within two days of the New Moon, with the Indifference of most people to what doth not concern themselves, and the Terror with which all honest Persons pass by Night through the Roads near this Town" to explain "the Want of all Interruption to these Men in their Conveyance of the poor Girl" (*A Clear State*, 16). Beals's story atmospherically supports Fielding's generalized social observation, but the question which, of course, remains is whether the young woman Beals saw was in fact Elizabeth Canning. Certainly Canning herself claimed no such memory, and Beals could not identify her; on the other hand, the date and time are suggestive, and the episode was outside Beals's usual experience.

If Canning's whole story had not later been called into question, it seems likely that we would now take Beals's observation as a legitimate part of it. The question was very soon raised, however, why two robbers should carry off their victim to a destination ten miles away, and many writers on the case found the proposition so irrational as to be simply impossible. As Allan Ramsay put it, appealing once more to the convention of a universal human nature: "Was it ever known that any plurality of human creatures ever acted conjunctly but from vulgar and obvious motives of inte[rest,] safety, or pleasure?" (A Letter, 7). Dr. John Hill was equally incredulous: "To what Purpose should she be forced away? She is not handsome; so that the Design could not be upon her Person" (The Story . . . Considered, 15).

No one was ever specifically charged with the assault in Moorfields, so these analyses of motivation are being offered not for two particular men in greatcoats but for hypothetical abductors, figures whose identity with the abstract ideal of man as a rational animal is perhaps easier to make. If, however, we take Canning's story to be true and Beals's evidence as applying to Canning, the insistence of the men Beals saw and heard on their captive's drunkenness then suggests something about themselves that might have impaired any native reasonableness they possessed—Canning's abductors, like the perpetrators of many eighteenth-century street crimes, may well have been drunk themselves, and their emphatic labeling of their captive as drunk merely a natural enough displacement aimed at satisfying the possible curiosity of occasional passersby or the odd turnpike-keeper. If they were drunk, they may have found this subterfuge not only clever but even funny.

One man, not charged because Canning would go no further than to say he resembled one of the men who had robbed her, was a gypsy named George Squires, the son of that Mary Squires who was charged with stealing Canning's stays (A Refutation, 8). Although he was never tried himself, Squires did figure prominently in Canning's trial, where the prosecutor for whom he was a shaky key witness labeled him "stupid" (19: 342). As Andrew Lang commented when he reviewed the case in 1904, "The more stupid was George, the less unlikely was he to kidnap Elizabeth Canning as prize of war after robbing her" (21). Lang, however, saw Canning as the "victim of the common sense of the eighteenth century. She told a very strange tale and common-sense holds that what is strange cannot be true. Yet something strange had undoubtedly occurred" (27). It may be easier for people in the late twentieth century to identify alcohol and irrationality—to use a kinder term than stupidity—as major determinants of human behavior than it was for Allan Ramsay, but this does not make them exclusively twentieth-century phenomena. In both cases, a view of the world is constructing the events of one dark night in January 1753.

When Elizabeth Canning did not return to Mr. Lyon's house by nine, he himself went twice, at nine and at ten, to Mrs. Canning's home to look for her. After his second visit, James Lord was dispatched to the Colleys but found the household gone to bed, able only to tell him that they had left Elizabeth at about half past nine "upon the other side Aldgate church, in Houndsditch. There was great inquiry about the neighbourhood all night long almost; I inquired of several neighbours that night" (Lord, in *State Trials*, 19: 490). There ensued the advertisements, the "tearing about," the "wandering thoughts," the recourse to the "cunning man," all of which Mrs. Canning would be questioned about later, but at the time every action was overshadowed by the fact that Elizabeth Canning, eighteen years old, not pretty, but a serious and responsible girl on whom her mother and employers depended with complete and affectionate confidence, had disappeared without leaving a clue to her whereabouts. In the absence of police, if her family and friends did not find her she would not, without the interventions of chance, be found.

Enfield Wash

At the trial of Mary Squires and Susannah Wells, Canning testified that the two men "took me to the prisoner Wells's house." At the time, of course—it was now the early hours of 2 January, "about four o'clock in the morning" (*State Trials*, 19: 263)—Canning knew no one's name in the case, but names were filled in soon after her return home. All later accounts use them, tending thereby to shed a misleading clarity on the actual obscurity of the scene upon which she and the two men in greatcoats arrived. I have, therefore, removed the names, along with some details that might have been observed on Canning's later visit to the house of Susannah Wells at Enfield Wash on 1 February 1753, from the account that follows.

The room the three entered was a kitchen, lighted primarily by a fireplace. An old woman

> was sitting in a chair, and two young women in the same room . . . were standing against a dresser. [The older woman] took me by the hand, and asked me if I chose to go their way, saying, if I did, I should have fine clothes. I said, No.

Did she explain to you what she meant by going their way?—No, Sir. Then she went and took a knife out of a dresser-drawer, and cut the lace of my stays, and took them from me.

Had you, at that time, any apprehensions of danger?—I thought she was going to cut my throat, when I saw her take the knife. . . .

Was any thing else taken from you?—There was not then; but [the older woman] looked at my petticoat, and said, Here, you bitch, you may keep that, or I'll give you that, it is not worth much, and gave me a slap on the face.

Had she the petticoat in her hand?—No, it was on me. After that she pushed me up stairs from out of the kitchen, where we were. . . . After she shut the door, she said, If ever she heard me stir or move or any such thing, she'd cut my throat. (19: 263–64)

Stripped of names and possible later observations, this is still a stark and nightmarish story. Continuing to work on the assumption that Canning is telling the truth, I find it redolent of bewilderment and terror. Canning has been stripped half-naked and dragged for hours through cold and darkness by two men who have already promised to "do" for her. Now she is thrust into a small, smoky kitchen and addressed, at first barely comprehensibly, then threateningly, by an old woman while the two bystanders, young women like herself, laugh (Woodward, in *State Trials*, 19: 508). From the kitchen, where she has been slapped, further stripped, and threatened, she is thrust up some stairs into darkness again and a door shut upon her. The journey to this place took perhaps six hours, although all estimates of time in this case must be taken as extremely approximate; the scene in the kitchen can have taken only a few minutes. Still, relying upon Canning's story, she was to spend twenty-eight days alone in the room upstairs where the old woman had put her. It seemed to Allan Ramsay that Canning had remarkably little to tell about all of this:

What happened to Elizabeth Canning during the six hours and a half that she was upon the road between Moorfields and Enfield? Her own account will inform your Lordship: NOTHING.

What happened in the whole hour[?] she remain'd in Mother Wells's kitchen? Next to NOTHING.

What happen'd to her during the 28 days that she was confin'd in Mother Wells's house? NOTHING.

What happen'd to her during the six hours that she was upon the road from Enfield to her mother's house? NOTHING.

Never sure was there a history that stood [less] in need of abridgment. (*Letter*, 13–14)

[Canning's story is] not an artful, but on the contrary, an exceedingly stupid story. An artful story, is such a story as *Tom Jones*, where the incidents are so various, and yet so consistent with themselves, and with nature, that the more the reader is acquainted with nature, the more he is deceived into a belief of its being true; and is with difficulty recall'd from that belief by the author's confession from time to time of its being all a fiction. But what is there plausible in the adventures of Enfield Wash? What is there strange or poetically fancied in the incidents of *robbing, knocking down—cry'd out murder— stopt my mouth with a handkerchief—you bitch, why don't you go faster?—carrying to a bawdy house—offer of fine cloaths—cut your throat if you stir?* (*Letter,* 16–17; emphasis in original.)

It would seem from Ramsay's argument that Canning's story could not be true on any grounds: it is not artful, but an artful story is equated with a fictional one in any case, while the story it actually is, artless, is "stupid," and therefore unbelievable. Canning ought to have been more artful—but then she would have been more deceptive. Her tale is not "poetically fancied," and that in some way proves its falsity; Canning was evidently too little "acquainted with nature" to invent a plausible story and so invented an implausible one—which is implausible precisely because it is *not* "strange." Once again, too, assumptions based on a universal human rationality are at work. A person in remarkable circumstances ought to be observing them closely. Canning claimed to have undergone remarkable events but was able to recount them only artlessly; the conclusion is that she was lying, and invented her story from the contents of too ill-stocked a mind to convince more sophisticated observers such as Ramsay.

If we make opposite assumptions, that the human mind is much at the mercy of physical causes, that terror produces confusion, and that stress impedes observation, Canning's story is once again plausible—in fact, a highly detailed story would now be the doubtful one, a reading supported by mathematical studies of probability as well, which suggest that "If we have no direct evidence or theoretical support for a story, we find that detail and vividness vary inversely with likelihood; the more vivid details there are to a story, the less likely the story is to be true. . . . [P]eople come to probability judgments in mundane situations [by] form[ing] representative mental models of the situation . . . and come to their conclusions by comparison with these models" (Paulos 85–86), a process certainly observable in Ramsay and many other writers on the Canning case as well but not one, despite their belief, really addressing the question of the probability of Canning's story at all.

Assuming still, then, that Canning was telling the truth, and that not only was she abducted and confined as she said she was but that the place of her confinement was indeed the house of Susannah Wells at Enfield Wash (a point on which separate evidence will also have to be considered later), let us shift the focus to the house and its inmates in January 1753.

Despite Ramsay's casual designation, Mrs. Wells's house was not a bawdy house in any very formal sense. Formally, it was nothing at all, although it had been variously in the past a carpenter's shop, a butcher's, and an ale-house. Mrs. Wells kept a sow and pigs and a horse and in some sense took lodgers, but the role of the lodgers in the house was ambiguous at best. Virtue Hall, the young woman identified by Canning as having been present in the kitchen during the early hours of 2 January, said at the trial of Wells and Mary Squires, "I went there as a lodger, but I was forced to do as they would have me" (19: 268). Hall later recanted her story, but no evidence suggests that she changed her assessment of Wells's house. William Howard, a part-time government employee and gentleman of leisure on a small scale who lived within fifty or sixty yards of Wells's house "g[a]ve all my neighbours privilege to come for water" to his pump but otherwise kept as clear of the Wells household as possible—it bore a character "as bad as can be" (19: 533).

Mrs. Wells had been widowed twice. Her first husband, Mr. Howit, had been a carpenter and the father of two now adult children, John and Sarah. Her second, Abraham Wells, had been, to use her own term, "unfortunate," having been hanged for theft, and she acknowledged at her trial that her own character was "indifferent" (19: 274). She had been imprisoned in 1736 for perjury in a bungled fraud in which she assisted her husband, who at that time kept "a butcher's shop and public house at Enfield-Wash," and, according to a witness at the 1736 trial, "harbour[ed] that sort of people"—thieves and other perjurers. According to another deposition, he was also a receiver of stolen property (Appendices 47 and 48, A Refutation, 39–40). His widow's continued survival after his death seems to have been equally hand to mouth and marginally legal, without even the support of the butcher's shop or ale-house sidelines to give it credibility.

Sarah Howit was living with her mother at the time the latter was arrested and claimed to have been there for about two years after five or six years of working away, presumably as a servant. In response to the question, "How do you get your living?" she replied, "I go out to get my bread, to work in the country, sometimes harvest work; I have no family affair with my mother; I used to be in the family, when I was not engaged another way" (19: 409), a rather murky answer that was neither elaborated nor subjected to cross-examination and may refer to household labor, casual prostitution, or both. John Howit, a carpenter like his father, was married, and, according to the parish register of St. Andrew, Enfield, the father of at least two small children. He lived about a quarter of a mile from his mother and claimed at Canning's trial to have visited her house "now and then," even leaving his tools in her loft—where Canning was then supposedly imprisoned—in the middle of January. His evidence was later called into question by Alice Howard, William Howard's wife, who deposed after the trial that John Howit had come to the Howards at some time after his mother's trial to borrow a ladder "and at the same time declared, that he had not been in the dwelling-house of the said Susannah Wells . . . for the space of two months before she and Mary Squires were taken up." Mrs. Howard would have included this information in her testimony at Canning's trial if she had not at the time been "an utter stranger to the evidence given by the said John Howitt" (Appendix 65, *A Refutation*, 51). Mrs. Wells's youngest child, twenty-two-year-old Elizabeth Long, was the daughter of Abraham Wells and herself a widow. She lived three houses from her mother and visited her daily, going "all over the house" and taking home ashes from the loft (19: 420, 422). She was not asked how she got her living.

The Wells/Howit family does demonstrate a sort of obscure solidarity. Only John had regular employment, and his statement to the Howards may show some initial wish to distance himself from whatever had gone on in his mother's house in January 1753, but by the time of Canning's trial his position was consistent with his sisters', that is, supportive of his mother's innocence. As Susannah Wells herself had acknowledged, however, her family's character was not good, and rumors about her house found a ready local audience.

One such survives in the depositions collected after Canning's trial by her supporters, the report of a "labourer" surnamed Barrison, who, with his unnamed daughter, told a strange story "to Mr. Gay, of Enfield, brewer, and Mr. Jarvis, of Enfield, farrier, who confirmed the . . . account to Nicholas Crisp and J. Payne," two of the "Friends of Elizabeth Canning," who put together the most elaborate of the publications in her defense, *A Refutation of Sir Crisp Gascoyne's Address to the Liverymen of England*. It is thus a secondhand account collected and preserved by interested parties, neither certainly true nor obviously false. For whatever its unsupported worth may be, then, the story claims that Barrison's unnamed daughter inquired late one night in 1752 for lodging at Susannah Wells's house, although "when she was admitted into the house, she told Wells that she had no money; to which Wells replied, that she would give her a lodging and a supper too, and that she did not want money." After she had eaten, the girl was introduced by Wells to "a gentleman in a laced waistcoat" whose advances she resisted so convincingly that he promised not to

attempt any thing against her consent.

That she then took courage, and, after much persuasion, drank a glass of wine.

That the gentleman and Wells drank the rest of the wine between them; and after he was gone, Wells was very angry with her for not having complied, and told her that it would have been better for her if she had; and that if she would yet comply, she should live well with them and be happy.

That upon her persisting to reject this proposal, and crying very much, Wells thrust her up into the room over the parlour, and locked her in, where she cried all night, being greatly terrified at her situation; and the next morning begged to be released: but Wells refused to let her go; and insisted, that she should either pay for the wine, her supper, and her lodging, or do as they did.—That the girl then declared, she would break out at the window: Wells replied, that she would then indict her for a robbery; and still kept her there by force, till nine o'clock; when seeing a young man, whom she knew, go by with a team, she made a noise and called out to him, telling him she was kept there by force. That the man then came to the house, and demanded the girl, whom Wells still refused to release, till he threatened to bring others to assist him and break open the door. (Appendix 52, *A Refutation*, 43)

It was the sort of thing that might have happened at "Mother" Wells's house: Whether it actually had, and if so, how accurately the girl and her father reported it, are matters now unknowable. The episode certainly never entered the legal system, and Canning's case is enough to show that if it had, the truth might still be uncertain.

Even without the later problems raised by the Canning case,

it can never have been easy to say who was, at any given date, living at Wells's house. On 1 and 2 January 1753, we may be sure of Wells herself, and apparently of Sarah Howit and Virtue Hall. There were also, however, according to Canning, an old woman later identified as Mary Squires, a gypsy, and—not identified by Canning but apparently inseparable from her mother—Squires's daughter, Lucy. The two men in greatcoats may or may not have been lodgers, and one of them may or may not have been George Squires. According to Virtue Hall's initial testimony, the men had gone off with Canning's stays after the girl was put in the loft (19: 267), and Squires identified himself on the morning of 1 February as a more recent arrival at the house. According to Joseph Adamson, however, George Squires had then behaved suspiciously like a man who had been present on the earlier occasion: "When he was first apprehended, he appeared to be under great terror, and trembled very much: [when] he was told the chaise was just at hand, with the girl upon whose account the warrant had been granted . . . his confusion visibly increased, and he immediately pulled off his great coat and hat. . . . [I]f he had not known, that he, who robbed the girl in Moorfields, had a great coat on, he would have had no motive to pull off his" (*A Refutation*, 8).

Although much of Canning's 1754 perjury trial was to deal with Mary Squires's alibi, which placed her in Dorset on the authority of a large number of witnesses at the time when she had allegedly been cutting off Canning's stays and shoving her up the stairs to the loft of Wells's house, there is remarkably little evidence for any other aspect of Squires's life. She was commonly referred to as a gypsy, but even that identification was sometimes questioned: "tho' Squires has been all along represented as one of the Clan and Fraternity of Gipseys, it is certain she never did belong to them; but is really a Pedlar, and has a Licence from the proper Office to travel the Country and sell Goods in the Pedlary Way. This was sufficiently prov'd, even upon her Trial, by the Abbotsbury Men, who depos'd, that she was selling her Goods about the Town" (*The Controverted Hard Case*, 13). In fact, nothing about a pedlar's license was ever put into evidence about Squires or her children, nor in any case would possession of such a license have canceled membership in an ethnically based "Clan and Fraternity." Nevertheless, gypsies were a socially despised group. Legal penalties for being a gypsy had been on the books since Elizabethan times and although seldom applied, would not be repealed until 1784, so that some of Squires's supporters may have felt that it would be in her interest to deny that she was one.

Squires herself had very little to say—even more than Canning, she is the sum of her representations by other people, and their accounts often disagree. She was a dark, tall, but stooping, elderly woman, with an estimated age ranging from sixty to eighty, sometimes depicted as exceptionally hearty, since her alibi pictured her as trekking tirelessly across the Dorset and Witshire countryside in mid-winter, and sometimes as touchingly infirm—"Upon account of the great concourse of people in the court, and the faintness of the gypsy, she was carried several times into an adjoining room, to receive the benefit of fresh Air, and was brought into court occasionally as her presence was necessary" ("The Genuine Trial of Elizabeth Canning," in *Canning's Farthing Post*, 165). All accounts do agree that she was an exceptionally ugly woman, with a very large nose and a lower lip swollen and disfigured by scrofula.

Virtue Hall referred to the son and daughter of Mary Squires as John and Katharine, and they were so named without contradiction in their mother's trial, at which they did not testify. Thereafter, however, they are regularly called George and Lucy: the confusion is never addressed, much less resolved. Virtue Hall also identified one of the persons who may have been present in Wells's house at the beginning of January, Judith Natus, as Sarah. The effect of this uncertainty over names is to suggest at least that Virtue Hall's status in the household was quite as marginal as her deposition before Fielding (see chapter 2) implies. Somewhat more speculatively, it can be seen as a kind of inadvertent evidence of the extreme liminality of all of the dubious activities and shifting inhabitants of the house at Enfield Wash—it was unquestionably, as Hall's deposition put it, "a very notorious ill-governed and disorderly house" (*A Clear State*, 46).

Captivity and Escape

Canning's various descriptions of her place of confinement were to play a principal part in the later controversy over her case. Were they either exact or consistent? How much exactness and consistency were required for credibility or, viewed oppositely, might be read as evidence of complicity of some sort? It was and is possible to interpret the evidence in differing ways, and arguments about it continued through the whole time the case was a matter of public interest and thereafter in every later study of it. For Canning's trial John Donoval, a builder, surveyed Mrs. Wells's hayloft and made a model of it to be shown in court. The room measured thirty-five feet, three-and-a-half inches long and nine feet, eight inches wide, and the scale model of it included, "drawn on the wall," such prominent features of the evidence as "the hole for the jack-line, a window on the opposite side to the stairs, another at the end, and a chimney in one corner, a chest of drawers, and saddles, and jack pullies, . . . etc." (*State Trials*, 19: 427). A "Ground Plot . . . of Mother Wells's House, Barn, and Garden" and a "Perspective View of Mother Wells's Kitchen" had already appeared in the *Gentleman's Magazine* in July 1753 (306–7); now, in April 1754 a more elaborate "Plan of Susanna Wells's House, with . . . a Perspective View of Canning's Prison" was printed for sale. All of the items mentioned above are present and labeled in the picture, but the overall effect is of an empty room, certainly not of a room either cluttered with accumulated lumber or suitable for human habitation.

If indeed this was the room in which Canning spent four weeks in January 1753, she came to it initially in darkness, probably doubly confused by her brief exposure to the threats and firelight of the kitchen. At the trial of Wells and Squires, Canning testified that she "saw nothing brought up[, but w]hen day-light appeared, I could see about the room; there was a fire-place and a grate in it, no bed nor bedstead, nothing but hay to lie upon; there was a black pitcher not quite full of water, and about twenty-four pieces of bread . . . about a quartern loaf" (19: 264). Nothing further was asked about Canning's initial impressions of her prison, but she was asked about what she had told her neighbors on the night of her return to her mother:

> I told them I had a jug which was not quite full of water; they asked me how much? and I said, I believed better than a gallon of it: they asked me also, how I got out? and I said, I broke out of the window, and had torn my ear in getting out, which bled all the way coming home.
>
> What things did you observe in this hayloft?—There was a barrel, a saddle, a bason, and a tobacco-mould.
>
> What do you mean by a tobacco-mould?—I mean such a thing as they do up pennyworths of tobacco with.
>
> . . . .
> Had you used to hear anyone in the kitchen?—I heard people sometimes blowing the fire, and passing in and out. There was an-

other room in which I heard a noise at nights, but the house was very quiet in the day-time. (19: 265–67)

Virtue Hall's evidence supported Canning's as to the contents of the room; she added that "about three hours after the young woman was put up, Mary Squires filled the jug with water, and carried it up" (19: 268). Canning denied having "any of [her] fits while in that room," but agreed that she was "fainting and sick" while in captivity (19: 266). If she collapsed into stunned sleep shortly after the door was shut upon her, she could easily have missed the arrival—still in the hours of darkness—of her bread and water.

Because Canning was taken to Enfield Wash on 1 February and there asked to identify not only the person who had robbed her of her stays but the room in which she was held, however, all of her subsequent descriptions, including the one given at Wells's and Squires's trial and her deposition before Fielding, are subject to suspicion—whether or not she actually did so, she was in a position to make her descriptions fit the evidence on the scene at that later date. Thus her report to her neighbors on 29 January and her statement to Alderman Chitty on 31 January ought to provide less potentially tainted evidence, but they, too, are problematic. As I have already related, Canning's return home created a neighborhood uproar—friends and bystanders poured into Mrs. Canning's small dwelling, full of solicitude and questions, but they were not primarily interested in establishing a verifiable description of the place where Canning had been confined. Suffering and survival were the phenomena that preoccupied them, and thus the pitcher and the bread were noticed by everyone while the size and shape of the room and any furnishings it might have possessed irrelevant to Canning's imprisonment were matters of indifference.

It was Canning's former employer, John Wintlebury, who began the process that led to the naming of Wells's house.[1] Referring to the night of Canning's return, he testified:

I took hold of her hand and said, Bet. She said, O Lord, Sir, you don't know what I have gone through! or something to that effect. Said I, You are at home now; and it is to be hoped, you have friends to assist you if you have been used ill. I asked her where she had been? she said, On the Hertfordshire road. I said, How do you know that? she said, she remembered seeing (through some cracks, when she was in the room) the coachman that used to carry things for me.
What coachman had you used to send things by?—By the Royston

or Hertford coach. I asked her, how far she was from London? She said, about ten or eleven miles. Then I said, Pray can you tell whose house you were at? She said, I cannot; but I heard the name Wills, or Wells, by people below stairs. (19: 510)

According to Wintlebury, there were "ten or a dozen people" in the room at the time of this exchange, but as Canning herself was barely audible and not everyone else was silent not everyone heard every part of it. Mrs. Woodward had already heard the Hertford road named but "knowing nothing of [it] asked her no more about it" (19: 508). Mary Myers and James Lord both testified that they had heard Elizabeth mention "Wills or Wells" (19: 505, 491), but so did Robert Scarrat, whose officious role in the case contributed considerably to its difficulties.

Scarrat was by occupation a hartshorn-rasper, presumably thus employed in the manufacture of smelling salts. He had once lived as a servant at Edmonton, near Enfield, but for some time previous to January 1753 he had worked in Old Change and lived and boarded "at Mr. Carlton's, a potter, in Aldermanbury-Postern . . . next door but one" to Elizabeth Canning's mother (19: 501). The "apothecary's maid" brought the news of Elizabeth's return to the Carlton household, and Scarrat, having followed the crisis of her disappearance along with the rest of the neighborhood, went like many others to see the phenomenon for himself. Since the apothecary's man arrived relatively late on the scene, it seems possible too that Scarrat's alerting by his maid was equally late in the evening's events, but a definite chronology of arrivals and questionings is impossible to establish. John Wintlebury definitely denied that it was Scarrat who came to tell him Elizabeth had come home, and while Scarrat might have been in the room when she said to him that she had heard the name "Wills or Wells," "I did not see him then." Asked further, "Do you recollect that Scarrat mentioned Wills or Wells to her?" Wintlebury replied, "To the best of my knowledge he did not" (19: 510).

Scarrat himself, however, at least on 29 January, seems to have felt that he held the key to the mystery of Elizabeth Canning's disappearance. He had, after all, during his servant days at Edmonton, actually visited Wells's house, though he denied ever taking a girl there and was, by the time of Canning's perjury trial, when he had married Mr. Carlton's daughter, evidently eager to present his acquaintance with the house as blandly as possible. Still, he knew the Hertford road, he knew Wells's house, and he "came to pitch upon" it "because I did not know any other house on that road so likely" (19: 498), and likelihood for Scarrat was apparently equivalent to certainty:

> Then you mentioned several things to her very familiarly?—I did.
> What were her answers to them?—Her answers were,—yes,—she believed,—or, she was sure, or to that effect.
> Did you, in the examination of this girl, recollect as many particulars of the house, and about it, as possibly you could?—I did.
> Were you able to describe the house, the road, the pond, etc.—I did not mention the pond, nor nothing in the house. I mentioned the tanner's house, and a little bridge that crosses the brook; and asked her about the road and the field, whether it was ploughed up.
> Did you mention one single particular, to which she answered in the negative?—That question is answered; she said the road was so, and the fields so.
> Did it never occur to you to ask about anything that you knew as not there, in order to be better satisfied, whether she had been there?—I don't know I thought of such a thing. (19: 498–99)

Scarrat denied ever having been in Wells's hayloft; otherwise, there were no necessary limits on the evidence he could inadvertently suggest. I do not myself believe that Scarrat intended anything more than to be helpful—and thereby important—in his intervention in the Canning case. His suggestions, however, had and still have the effect of tainting Canning's own evidence. Ill and exhausted, she may even scarcely have heard him, much less have carefully heeded what he said, but his voice thereafter insistently mingles with hers.

We know remarkably little, then, about the room as Canning perceived it. It was dark when she was thrust into it, and it remained in her memory as dark, although there were two windows and the unfinished ceiling let in more light through chinks in the pantiles of the roof. It was January, however, a month with little daylight, and the snow, too, may well have lain on the roof much of the time as the room was not heated. Certainly the room was cold, and Canning continued to be half naked. She found "an old sort of bed-gown and a handkerchief" lying in "the grate in the chimney" in the room—when the room was visited later there was no grate in the fireplace—and wrapped herself in the former (19: 265), but, questionable as Ramsay and some later writers on the case have found the assertion, she seems to have done little more by way of studying the accoutrements of her prison.

I will consider the limitations of Canning's evidence further when I come to the minutes taken on her case by Alderman Chitty, but there is, meanwhile, one other observation on the room which has been given little or no weight by other writers on the case but which seems to me suggestive. Mary Myers, one of the first neighbors summoned by Canning's mother after her return home, accompanied the party that went to Enfield Wash on 1 February and was in the hayloft when Canning identified it as her prison:

> She took her foot, and put the hay away, and shewed the gentlemen two holes; and said they were in the floor, when she was in it before.
> Had you heard her mention them two holes before?—No, I never did. (19: 506)

For legal purposes, the holes in the floor are negligible—if Canning had sworn to their existence before seeing the room "the gentlemen" might have taken more interest in them, but she does not seem to have been trying to make a case for herself. Instead, transported once more to the room in which she had just spent a month sitting or lying on the floor and still dangerously weak and disordered, she seems to me to look with a certain bewilderment on an otherwise insignificant aspect of the room that had nevertheless sunk surprisingly deeply into her awareness, two small holes in the floor.

So much, and so inconclusively, for the room in which Canning was imprisoned. Many of her critics objected in disbelief to her continuing so long in a place from which escape ultimately proved easy, and Canning herself gave no other reason than her initial belief that "they might let me out" (19: 266). No one asked her how she kept track of time during her isolation, and it is likely that she learned how long she had been gone only after her return, although she later felt able to testify about times and dates. The objection to her story noted by Fielding, "That she should so well have husbanded her small Pittance as to retain some of it till within two days of her Escape" (A Clear State, 13), is thus an overrationalized presentation of Canning's actions that indeed renders them incredible, as if she had first decided to stay in the hayloft for four weeks and then calculated how to divide the available bread and water. Fielding's own analysis, that Canning lay on the floor of the hayloft until "Despair" (18) at length motivated her to escape, now seems more plausible than the objection he is attempting to meet. Escape, in fact, once Canning determined upon it, did turn out to be within reach: "I broke down a board that was nailed down at the inside of a window and got out there" (19: 264). The window was at the north end of the hayloft, just over nine feet from the ground, above a cellar door flush with the wall of the house, and the jump itself, though awkward—"First I got my head out, and kept fast hold by the wall, and got my body out; after that I turned myself round, and jumped into a little narrow place by a lane, with a field behind it"—was not particularly dangerous, as the ground was "soft clay," but the maneuver through the window did catch Canning's ear on some projection, tearing it and causing bleeding (19: 265).

It was, she thought, about four thirty in the afternoon of 29 January, the light waning and the nocturnal household still silent, as good a time as Canning could have chosen for her escape, but she did not linger to study the scene.

> I went on the back-side of the house up a lane, and crossed a little brook, and over two fields, as I think, but I did not take notice how many fields; the path-way brought me by the road-side. Then I went by the road straight to London.
> Did you know the way?—I did not.
> Did you call at any house?—No, I did not. It struck ten o'clock just as I came over Moorfields. I got home about a quarter after to my mother's house in Aldermanbury.
> Did you acquaint anybody with your misfortune coming along?— No, I did not. . . .
>
> [Cross-examination]
> Did you not pass many houses in your way home?—I did, and asked my way of people on the road.
> How came you, being in that deplorable condition, not to go into some house, and relate the hardships you had gone through?—I thought, if I did, may be I might meet some body belonging to that house. (19: 265–66)

This is the account Canning gave at the trial of Squires and Wells, three and a half weeks after her escape—it seems still fresh in her mind, and more questions might have elicited more corroborative detail, but they were not asked. Thus only at her own perjury trial over a year later were three witnesses called who believed they had actually met Canning during her return to London.

The first, Thomas Bennett, had a shop "near Mrs. Wells's

house" and between there and "the ten-mile stone," between four and five o'clock on 29 January, he encountered "a miserable poor wretch." This figure "had neither gown, nor stays, nor cap nor hat on, only a ragged dirty thing, a half-handkerchief like, and a bit of something that reached down below her waist, and no apron on, and her hands lay before her." Recounting his conversation with this person, Bennett said,

> She asked me the way to London; I told her; she said she was affrighted by the tanner's dog. I bid her turn on the right hand, and then on the left, and that would bring her to London. She was going to turn out of the great road into the foot way.
> Whereabouts is the tanner's house?—That is a little nearer London.
> Which way did she come?—I can't tell which way she came; I saw her first coming in there; but she went for London: if she had not spoke to me, she would have gone the wrong way for London. (19: 527)

In his closing argument, prosecuting attorney William Davy first cast doubts on Bennett's evidence as "coming from the mouth of a witness in so low a station of life" whose "appearance" could warrant little credit but then claimed that it was in any case impossibly self-contradictory since Canning could not have known that the dog belonged to the tanner. Bennett, however, was paraphrasing Canning, not quoting her directly, and it seems likely that he himself, knowing the dog to be the tanner's, included the information as if it were self-evident. As often in reading Canning's long trial, one wishes it were even longer, and that someone, probably one of the defense counsel, although they were not always very alert and sometimes not even present, had asked Bennett if Canning herself had used the phrase "the tanner's dog."

Bennett was succeeded on the witness stand by David Dyer, an Enfield laborer who lived near the ten-mile stone and was "chopping some rotten bushes" near the door of his cottage on 29 January when he saw "a poor distressed creature come by me out of the common field, from Mrs. Wells's-ward, for London. . . . [S]he had a thing tied over her head like a white handkerchief, with her hands before her; she walked very weakly. She was a shortish sort of woman, and had a shortish sort of thing about her. I looked at her face as she came by me: I said, Sweetheart, do you want a husband? She did not speak to me" (Trials, 19: 528).

Davy cross-examined Dyer with a view to casting doubt either

on his identification of Canning or on Canning's reported appearance on her arrival at her mother's or both:

> Was she a likely girl in the face?—The girl was a likely girl enough
> to look at, but her clothes were not; she looked as if she wanted
> some victuals.
> You did not mistake her for a blackamoor?—No, I did not.
> Was she not black in the face?—No, she was not.
> Was she fresh-coloured?—No, I did not see any red in her face;
> she looked thin and weakly; she had not much colour.
> Did she look pale in the face?—She looked whitely.
> Then she was not red?—No.
> Nor yet black?—No.
> Then she was white?—Yes.
> Was it pretty late at this time?—It was not dark; I saw her face
> very plain.
> Did you take particular notice of her face?—I did; I took particular
> notice of her, I looked at her very wishfully. [curiously?]
>
> . . . .
>
> Are you sure the prisoner is she?—I am pretty sure; I am partly
> positive; I will not be punctual.
> You say, she had her hands before her?—She had.
> Had she a pretty hand?—I did not handle them; they were as other
> people's are.
> A white hand?—Yes. (19: 529)

The third witness to testify to meeting Elizabeth Canning on
her journey to London was Mary Cobb, a mantua-maker who
claimed to have seen her "between the five and six-mile stones"
(19: 531) and found her a disturbing figure:

> The first sight I had of her, she was getting over a stile, and looked
> at me, and made a slip, but did not fall: she came up directly towards
> me, and looked at me, and I at her: I was afraid and moved slowly. I
> turned about, as she came up to me, and looked at her: I thought she
> would have asked me charity; I put my hand in my pocket, and had
> no half-pence. I had a mind to have spoke to her; but having nothing
> to give her, I did not. I perceived her to have a young face. She
> appeared to be in a very wretched, miserable condition, as ever I saw
> a person in all my life. She walked creeping along. I could not tell
> what to make of it, whether she was afraid of me, or what. (19: 530)

Cobb positively identified Canning as the person she had seen,
although now, over a year later, the points of resemblance she
found worth mentioning were her height—"much about a head
shorter than myself"—and "the tip of her nose" (19: 530). She

also gave a confused account of the times involved in her own occupations that day, resulting in her claiming to have met Canning earlier than Canning could have arrived at that point in her journey, leaving an opening for Davy to observe in his closing argument, "Let her be as slow in walking as she appears in invention, she could not eke out the time so as to meet the defendant" (19: 625). Davy often insinuated that defense witnesses might be perjured and had earlier claimed that Dyer's description of Canning as pale rather than black proved that the woman he saw was not Canning, although Bennett had been asked no questions about the complexion of the woman he spoke to, while Cobb had described her face as "dismal and black, in a dirty way" (19: 531). Now, however, he made an odd concession: "If it were possible to admit [these witnesses] saw any person in the manner they have sworn, it appears, by every circumstance, they all saw one and the same person, and [sic: "but" would make more sense] the evidence of Dyer fully proves, that woman was not the defendant" (19: 625).

If anyone's evidence had that effect, it would probably be Mary Cobb's, since she placed Canning at around five at a spot she could not have reached—provided her own estimate of the time when she left the hayloft was correct—until after six, but all of the time evidence is vague, referring to outdoor encounters between people who certainly did not carry watches.[2] In fact a pale face is compatible with Canning's having been shut up indoors and nearly starved until only a half-hour or hour before she was seen by Bennett and Dyer. If she met Cobb an hour or more later, some of the lividity that made her so horrific an object to James Lord and the rest of Aldermanbury Postern might well be beginning to mark her features, causing Cobb to perceive them as "dismal and black, in a dirty way." All three witnesses saw her movements as creeping, as did her mother later that night, and her hands as held before her or—Mary Cobb—"wrapped up" (19: 531). It seems extremely unlikely—and in spite of the dubious role that claims of probability have played in supporting or undermining other interpretations of the Canning case I find it impossible to state this conclusion in other terms—that Canning invented her story of an escape and ten-mile walk to London but at the same time she claimed that this had occurred some other half-naked young woman was visibly pursuing the same journey. I believe that Bennett, Dyer, and Cobb did meet Elizabeth Canning on the way to London on 29 January. Their evidence does not prove her imprisonment in Well's hayloft, but does place her very nearby, in a visibly distressed condition, and in those respects corroborates her story.

The Friends of Elizabeth Canning

As Canning said at the trial of Squires and Wells, she was too frightened to stop at any strange house on her way to London—the only place that seemed safe to her was home, and she expended nearly all the energy left in her body to arrive there, "e'en almost dead" (Lord, in *State Trials*, 19: 491). It is doubtful whether she had any plan beyond that moment when she lifted the latch and staggered into the room. From that moment, though, "the friends of Elizabeth Canning" came into being.

It is arguable that Canning's friends came to have as much or more control over her life and destiny that ever her kidnappers did. When John Wintlebury, moved by his former maidservant's condition, said encouragingly, "You are at home now, and it is to be hoped, you have friends to assist you if you have been used ill" (19: 510), he was proposing to go beyond the domestic security Canning had regained by her own desperate effort and to seek redress as well.

This might seem to late twentieth-century readers a totally unremarkable sequence of events, but the pattern was by no means automatic in 1753. Although "assault [was] by far the most common form of violence brought before the courts," it was a "category of offense" including a "wide variety of events and behaviors," and it was "commonly treated . . . as though it were a civil action between two disputing parties rather than as a breach of the peace that engaged the public interest" (Beattie, 75–76). This meant in practice that Canning would have to undertake not only the prosecution of the persons who had injured her but all investigation of the crime as well, a considerable commitment of money and time with no guaranteed outcome. Considering that her mother had been able to advertise for her only with help from the neighbors, it becomes obvious that the same sort of help would be required if the assault was to be pursued as a crime. Furthermore, "[a] justice's response to an accusation made before him would depend to a considerable extent on the offense being alleged. Assaults and trespasses and other misdemeanors were frequently settled by the justice's mediation: they were clearly encouraged to reconcile the disputing parties in such cases rather than sending the matter to trial" (Beattie, 268).

Thus, although Canning's physical condition was the incitement to her friends to bring charges, the theft of her stays—and, probably, their rather high valuation at ten shillings, bringing the offense under a capital statute—was the factor that had to be emphasized in order to make the assault charge worthy of legal attention.

On 30 January Elizabeth Canning was visited by the apothecary, who found her so weak he could "scarcely hear her speak," with a faint pulse and cold sweats. Since her bowel functions had ceased during her period of starvation, he administered first "a purging medicine; but her stomach was too weak," causing her to vomit it up, then, that evening, "a glyster [enema]," a process that would be repeated several times before it had satisfactory results (19: 271, 522). On the same day, a paragraph was submitted to the London Daily Advertiser, presumably by Wintlebury and others who had been present at Mrs. Canning's home on the evening of the 29th:

> On Monday night the young woman, who was advertised as left in Houndsditch on New Year's Day last, about nine in the evening, came home to her mother, who lives in Aldermanbury Postern, and gave the following extraordinary account of her being forced away and detained.
>
> She had been at Saltpetre Bank near Rosemary Lane, to see her uncle and aunt, who came with her as far as Houndsditch, in her way home, where she desired them to return. She went from thence into Moorfields by Bethlehem-wall, as the nighest way home; there she was met and attacked by two fellows, who pulled off her hat and gown, cut off her apron, then gagged her, and threatened her with bitter imprecations if she cried out to cut her throat. They then forcibly carried her to Enfield, to a house kept by one mother Wells, near the Wash by the ten mile stone, which place they reached about four o'clock in the morning. The fellows left her in that house, and she has not seen them since. The woman of the house immediately cut off her stays with her own hands, and with the horridest execrations forced her into a room, where she was kept upon bread and water. She broke her way through a window almost naked, and in that wretched condition came home. She left several unhappy young women in the house, whose misfortune she has providentially escaped. (Rpt. in Ramsay 27–28)[3]

This paragraph appeared on 31 January, the same day on which, in a physical state that by now should need no further description, Canning was carried by a body of friends and neighbors before Alderman Thomas Chitty, who later estimated that "about fifty" people (19: 376) were present in the Guildhall's justice room. It is clear from the newspaper paragraph that within hours the identification of Wells's house as Cannings's prison had become a certainty, and it was to secure a warrant against Wells that the application to Chitty was made. Chitty himself was not called at the trial of Wells and Squires, and his testimony to his own actions at Canning's trial thus cannot be checked against any earlier record, a fact he himself reinforced by his statement then that "as it [was] about a year and a half ago, I cannot give a distinct account of it." Alderman Chitty's account is indeed indistinct:

> There were a few notes taken for my own memorandum, which I believe are in court, which are the substance of what passed.
> Were they signed by [Elizabeth Canning]?—No; I took it on paper, as I generally do; but not thinking it would have been the subject of so much inquiry, I did not take it so distinct as I could wish. (He produces a paper.)
> Is this your hand-writing?—It is; this is not what I had taken at that time, but what I took since from that paper I took then of her's, and other persons that were brought before me.
> Then is this the substance of that account of her's you took?—It is. (19: 373)

It would appear that the paper which Chitty produced in court, which was about to be introduced into the trial record under the title, "A Copy of the Minutes taken by Thomas Chitty, upon the Examination of Elizabeth Canning, at Justice-Room, Guild-Hall, January 31, 1753," is not quite what it claims to be but rather a later version of some personal notes now evidently no longer in existence, incorporating not only what Canning said but "other persons" as well, not signed by Canning, or, apparently, read to her for her approval. It is at best a selective summary: "There were a great many questions asked her, which are not down here. There was an examination for I believe near an hour" (19: 375), while the document incorporating its results, which follows, takes about two minutes to read aloud:

> Elizabeth Canning swore, that on last New-year's day, as she was returning from her uncle's, about Saltpetre-bank, as she came along by the dead wall against Bedlam, in Moorfields, about or near ten o'clock at night, she was met by two men, who stripped her, and

robbed her of half-a-guinea, three shillings, and a halfpenny. [An interpolated question and response are omitted here.] A hat from her head; she struggled and made a noise; one stopped her mouth with something like a handkerchief; and swore, if she made any noise or resistance, they would kill her, and then hit her a blow over the head, and stunned her, and forced her along Bishopsgate street, each holding her up under her arms; but did not remember any thing more that passed, and did not come to herself till about half an hour before she came to Enfield-Wash, as she had learned since, to Wells's house there, and there were several persons in the room; they said, she must do as they did, and if so, she should have fine clothes, etc. She said she would not, but would go home, and refused compliance; and then a woman forced her upstairs into a room, and, with a case-knife she had in her hand, cut the lace of her stays, and took her stays away, and told her there was bread and water in the said room, and if she made any noise, she would come in and cut her throat; then went out, and locked the door; and never saw her nor any one of them since, till after her escape; which bread was in quantity about a quarter of a peck loaf in pieces, and three quarters of a gallon of water, or a little more, in a pitcher, as she supposed, on which only she subsisted, and one penny mince-pye she had in her pocket, till she got away, which was on the 29th of January, about half an hour after three o'clock or four in the afternoon, and then made the best of her way to town to her mother's, at the bottom of Aldermanbury. She further said, on inquiry, she had no stool all that time, only made a little water and said, there was an old stool or two, an old table, and an old picture over the chimney, two windows in the room, one fastened up with boards, the other, part ditto and part glass, in which latter she made a hole by removing a pane, and forced part open, and got out on a small shed of boards or pent-house, and so slid down and jumped on the side of a bank on the backside of the house, and so got into the road, and proceeded to her mother's that night, which was about ten o'clock. Her mother said she was faint, so she got her some wine and water, but it would not go down, the passages being swelled, therefore sent to the apothecary for advice. Mr. Lyon, her master, gave her an exceeding good character, and so did her late master, Mr. Wintlebury. (19: 374–75)

This account is less coherent than the deposition Canning gave before Fielding or her testimony at Wells's and Squires's trial, and it also includes details not mentioned in other versions or by anyone testifying to Canning's story as she told it on 29 January—the contents of the room particularly are different, and the "shed of boards" appears nowhere else. Some parts of the story seem jumbled together out of sequence—Canning's being forced along Bishopsgate after being knocked unconscious and her being robbed of her stays after being shoved upstairs—but this is at least as likely to be the product of Chitty's narrative style as of awkward prevarication on Canning's part: Chitty also has evident trouble with pronoun references and sentence structure. Probably the most telling phrase in these minutes, however, is "and never saw her nor any one of them since, till after her escape," words that suggest that Chitty did not actually write down his summary of Canning's evidence until at least after 1 February, when the prosecutorial party, armed with his own warrant (see appendix), descended on Enfield Wash, and, after Canning's identification of her, arrested not Susannah Wells but Mary Squires as the woman with the knife.

Bamber Gascoyne, examining Alderman Chitty for the prosecution at Canning's perjury trial, focused his questions not on the adequacy, or even the date, of Chitty's minutes but on discrepancies which the prosecution now saw as evidence that Canning's entire story was a lie:

> During the time of this examination, did she mention any hay?— She said, there was nothing in the room but those things she had mentioned, not one tittle of hay, neither do I remember what she said she lay upon.
> Did she describe any gypsey, or any remarkable woman?—I asked her, whether she should know the woman again? she said, she believed she should; but she did not make mention of any extraordinary woman doing this.
> Did she say when she drank all her water?—She said, a little water was left when she made her escape. I asked her, whether she knew what the quantity of a quartern loaf was? she said, she did, for her former master kept a public house. I asked her, what sort of bread this was? she said, there were four or five pieces, to the quantity of a quartern loaf.
> Are you sure she said four or five pieces?—I am sure she said four or five, or five or six pieces.
> Mr. Davy. Did she mention any such thing as a tobacco-mould, a bason, a saddle, hay, or a barrel?—Ald. Chitty. I heard of no such things: she said there was nothing in the room but what things she had mentioned: she apprehended then, it might be the woman of the house that had served her thus, but it appears, as it comes out, she had no notion who that woman was. I asked her, whether or no she had seen anybody in all that time? She said, she had not but once; she looked through the key-hole, and saw some one person pass below. (19: 365)

Questioning now focused on "the woman of the house," Susannah Wells, for whom Chitty had issued his warrant, although he now testified that he was "a little unwilling, at this extraordinary account, to grant" it, justifying himself in retrospect as having warned Canning, "Be sure what you say; say nothing but what you can swear to," and concluding on both sides of the question, "and as she swore all to be true, upon this information I granted her a warrant, but told her I could not believe the story she had told me" (19: 375). Chitty did not believe that Canning had mentioned the name of Wells, but that "they had got that name before they came to the justice room" (19: 376), although he could not recollect who had mentioned it. If this is actually what happened—and certainly the name of Wells had already appeared in the London Daily Advertiser paragraph—it does seem questionable for Chitty to have issued a warrant against a person whose name had been produced by processes completely mysterious to him but certainly excluding any contribution of evidence from the only eyewitness present in the justice-room, but whether Chitty's memory is accurate is by no means certain. By the time of Canning's trial the lines between the friends of Elizabeth Canning and her opponents had been drawn with unmistakable clarity, and Chitty both by class and professional associations was on the side of the opponents.

Chitty's evidence was apparently flimsy enough, however, for prosecution counsel to feel that it needed some reinforcement. Thus William Davy included the following dramatically enhanced summation in his closing argument: "Mr. Alderman Chitty swears, she was under examination above an hour, with all her friends, and none else about her;—and that after recounting all the particulars she thought fit to mention, she, apprized of the dangers of omitting any thing, was again asked, 'Whether there was any thing else in the room?' To which she coolly and deliberately answered, 'Nothing but the things in the paper'" (19: 603–4). As Chitty's actual evidence makes clear, of course, there probably was no such exchange, and there certainly was no such paper. William Moreton, Recorder of London, also gave a summary to the jury—standing in, strangely enough, for defense counsel but recommending the jurymen to disregard his personal opinion, should he "accidentally disclose" it—telling them that Alderman Chitty's evidence showed that Canning's "information laid before him . . . differ[ed] in many remarkable circumstances" from her testmony at Wells's and Squires's trial, "both as to the size of the room she was confined in, the furniture of it, as well as the bread and the water she swears she found and left there" (19: 633, 643). Alderman Chitty's minutes, however, make no reference to the size of the room, and his testimony on the number of pieces of bread in it is from memory, not from his notes—although it is not at all obvious in any case why a discrepancy in the reported number of pieces the same quantity of bread was broken into (if it indeed originated with Canning and not with Chitty) could constitute wilful and corrupt perjury, part of a design to incriminate innocent people. If Canning's friends came to define themselves more and more as a group characterized by a considerable skepticism about, even antagonism to, duly constituted authorities, their experience with Alderman Chitty may well have fueled them.

Having obtained the warrant, however, Canning's friends arranged next to take her to Wells's house to identify her prison, confront her kidnappers, and bring the guilty to justice. Considering Canning's physical condition—the first physician to see her, Dr. John Eaton, "was very apprehensive she would die" (State Trials, 19: 522)—this may seem both cruel and dangerous, but the danger of death was in fact a part of the motive for haste: if Canning's captors turned out to have killed her by their treatment, she might at least have identified them before succumbing.

On 1 February, then, the day after their appearance before Alderman Chitty, a large party set off for Enfield Wash. Owing to the variety of their transportation and the badness of the roads, they arrived in at least three successive stages. The first consisted of three men on horseback, John Wintlebury, Robert Scarrat, and Joseph Adamson, an Aldermanbury neighbor who had known Elizabeth Canning "ever since she was big enough to play about her mother's door" but had not seen her for three months prior to 1 February. He had heard of her disappearance before, but learned of her return only on the night of the 31st, "when spending the evening with . . . Mr. Lyon and Mr. Wendleborough [sic], and some other neighbors, they were discoursing of their intention to go to Enfield Wash, in order to search after the house where it was suspected Elizabeth Canning had been confined, and desired him to accompany them."

Wintlebury seems to have had his own horse, but Scarrat and Adamson borrowed the ones they rode; the rest of the party traveled in a hired coach and chaise. All were to rendezvous at the Rose and Crown in Enfield Highway, but since the party on horseback arrived first, they went on to the Sun and Woolpack at Enfield Wash, where they encountered William White, the officer with the warrant, and other peace officers. The group watched until they saw Susannah Wells enter her house, then went across the way and "secured" everyone in the building—"Mary Squires, her reputed son and two daughters, Susannah Wells, Vertue Hall, and a reputed daughter of Susannah Wells." Adamson questioned the Squires family about how long they had lodged there, reporting in his deposition that "they varied in their answers, the son pretending to be a traveler, and to have lodged there accidentally, and all of them denied their having been there above a week" (Appendix 10, *A Refutation*, 9).

William White meanwhile looked over the rest of the house and added Judith Natus, whom he found in the hayloft, to the group in the parlor. When he went up into the hayloft and looked it over, he saw some "hay, and two windows, some saddles, a chest of drawers, an old barrel, a musket, and a tub, and a great deal of lumber that I can't particularly describe." He reported himself as "a little surprized, and thought the girl was mistaken," so he went downstairs and looked under the north window, but although the ground was soft he could find no suggestive impressions on it (19: 395). He did not apparently look for or expect to find a "shed of boards or pent-house."

This first phase of the investigation and arrest took place, according to White, at about nine o'clock in the morning. Wintlebury rode back to encourage the rest of the party and met the coach, which contained Edward Lyon and three goldsmiths, Gawen Nash, Edward Aldridge, and John Hague. Lyon had done carpentry work for the Goldsmiths' Company "for about sixteen years," and was at that time "very intimate" with Nash and Aldridge although less well acquainted with Hague; their relations would be destroyed over the Canning case, but according to Lyon there was discussion but no serious disagreement on 1 February:

> We all came home together in the coach; [Nash] seemed very well satisfied; I could see but very little otherwise.
>   Did he say any thing at all, whether he was satisfied or not?—I cannot say but he did say something, but I cannot recollect what: I can recollect Mr. Hague said, he did not see any grate in the chimney, not pictures in front of it. I said, I never heard that mentioned, but these things are moveables, and may be moved: we had a little talk; after that we had a beef-steak at the Three Crowns at Newington, and were good friends. (19: 468–69)

Lyon and the goldsmiths inspected the hayloft. Since the chaise with Canning in it still had not arrived, the three men with horses had a small dispute over which of them ought to go back and meet it. Wintlebury had already run one errand, so Adamson and Scarrat, who did not otherwise know each other, reluctantly tossed a half-penny to see who would go this time. Adamson, who admitted in court that he had borrowed the horse he was using without leave, was finally obliged to go. At this time White, Wintlebury, Adamson, Scarrat, Lyon, Nash, Hague, and Aldridge had all been over the house and hayloft. None of them, according to their own testimony, saw or, later, remembered quite the same things or recollected Canning's earlier accounts of the place, whether on 29 or 31 January, in quite the same way. Some of them believed they had heard Canning say there was hay in the room; others were surprised by the hay and felt it needed an explanation. Thus one of Canning's attorneys, John Morton, asked Adamson directly, "Did you tell Canning there was hay in the room?" and Adamson replied firmly:

> I did not, either directly or indirectly, from first to last; nor have I asked her a question since, only when we were in the room. After I had spoke to the coachman to make what haste he could, they [the party in the chaise: Canning, her mother, Mrs. Myers, and a Mrs. Garret not otherwise named in the case] asked me if we had taken any people up? I said, we had; and some of the people were uneasy to be gone. Then I asked, what sort of a place was she confined in? She said, an odd, or a wild sort of place; some hay, and something else which I can't remember: I think it was a chimney in the corner.
>
> Did you mention hay to her?—I never did, to my knowledge. I then rode on; and as her master Mr. Lyon and the others were going from the ale-house to Mother Wells's, I halooed to them, and told them what the girl had told me, that is, that there was some hay in the room, and a fire-place, or a chimney, I can't tell which. (19: 516)

Although Lyon believed that Nash seemed to be in agreement with the justice of Canning's complaint on 1 February, changing his mind later, Nash's own account at Canning's trial was quite different. He claimed to have said, "Gentlemen, this cannot be the room, for the girl gave no account of any hay being in the room," before Adamson's ride back to meet the chaise, and then described Adamson's return, "seemingly with a good deal of pleasure, waving his hat with his left hand, and say[ing], We are all right yet, for she says there is a little hay in the room" (19: 382). Davy asked Adamson on cross-examination, "What did you mean, when you came back, in saying, We are all right, shaking your hat?" Adamson replied with some chagrin, "Going through the Wash, my horse got away from me. (I believe I had my hat in my hand.)" He was neither "rejoiced" nor "surprised" by what Canning had told him and reported it simply "because she said so," reminding Davy that he had not himself heard a description of the room but had joined the group at Wintlebury's request: "I had just come off a journey, and took a friend's horse without leave" (19: 519–20).

Again according to White, it was twelve or one o'clock before the chaise arrived. Even if the elapsed time was less, it was certainly long enough for everyone present earlier to handle the evidence, converse with the rest of the party, revisit the Sun and Woolpack, and repeat these activities until both boredom and confusion set in together, while the group shut up in the parlor were free to speculate and, perhaps, begin to plan their defense.

Canning, "wrapped up in two cloaks," and her mother and the baby "sat forward under cover" in the chaise "with the curtains drawn before them," while Mrs. Myers and Mrs. Garret "sate backwards, exposed to the weather" (A Refutation, 7). The journey must have been an additional drain on Canning's depleted stamina. When the chaise arrived at Enfield, Joseph Adamson carried her into the house—"she was then very weak. I took her in my arms like a child"—and "set her on the dresser" in the kitchen (19: 270). Canning was asked no questions at the trial of Squires and Wells about the 1 February trip to Enfield or her identification of Wells's hayloft as her prison and of Mary Squires as her jailer; at her own trial she was, as the defendant, prohibited from testifying. There is thus no direct evidence of her own sensations or observations on 1 February, and there is if anything too much evidence from everyone else. Not only were her own supporters present in force, including some, like the Aldermanbury Postern baker Edward Rossiter and Canning's uncle, Thomas Colley, who seem to have traveled separately from the three distinct groups of the horseback, coach, and chaise parties, but there were besides White an unspecified number of other peace officers, and, by now, quite a crowd of Wells's own neighbors who wanted to see what was happening. When asked, any one of these people might have a different idea of what Canning herself saw or did not see, said or did not say, and the picture that emerges is unsurprisingly incoherent.

It seems, however, that Canning said little or nothing in the kitchen, and certainly did not point out the door to the hayloft. After some interval of confusion—Gawen Nash, a hostile witness, says twenty minutes passed while a pint of wine was fetched and mulled, but his fellow goldsmith, Edward Aldridge, also a prosecution witness, said the time spent in the kitchen was "not long," and that Canning was "faint and ill" (19: 393)—it was decided to carry her into the parlor to see if she could identify the person who had cut her stays off, and there the would-be prosecutors were more successful, although they were also surprised: Canning passed over Susannah Wells and instead, "as soon as she saw Mary Squires," according to Adamson, "charged her with being the person who took a knife out of a drawer, and cut off her stays; and declared, that a person, who was said to be one of the daughters of the said Mary Squires, and . . . Virtue Hall were in the room at the same time. . ." (Appendix 10, *A Refutation*, 9). Aldridge, still testifying for the prosecution, thought she "sp[oke] of her own accord. . . . I saw nobody talk to her then" (19: 393).

Canning was then taken up the main staircase of the house and, according to Adamson, said "she thought they were the stairs she was pushed up, but when she had been in all the [upstairs] chambers, declared, that neither of them was the room wherein she was confined." Canning was then—still in the friendly Adamson's words—"carried into the [hayloft] backwards, and as she was at the top of the steps . . . she looked about it some time, and said, here is more hay in the room than there was when I was confined in it" (Appendix 10, *A Refutation*, 10).

All of these small rooms were, while this sequence of events was being enacted, crowded and noisy. Gawen Nash, as concerned at Canning's trial to question her veracity as Adamson was to support it, testified that it was his idea to show her the whole parlor full of people and ask her to pick out the guilty ones. Mary Squires, he said, "sat on the right hand of the chimney, upon a low chair, almost doubled together, with a black bonnet on; I am sure I could not see her face . . ., but I will not pretend to say what [Canning] could see" (19: 383). Some witnesses—John Hague, Edward Aldridge, William White—were doubtful whether Canning could have seen Squires's face before identifying her; others—Edward Lyon, Robert Scarrat, John Wintlebury—thought she could. What all of them who described Squires at all from their own perspective, however, emphasize is not her strikingly ugly face but her characteristic posture. As Wintlebury put it, "The old gypsey had a little pipe in her hand, sitting crouching, with her head and her knees together; and as Canning looked round, she said, 'That is the woman that cut my stays off'" (19: 511–12).

At Squires's trial, Canning would state that when she was

dragged into the firelit kitchen at four in the morning on 2 January, Squires "was sitting in a chair," and Elizabeth Long, Mrs. Wells's younger daughter and a witness for the prosecution at Canning's trial, would testify in response to the question, "Did she sit upright?—I think she did not, she is not an upright woman." Squires's characteristic posture, in fact, may have been a more identifying feature in Canning's eyes than the grotesque features she seems to have habitually kept partially covered. Thus according to Long, Squires did not at first hear (or at least heed) Canning's accusation and one of her daughters said to her, "'Mother, the young woman says you cut her stays off.' Then she got up, and said to the young woman, 'Young woman you are mistaken. I am a very remarkable woman, and have got the evil [scrofula] in my face, and you may know me by night or by day. She showed her face by putting her hand up to her clout on each side to make her face bare." Davy asked Long, "Did you hear the young woman mention the time of the robbery?" and she replied, "I can't say I did, or any body else" (19: 421). I am unsure why Davy asked this question, but the answer seems to suggest that Squires knew or suspected that she had been accused of a crime that took place at night. If my reading of the situation in the parlor is correct, however, everyone present must have had a good idea of what they might be accused of long before Canning arrived in the chaise. The only element of suspense would have been what identifications she would make.

At any rate, the next step in the proceedings was to carry Canning into the hayloft, which, of course, had already been considerably explored by the earlier arriving members of the party. If it was indeed the place where she had been held prisoner, the occupants of Wells's house had had two days in which to change its appearance, something they might have done most simply by changing its contents. Certainly the room now contained the bed, "made of hay and straw mixed together" (Fortune Natus, in *State Trials*, 19: 398), from which William White found Judith Natus just getting up, and the Natuses would eventually swear that they had slept there for over a month. That very morning, too, Canning's supporters had themselves made changes in their search for clues: Adamson and Colley had pulled the boards down from the north window, and Adamson had "called all the gentlemen to see that it was not in the same condition with the rest of the things in the room, with cobwebs. . . . The wood was fresh split with driving a great nail through it, and appeared as fresh as it could be" (19: 517). Meanwhile, Gawen Nash had discovered a hole in the wall of the hayloft stuffed with hay to keep out the wind; he removed the hay and found that the hole had at one time served for the operation of a jackline and over-looked the kitchen, "except just under it" (19: 380).

Canning's identification of the hayloft as her place of impris-onment was both confirmed and called into question for different witnesses by her response to various questions put to her there. Adamson stood in front of the casement window and asked what could be seen from it, and Canning "described fields, and a hill at some distance, and some trees; [with] some houses to be seen on the left-hand side of the lane" (19: 517). John Hague asked Canning if she remembered the pulley for the jackline on the wall above the hole and Canning said she had never seen it. Hague continued,

> There was an old casement over the chimney that was very dirty and dusty. I said to Canning, Child, did you take this for a picture? she said, No. . . . [S]omebody asked her, if she knew [the tobacco-mold]? she said, she did. There were two women's saddles, and a man's saddle. I asked her if she saw them? she said, she believed there was one; they all appeared to have been there a long while, they were very nasty and dusty. . . . I said to the girl, Zounds, child, I cannot think you were ever here at all.
>
> What answer did she make to that?—She made me none at all. (19: 388–89)

Although Nash, Hague, and Aldridge swore at Canning's trial that they had arrived at complete disbelief in her story on 1 February, they seem not to have argued the point with the rest of the party. Hague, indeed, claimed under oath that "When we were in the coach going home, Mr. Nash, and Mr. Aldridge, and I gave our opinion to Mr. Lyon, . . . [and] he was so angry at it, that he did not speak to us all the way home" (19: 389). But this squares neither with Lyon's testimony about the coach party's shared beefsteak and unimpaired friendship nor with Aldridge's response to the question, "Did Mr. Lyon and you all return very good friends?—They went before justice Tashmaker [sic]; and I was quite tired of the thing. I went to an ale-house, and got some mutton chops, and half a pint of wine: I thought it was not worth hearing" (19: 393).

What certainly happened next, whoever participated and what-ever reservations were felt, was the transportation of the party rounded up in Wells's parlor to be interrogated by a nearby jus-tice of the peace, Merry Tyshemaker, who, according to Fielding, "first examined Elizabeth Canning alone, but without taking any Information in Writing," then examined all of the people brought to him from Wells's house, "and in the End committed the Gipsy Woman and Wells, the former for taking away the Stays from Elizabeth Canning, and the latter for keeping a disorderly House" (*A Clear State*, 29). The other residents of the house, including especially George Squires and Virtue Hall, who "at that Time, absolutely den[ied] that she knew any Thing of the Matter" (*A Clear State*, 30), were set free, and Elizabeth Canning, too, was now free to return home and attempt to recover her health, while her friends, carried on the wave of triumph given impetus by Alderman Chitty's warrant and moved forward by Justice Tyshemaker's commitment of Squires and Wells to Newgate and Clerkenwell Bridewell respectively, were now faced with the practical task of bringing about a successful prosecution.

In order to finance their effort, therefore, they now compiled and published a document entitled "The Case of Elizabeth Canning." Its first two paragraphs recounted the now widely known story of Canning's robbery, abduction, imprisonment, and escape. It then continued more polemically:

> The house of that notorious woman, well known by the name of mother Wells, between Enfield Wash and Waltham Cross, was immediately suspected; and from many circumstances, appears to be the dismal prison of this unhappy sufferer, whose melancholy situation since her miraculous escape, is worthy the compassion and charitable contributions of all public-spirited people, and everyone who has any regard for the safety of their own children and relations, who are equally liable to the same inhuman and cruel usage, as the before-mentioned young person; who since her escape from the house of that monster of a woman, has been in a most deplorable condition; the whole course of nature, having as it were been put out of its usual action; she has through her uncommon and cruel usage, been deprived of the natural effects of food, nothing having passed through her, since being first hurried away in the manner before mentioned, but by the art and indefatigable pains of the physician and apothecary who attended her, till the 7th of February, when she had an urinary evacuation. All these circumstances being duly considered, it is not doubted but a subscription, or contribution will soon be raised, to enable the persons who have undertaken to detect this notorious gang, to prosecute their good intention with the utmost vigour, as such a nest of villains is of the greatest danger to the safety of all his majesty's good subjects.
>
> The truth of the above mentioned facts, we whose names are under written (inhabitants in and about Aldermanbury Postern, who have

known the above Elizabeth Canning from her birth, to have always been a very sober, honest and industrious girl) are ready to attest.

Francis Roberts.
Thomas Miles.
John Marshall.
Robert Gerrard.
Jasper Brydon.
Thomas King.

Cases may had gratis, and donations are taken in at the Royal-Exchange Coffee-House in Threadneedle-Street; at Lloyd's Coffee-House in Lombard-Street; at St. Dunstan's Coffee-House in Fleet-Street; at Mr. Say's, Printer in Newgate-Street, and at Mr. Francis Roberts's in Aldermanbury Postern, who is appointed Treasurer for carrying on the Prosecutions.

Feb. 8th 1753. Virtue Hall, one of the women sworn to by Elizabeth Canning, made a confession before the worshipful Justice Fielding. (Rpt. in Ramsay, 25–27)

While Canning herself continued under medical treatment, at first with her mother, then with Mrs. Woodward, the zealous but loosely organized group who had constituted themselves her "friends," a term of somewhat more public weight then than now, signifying not a group bound by personal affinities but a body of supporters who, in the case especially of a young woman, had also some powers of control and direction, pursued her cause in the manner that seemed best to them. There is no evidence that they consulted Canning, or even her mother, over the actions that they took, but there is also no evidence that either Canning or her mother was ever anything but grateful to them for their efforts. The legal conflict between the one young woman, Elizabeth Canning, on the one side and the two old ones, Mary Squires and Susannah Wells, on the other would be carried out in practice by two increasingly antagonistic and vehement bodies of men, the friends of Elizabeth Canning, or, as they were sometimes called later, the Canningites, and the supporters of Mary Squires, whose identification as a gypsy led to the label "Egyptians." All of the women and none of the men would suffer legally before the battle was over.

The Prosecution and Trial of Mary Squires and Susannah Wells

Canning's friends now consulted a solicitor, Mr. Salt, who advised them to get the opinion of the Magistrate Henry Fielding, and accordingly, on 6 February, Salt visited Fielding with what may have been merely a version of the printed "Case," which was "indorsed at the Top, The Case of Elizabeth Canning for Mr. Fielding's Opinion" (*A Clear State*, 30). Fielding sent a message to Salt that he would take the document along with him on a proposed day's trip to the country and get back to him about it on his return, but Salt persisted, and Fielding's clerk, Joshua Brogden, brought him upstairs. Salt argued that "the Question would be of very little Difficulty" but was urgent because, "being of a criminal Nature, . . . he feared the Parties would make their Escape" (*A Clear State*, 31). Once tea was finished Fielding read over the case, and Mr. Salt requested him to hear Canning's information sworn—although the point is tactfully not made by Fielding, neither Chitty nor Tyshemaker had fully done this, since neither had produced a written and signed deposition—"and added, that it was the very particular Desire of several Gentlemen of that End of the Town, that Vertue Hall might be examined by me relating to her Knowledge of this Affair."

Fielding was initially reluctant to comply. Enfield was a long way from his home territory of Bow Street, and furthermore he held a good professional opinion of Tyshemaker. More importantly for himself he was "almost fatigued to Death" (*A Clear State*, 32) and wanted his holiday, but the combination of Salt's "Importunities" and his own "some Curiosity" and "great Compassion" eventually led him to agree. The next day, therefore, 7 February, Elizabeth Canning was brought to his house in a chair and half carried up the stairs "between two" (*A Clear State*, 33), and her information was read over to her and signed by her with her mark, the initials E. C. On the basis of this document Fielding issued "a Warrant, against all, who should be found resident in the House of the said Wells, as idle and disorderly Persons, and Persons of evil Fame, that they might appear before me, [and] give Security for their good Behaviour; upon which Warrant, Vertue Hall and one Judith Natus were seized and brought before me, both being found at Mother's Wells's" (*A Clear State*, 38). Evidently George Squires and his sisters and Wells's daughter Sarah Howit, perhaps even Fortune Natus, Judith's husband, had by now gone elsewhere.[4]

There is some confusion over when the warrant was served and Hall and Natus questioned. According to *Canning's Magazine*, an anti-Canning source, a newspaper paragraph reported that Hall was apprehended at once, on 8 February, and her questioning begun then, although "by Mr. Fielding himself we are told, she could not be prevailed on to make this Information 'til the 13th or 14th" (40). Hill says, "'Twas on the fourteenth of February, and not before, that she was examined by Mr. Fielding" (*Story . . . Considered*, 36), while Fielding himself dates Hall's deposition 14 February but seems to imply that her examination took place on the same day she was apprehended, though he does not say that it took several days to prevail upon her. Allan Ramsay, however, does quote the *Public Advertiser* of Friday, 9 February, as reporting that Hall had been "under examination from six till twelve at Night [on the 8th] when, after many hard struggles and stout denials of the truth, she at length confessed the whole; by which means it is not doubted, but that all the actors of that cruel scene will be brought to the fate they deserve" (36). Fielding's own account implies one continuous action, immediately subsequent to Hall's apprehension:

They [Hall and Judith Natus] were in my House above an Hour or more before I was at leisure to see them, during which Time, and before I had ever seen Vertue Hall, I was informed [Fielding does not say by whom], that she would confess the whole Matter. When she came before me, she appeared in Tears, and seemed all over in a trembling Condition; upon which I endeavoured to soothe and comfort her: The Words I first spoke to her, as well as I can remember, were these, Child, you need not be under this Fear and Apprehension; if you will tell the whole Truth of this Affair, I will give you my Word and Honour, as far as it is in my Power, to protect you; you shall come to no Manner of Harm. She answered, that she would tell the whole Truth, but desired to have some Time given her to recover from her Fright; upon this, I ordered a Chair to be brought her, and desired her to sit down, and then after some Minutes began to examine her; which I continued doing, in the softest Language and kindest Manner I was able, for a considerable Time, till she had been guilty of so many Prevarications and Contradictions, that I told her I would examine her no longer, but would commit her to Prison, and leave her to stand or fall by the Evidence against her, and at the same Time advised Mr. Salt to prosecute her as a Felon, together with the Gipsy Woman; upon this, she begged I would hear her once more, and said that she would tell the whole Truth, and accounted for her Unwillingness to do it, from the Fears of the Gipsy Woman and Wells. I then asked her a few Questions, which she answered with more Appearance of Truth than she had done before; after which, I recommended to Mr. Salt, to go with her and take her Information in Writing; and at her parting from me, I bid her be a good Girl, and be sure to say neither more nor less than the whole Truth. During this whole Time, there were no less than ten or a dozen Persons of Credit present, who will, I suppose, testify the Truth of this whole Transaction as it is here related. (*A Clear State*, 38–40)

Even if the discrepancy over the date were to be cleared up, this would still seem to be a cavalier proceeding, although Fielding himself obviously saw nothing wrong with it. In the long term, however, it would fuel accusations that Hall's testimony was the result not only of bullying and intimidation but of collusion of the magistrate with Canning's own counsel and supporters. In the short term, meanwhile, it produced what seemed to be very satisfactory confirmation of Canning's whole story:

> The Information of Virtue Hall, late of the Parish of Enfield in the County of Middlesex, Spinster, taken upon Oath this 13th day of February, 1753, before me, Henry Fielding, Esq., one of his Majesty's Justices of the Peace for the County of Middlesex.

This Informant, upon her Oath, saith, That on Tuesday, the second day of January, last past, about four of the Clock in the Morning, a young Woman, whose Name, this Informant hath since heard, is Elizabeth Canning, was brought (without any Gown, Hat, or Apron on) to the House of one Susannah Wells of Enfield Wash, in the County foresaid, Widow, by two Men, the Name of one of whom is John Squires, the reputed Son of one Mary Squires, an old Gypsy Woman, who then, and some little time before, had lodged at the House of the said Susannah Wells, but the Name of the other of the said two Men this Informant knows not, she, this Informant, never having seen him before or since to the best of her Knowledge. And this Informant saith, That when she the said Elizabeth Canning was brought into the Kitchen of the said Wells's House, there were present the said Mary Squires, John Squires, the Man unknown, Katherine Squires, the reputed Daughter of the said Mary Squires, and this Informant; and this Informant does not recollect that any one else was in the said Kitchen at that time: and saith, That immediately upon her the said Elizabeth Canning's being brought in, the said John Squires said, here Mother take this Girl, or used Words to that Effect; and she, the said Mary Squires, asked him where they had brought her from? and John said from Moorfields; and told his said Mother that they had taken her Gown, Apron, Hat, and half a Guinea from her, to the best of this Informant's Recollection and Belief; Whereupon she the said Mary Squires took hold of the said Elizabeth Canning's Hand, and asked her if she would go their Way, or Words to that Effect; and upon the said Elizabeth Canning's answering no, she, the said Mary Squires, took a Knife out of the Drawer of the Dresser in the Kitchen, and therewith cut the Lace of the said Elizabeth Canning's Stays, and took the said Stays away from her, and hung them on the Back of a Chair, and the said Man unknown took the said Cap off the said Elizabeth Canning's Head, and then he, with the said John Squires, went out of Doors with it. And this Informant saith, That quickly after they were gone, she, the said Mary Squires, pushed the said Elizabeth Canning along the Kitchen towards and up a Pair of Stairs leading into a large Back-room like a Loft, called the Workshop, where there was some Hay; and whilst she the said Mary Squires was pushing her the said Elizabeth Canning toward the Stairs, she the said Susannah Wells came into the Kitchen and asked the said Mary Squires what she was going to push the Girl up Stairs for, or Words to that Effect, and to the best of this Informant's Recollection and Belief, the said Mary Squires answered—What is that to you? you have no Business with it. Whereupon the said Susannah Wells directly went out of the Kitchen into an opposite Room called the Parlour, from whence she came, as this Informant believes. And this Informant saith, That the said Mary Squires forced the said Elizabeth Canning up Stairs into the said Workshop, and buttoned the Door at the Bottom of the Stairs in the Kitchen upon her, and confined her there. And this Informant saith, That about two Hours after, a Quantity of Water in an old broken-mouthed large black Jug was carried up the said Stairs, and put down upon the Floor of the said Workshop at the Top of the Stairs, to the best of this Informant's Recollection and Belief. And this Informant saith, soon after the said Elizabeth Canning was so put into the said Workshop, and the said Susannah Wells was returned into the Parlour, the said John Squires returned again into the Kitchen, and took the Stays from off the Chair and went away with the same, and in about an Hour's time returned and went into the Parlour to the said Susannah Wells; he, the said John Squires, came again into the Kitchen, and then this informant went into the Parlour to the said Susannah Wells, and the said Susannah Wells there said to the informant Virtue, the Gipsy Man (meaning the said John Squires) has been telling me that his Mother had cut the Girl's (meaning the said Elizabeth Canning's) Stays off her Back, and that he has got them; and further said I desire you will not make a Clack of it for fear it should be blown, or used Words to that or the like Effect. And this Informant saith, That from the Time of the said Elizabeth Canning being so confined in the Morning of the second day of January in manner as aforesaid, she the said Elizabeth Canning was not missed or discovered to have escaped out of the said Workshop until Wednesday the 31st Day of the same Month of January, as she this Informant verily believes; for that to the best of this Informant's Recollection and Belief, she was the Person that first missed the said Elizabeth Canning thereout. And this Informant saith, That the said

Susannah Wells harboured and continued the said Mary Squires in her aforesaid House from the Time of the said Mary Squires robbing the said Elizabeth Canning of her Stays, until Thursday, the first Day of February last past, when the said Susannah Wells, Sarah, her Daughter, Mary Squires, John Squires, his two sisters, Catherine and Mary Squires, Fortune Natus, and Sarah, his Wife, and this Informant, were apprehended on account thereof, and carried before Justice Tyshemaker. And this Informant said, that Fortune Natus and Sarah his Wife, to the best of this Informant's Recollection and Belief, have lodged in the House of the said Susannah Wells about eleven Weeks next before Monday, the fifth Day of February Instant, and layed on a Bed of Hay spread in the Kitchen at Night, which was in the Daytime pushed up in a Corner thereof, and continued lying there, when at home, until Thursday, the said first Day of February, when, before the said Mr. Tyshemaker, all, except the said Susannah Wells and Mary Squires were discharged, and then that Evening the said Fortune Natus and Sarah, his wife, laid up in the said Workshop where the said Elizabeth Canning had been confined, so that, as this Informant understood, it might be pretended that they had lain in the said Workshop for all the time they had lodged in the said Susannah Wells's House. And saith, That on the Day on which it was discovered that the said Elizabeth Canning had made her Escape out of the said Workshop, by breaking down some Boards slightly affixed across the Window-place, the said Sarah, Daughter of the said Susannah Wells, nailed up the said Window-place again with Boards, so that the same Window-place might not appear to have been broke open. And lastly, this Informant saith, That she, this Informant, hath lived with the said Susannah Wells about a Quarter of a Year last past, and well knows that the said Susannah Wells, during that time, hath kept a very notorious, ill-governed, and disorderly House, and has had the character of doing so for many Years past; and that the said Susannah Wells well knew and was privy to the Confinement of the said Elizabeth Canning.

Sworn before me, this	her
14th February 1753.	Virtue + Hall
H. Fielding.	mark
	(*A Clear State*, 41–47)

Every part of Hall's deposition that can be compared to Canning's either corroborates it exactly or supplements it in a way that supports it, as for instance in "John" Squires's "Here, Mother, take this girl," and Mary Squires's carrying the jug of water upstairs before daybreak. Those parts, which could be known only to Hall, demonstrate Wells's knowledge of Canning's imprisonment and her at least tacit connivance in it—Hall says she was told "not [to] make a Clack of it." For Fielding, Hall's deposition thus completely confirmed Canning's story, and since Hall had not, he believed, been present when Canning gave her evidence to Justice Tyshemaker, how other than by truth could this consistency have been arrived at?

Other writers were not persuaded, and in this case it is easy to see why. Even apart from the discrepancy of date over Hall's examination, she seems certainly to have been frightened by someone, perhaps by figures on both sides of the issue, and even if her anxieties were not allowed to develop from 8 to 14 February, the period from the 1st to the 8th would have been ample for the purpose. Considering the "above fifty" people crowded into the Guildhall for Alderman Chitty's examination of Canning and the "ten or a dozen Persons of Credit" present for no apparent reason while Hall herself was questioned by Fielding and Salt, it seems at least improbable that Justice Tyshemaker should have questioned Canning in conditions of strict privacy. Even if he did, a good deal of more or less coherent repetition of Canning's charges must have gone on during the morning of 1 February, when Canning's friends tramped over Wells's house examining the evidence while the residents clustered in suspense in the parlor. Dr. John Hill drew the most sweeping conclusion: "Can two persons who swear the same thing agree in all Particulars, and yet that thing be false? Yes, certainly, if one has heard the other's Story. As certainly if the same hand drew up both the Informations, and both that swear are perjured" (Story . . . Considered, 37). The last clause does not necessarily follow, but certainly nothing in Virtue Hall's information renders it impossible.

Judith Natus claimed to have slept in Wells's hayloft throughout January. Fielding believed she was lying and warned her to consider "the Truth of what she said, if she intended to give that Evidence at the Old Bailey" (A Clear State, 48), but he could not charge her with perjury since it was merely Hall's word against hers, and she was not in fact ever charged with anything.

Fielding now considered his involvement in the case at an end. He went out of London, perhaps for his deferred holiday, and returned to hear from his clerk "that several Noble Lords had sent to my House in my Absence, desiring to be present at the Examination of the Gipsy Woman" (A Clear State, 49). Fielding had not intended to interview Squires or Wells at all, but he now obligingly arranged to do so, having Mr. Salt bring Canning and Hall as well to re-swear their depositions at the same time—

Hall was easy to lay hands upon as she had been committed to the Gatehouse, a Westminster prison whose keeper was Salt's brother. Her maintenance there—she was not exactly a prisoner, being charged with no crime, but it was evidently undesirable to leave her in Wells's house—was paid for by Canning's friends, a proceeding which will now probably strike most readers as tantamount to witness-tampering and which was later questioned by Canning's enemies (Gascoyne, 9), but which again did not seem extraordinary in the context of the time, no more so than did the presentation of Squires, Wells, Hall, and Canning as in effect an entertainment for "several Gentlemen of Fashion" (A Clear State, 49).

Fielding saw Canning and Hall another time when they appeared before him to "see a Man who was taken on Suspicion of the Robbery"—presumably neither identified him, since no more is said on the subject—and Canning still once more when "some Gentlemen" asked him for advice on how best to lay out some money they had collected for her, and he sent for her to meet with one of these benefactors at his house. In his view, however, the evidence was conclusive and untainted and the matter could safely go to trial without further involvement on his part.

The printed "Case" and newspaper publicity had already created unusual interest in the impending trial, as the various applications to Fielding by "Noble Lords" and charitable gentlemen demonstrate. On 15 February, consequent to Virtue Hall's information, a notice appeared signed by Francis Roberts, the treasurer of the funds raised on Canning's behalf by public appeal, and Mr. Lyon that offered a reward for the apprehension and conviction of "John" Squires and the other, unnamed robber—£10 for the conviction of one, £20 for both—and listed again the places where donations could be left. The conclusion of the notice, "That any Sum, ever so small, would be very acceptable, and be either applied to the carrying on of the Prosecution, or given to the poor Girl as a Recompence for her Virtue, and Miseries she has gone through" (Appendix 7, Canning's Magazine, 77)—establishes a theme that later became central to much of the writing on the case: Canning's sexual purity.

Squires himself, however, was nowhere to be found. It would later be established that he had gone to Dorset, where he was occupied in procuring witnesses for his mother (A Refutation, 10). Three were to testify at her trial and offer an alibi for her whereabouts at the beginning of January, but he himself did not appear in or around the court, and, like Judith Natus, was never actually charged with any crime.

In the meantime Susannah Wells and Mary Squires duly appeared before Fielding and the noble lords and "stoutly denied" any knowledge of Elizabeth Canning and her misfortunes. A highly colored account was sent to the press, perhaps by John Myles, the rather flamboyant solicitor who about this time replaced the more cautious Salt as Canning's friends' chief legal adviser, although the date at which he did so cannot be fixed:[5]

> Mother Wells expressed herself with all the Art and affected Innocence of those wicked Wretches, who are deliberately and methodically taught the methods of evading Justice; and the old Gipsy behaved as a Person traditionally and hereditarily versed in the ancient Egyptian Cunning, making the most religious Protestations of her Innocence; though she was afterwards heard to say, Damn the young Bitch! It is not in the least doubted, but this Affair will be traced to the very Root, and many secret Works of Darkness brought to Light, greatly to the Honour of those publick-spirited and humane Gentlemen, who have supported the Cause of a poor, injured innocent Girl, and done such singular Service to their Country, by their Endeavours to eradicate a gang of desperate and cruel Villains, of the greatest Danger to a civilized Nation. (Rpt. as Appendix 10, dated 16 February 1753, in *Canning's Magazine*, 79).

The trial itself, despite the public excitement kept up at least in part by the widespread distribution of the "Case" even around the court, was necessarily something of an anticlimax. Held on Wednesday, 21 February, with sentencing held over until Monday, the 26th, it can have taken no more than an hour from start to finish, and was typical in length and format of almost all eighteenth-century jury trials:

> Virtually every jury trial . . . began with the prosecutor, who was usually the victim of the offense, telling his [sic] story to the jury. He was followed by the witnesses for the Crown . . . [who] gave their evidence under oath. . . . [T]here was a certain hectic quality produced by interventions from other quarters besides the bench while the prosecution evidence was being given. The prisoner was allowed to ask questions of the witnesses as they gave their evidence. . . . But his [sic] observations on this evidence and his responses to it were meant to come when the prosecution case had been completed. Jurors occasionally intervened too, asking questions or making comments, sometimes directed to the judge but often apparently simply fired at the witness during his testimony. (Beattie, 342–44)

The trial of Mary Squires for assault and theft and of Susannah Wells for "well-knowing" what Squires had done and thereafter harboring and concealing her (*State Trials*, 19: 262) was held at the Session House of the Old Bailey before the Lord Mayor of London, Sir Crisp Gascoyne, and a panel of other justices including the Recorder, William Moreton. No counsel are named either for the prosecution or for the defense and some of the testimony, Mrs. Canning's, Edward Lyon's, and Joseph Adamson's, among others, is reported in large chunks rather than in question and answer form—the latter format indeed predominates but the questioner is seldom identified and at one point repetitive testimony is summarized without even the names of the witnesses being given: "Each of the persons that said they went down to take the prisoners, were asked where they went to? and answered, to Enfield-Wash, the house of the prisoner Wells" (19: 271). The shorthand writer, Thomas Gurney, was asked later, at Canning's trial, how exact his record was of the various witnesses' words. He replied—the specific reference here is to Mrs. Canning—"I will not take upon me to say these are the very words she made use of, or that she made use of no more words; it is my method, if a question brings out an imperfect answer, and is obliged to be asked over again, and the answer comes more strong, I take that down as the proper evidence, and neglect the other. . . . It is not to be expected I should write every unintelligible word that is said by the evidence" (19: 488).

According to J. M. Beattie, as late as "1800 at the Old Bailey something like seven of every ten defendants, including many on trial for their lives, apparently had no counsel to assist them" (375), and this seems to have been the case with Squires and Wells. Elizabeth Long, Wells's younger daughter, did get an attorney, George Talmash, to issue eight subpoenas to witnesses including Fortune and Judith Natus, but none of them were called in the trial, and Talmash himself, asked at Canning's trial if he could explain "why these people did not appear," replied, "No, no more than what they told me; I was concerned no more in it" (19: 425). Long's explanation, accepted without question by most later writers on the case, was that the Canningite mob outside the court intimidated the witnesses. As Arthur Machen luridly put it, "The Canning fever was at the mad height of its delirium, the mobs were furiously for Canning, and the London mob of the seventeen-fifties was a terrible thing" (62). Long herself said that when she came into the yard of the Old Bailey "the people would not let me come in. . . . [S]omebody knowed me to be mother Wells's daugher, and they pushed me out and would not let me come in; they frightened me very much, and I went back again, and up two or three pair of stairs in a house in the Old-Bailey, and heard the mob cry out, Mother Wells's daughter!" Long could not remember, however, all of the potential witnesses she had had subpoenaed, and she was not sure that one of them who was with her, Giles Knight, "was refused being in the yard" when she was (19: 421–22). His own testimony on the point was merely that he was not called. Asked pointedly, "Was it in your power to come in, if you had a mind?" he replied, "I did not know for that: I did not know the way of it" (19: 413), apparently meaning that legal procedures were unfamiliar to him but not suggesting the presence of a dangerous mob.

Fortune Natus, questioned at Canning's trial by prosecution counsel William Davy, testified first that the only thing preventing his testimony at Squires's and Wells's trial was not having been called, "no other reason," leaving Davy to remind him:

> Were you not assaulted?—I was, at the place that turns out of the Old-Bailey yard, three or four times, and I showed my subpoena.
>
> Who assaulted you?—There was a tallish man that kept the gate, pitted very much with the small-pox, he was the only person that turned me out of the yard.
>
> Did any other person use you ill?—There were several other people, but none touched me to turn me out.
>
> Were you alone?—I was with the other witnesses; they stood upon the steps; two or three of them were turned out of the yard.
>
> What were the other witnesses attending for?—For the same as I did.
>
> What are their names?—I cannot say half their names.
>
> Name some of them.—There was the widow Long was one; they wanted to mob her.

At this point, rather belatedly, one of Canning's counsel objected on the grounds that even if defense witnesses had been excluded, "it cannot be proved that [Canning] was privy to it" (19: 402–3). Machen later interpreted Natus's evidence as showing "that the very officers of the Court were either infected with the Canning delirium, or, more probably, heavily bribed by Elizabeth's friends to keep out all witnesses averse from the great cause of purity" (70), but this seems to go far beyond the rather tenuous evidence. Since three West Country witnesses appeared for the defense without any suggestion that they had been intimidated, it seems likely that the tallish man pitted with smallpox was, as Natus describes him, keeping order. Certainly nothing in the record of Squires's and Wells's trial suggests that any expected witnesses were missing, and there is no independent contemporary record of disturbances around the court, although rioting of any magnitude was always a topic of interest to the press. The trial may well strike a twentieth-century reader as a very summary proceeding, with little attention to what we now call the rights of the accused, but it met eighteenth-century standards of fullness and fairness.

Testimony began conventionally with Elizabeth Canning once more recounting her story in response to questions, with one recorded interruption from Mary Squires: "I never saw that witness in my lifetime till this day three weeks" (19: 266). She was succeeded by Virtue Hall, who also repeated substantially the contents of her information before Fielding. Mary Squires interrupted once more—"What day was it that the young woman was robbed?"—and the Court, not Hall, replied, "She says on the morning of the 2nd of January." Squires responded, "I return thanks for telling me, for I am as innocent as the child unborn," and Susannah Wells then asked, "How long were these people (meaning the gypsies) at my house in all, from first to last?" This time Virtue Hall and not the Court answered: "They were there six or seven weeks in all; they had been there about a fortnight before the young woman was brought in" (19: 268).

Hall was followed by Thomas Colley, Mrs. Canning, John Wintlebury, Joseph Adamson, Edward Lyon, Robert Scarrat, Edward Rossiter, Sutherton Backler, and apparently a further group of witnesses who all testified to having gone to Wells's house at Enfield Wash. All of these witnesses, in comparison to Canning and Hall, testified only very briefly, and at this point, three quarters of the way through the printed record, the annotation appears, "Mary Squires said nothing in her defense, but called the following witnesses"—none from Enfield but three-men from Dorset and Wiltshire.

The first, John Gibbons, was the master of the Old Ship public house in Abbotsbury, six miles from Dorchester. He testified that Squires, together with her son and daughter (whom he knew as George and Lucy, not John and Katherine) had come to his house "with handkerchiefs, lawns, muslins, and checks, to sell about town" from 1 January to 9 January. He had kept the Old Ship for two years but had known Squires for three (19: 271–72). He was corroborated by William Clarke, a cordwainer, who had lived in Abbotsbury for seven years and had last seen Mary Squires, whom he too had known for three years, on 10 January, when, as he was "carrying goods" that way, he went along the road to Portisham with the Squires family, whose clothing he described (19: 272–73). Squires's third witness was Thomas Greville, who kept a public house at Coombe, three miles from Salisbury, who said he had seen Mary Squires and "her sister and her brother" on 14 January. "[T]hey sold handkerchiefs, lawns, and such things" and spent one night under his roof. All three witnesses "shewed their subpoenas, as the cause of their coming to give their evidence" (19: 273).

One further witness, John Iniser, who sold fish and oysters around Waltham Cross and Theobalds, near Enfield, testified that he knew Mary Squires very well by sight and had seen her about the neighborhood of Wells's house for three weeks prior to her arrest, not selling goods but telling fortunes, including his (19: 273–74).

It was now time for the defendants to speak for themselves: "Wells being called upon to make her defence, said, As to her character, it was but an indifferent one; that she had an unfortunate husband, who was hanged; and added, she never saw the young woman (meaning E. Canning) till they came to take us up; and as to Squires, she never saw her above a week and a day before they were taken up" (19: 274). The jury, evidently more impressed by the testimony of Canning and Hall than of Gibbons, Clarke, and Greville, pronounced both Squires and Wells guilty, and on Monday, 26 February, five days later, Squires was asked "what she had to say before she received sentence." She responded with a rather rambling statement which notably failed to square with the evidence earlier brought on her behalf:

[O]n New-year's day, I lay at Coombe at the widow Greville's house; the next day I was at Stoptage; there were some people who were cast away, and they came away with me to a little house on the top of the moor, and drank there; there were my son and daughter with me. Coming along Popham-lane, there were some people raking up dung. I drank at the second ale-house in Basingstoke on the Thursday in the New-year week. On the Friday I lay at Bagshot-heath at a little tiney house on the heath. On the Saturday I lay at Old Brentford at Mrs. Edwards's, who sells greens and small-beer. I could have told this before, but one pulled me, and another pulled me, and would not let me speak. I lay at Mrs. Edwards's on the Sunday and Monday, and on the Tuesday or Wednesday after, I came from thence to Mrs. Wells's house at Enfield. (19: 274)

It is unlikely that if Squires had "told this before" it would have helped her case—not only did it conflict immediately with her own alibi witnesses' testimony, it was also not resurrected and supported at Canning's trial over a year later, suggesting that it was at best the product of a confused memory, at worst of intentional obfuscation. The public house at Coombe was kept not by Thomas Greville but by his mother, as Squires herself evidently knew, but Greville himself seems to have known little of the Squires family, representing George and Lucy, who were reported by the Abbotsbury Churchwardens and Overseers of the Poor to be approximately thirty and twenty-six years old respectively, as peers of their elderly mother, who was "about seventy" (Gascoyne, 7). The distances Squires represents herself as traveling in a day, eighteen miles from Coombe to Stoptage, nineteen from Basingstoke to Bagshot, another nineteen from Bagshot to Old Brentford (Appendix 18, *A Refutation*, 21), are remarkable for an elderly woman on foot in mid-winter, particularly with so many pub stops along the way. The only person specifically named besides Thomas Greville's widowed mother is Mrs. Edwards of Old Brentford—the three witnesses who had actually testified for her went unmentioned.

The Canning case stood in no need of further obscurity, but it received it in the wholly gratuitous shape of the calendar reform of 1752, which in that year cut the eleven dates between 2 and 14 September in order to bring England onto the Gregorian system and began the year henceforth on 1 January rather than 25 March. Thus New Christmas, 25 December 1752, and Old Christmas, Friday, 5 January 1753, are distinct but constantly confused and confusing reference points. The days and dates in Squires's statement are compatible with New Style, but only by translating them into a very rough approximation of Old Style could they be made even to come close to Gibbons's, Clarke's, and Greville's dates. It was a confusion which would eventually be used more effectively against Canning's witnesses than against Squires's, but it was with reference to Squires that it surfaced first.

In any case, Squires was now sentenced to death by hanging and Wells to be branded in the hand and imprisoned for six months. The branding was evidently carried out immediately, and though I have been unable to find a contemporary account of it later writers have reconstructed it vividly enough—Lillian de la Torre invokes "the vicious howls of the mob" and reports that "the odour of burning flesh carried the news to the end of the street" (95), which seems unlikely in the case of a brand on the thumb. Both prisoners were returned to Newgate, and probably most observers, most certainly Canning's friends, felt that justice had been done.

ELIZABETH CANNING
From a Sketch taken in the Sessions House During her Tryal

This sketch appears to be the basis for all later images of Canning. Courtesy of The British Museum.

A View of the Front and Back of S. Wells's House at Enfield Wash: where E. Canning deposed, she was confined from y[e] 1st to y[e] 30th of January, 1753. R.R. the great Road to Hertford. L.a. Lane. O. the Window thro' which she said she escaped. W.W. the Loft, her pretended Prison.

Note the cellar door beneath the escape window and the height of the trees behind the house. Courtesy of The British Museum.

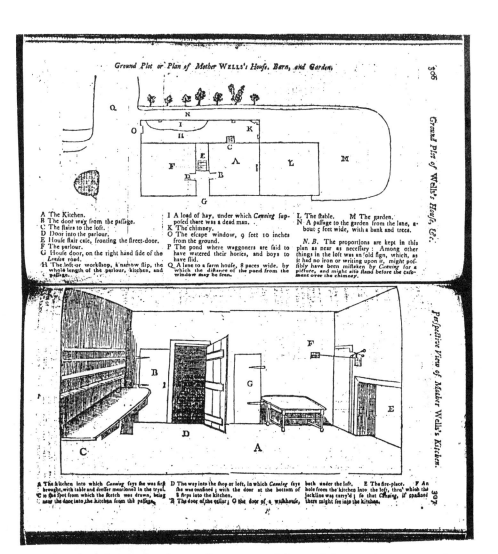

Ground Plot or Plan of Mother WELLS's House, Barn, and Garden.

305

Ground Plot of Wells's House, &c.

A The Kitchen.
B The door way from the passage.
C The stairs to the loft.
D Door into the parlour.
E House stair case, fronting the street-door.
F The parlour.
G House door, on the right hand side of the London road.
H The loft or workshop, a narrow slip, the whole length of the parlour, kitchen, and passage.

I A load of hay, under which *Canning* supposed there was a dead man.
K The chimney.
O The escape window, 9 feet 10 inches from the ground.
P The pond where waggoners are said to have watered their horses, and boys to have slid.
Q A lane to a farm house, 8 paces wide, by which the distance of the pond from the window may be seen.

L The stable.   M The garden.
N A passage to the garden from the lane, about 5 feet wide, with a bank and trees.

N. B. The proportions are kept in this plan as near as necessary: Among other things in the loft was an old sign, which, as it had no iron or writing upon it, might possibly have been mistaken by *Canning* for a picture, and might also stand before the casement over the chimney.

A The kitchen into which *Canning* says she was first brought, with table and dresser mentioned in the tryal.
C is the spot from which the sketch was drawn, being near the door into the kitchen from the passage.
D The way into the shop or loft, in which *Canning* says she was confined; with the door at the bottom of 8 steps into the kitchen.
B The door of the cellar; O the door of a washhouse, both under the loft.   E The fire-place.   F An hole from the kitchen into the loft, thro' which the Jackline was carry'd; so that *Canning*, if stationed there, might see into the kitchen.

Perspective View of Mother Wells's Kitchen.

307

The plan's left and right are the reverse of those of the exterior views in the previous illustration. Courtesy of *Gentleman's Magazine*.

To the Kings Most Excellent Majesty

The Petition of Elizabeth Canning Spinster

Most Humbly Sheweth

That Your Majesties Petitioner submitting herself to Your Majesties Royal Pleasure, prepares to meet the Execution of the Sentence passed upon her, with the Patience and Resignation that become a Dutiful Subject.

That Nevertheless Your Majesties Petitioner humbly hoped She might be favoured with all the alleviations Humanity could Indulge, and all the Liberty the Law can Authorize.

That therefore Your Majesties Petitioner applied by her Friends, to the Contractor for Conveying the Convicts under Sentence of Transportation to Your Majesty's Plantations for leave to be Indulged with a Companion of her own Sex during her Voyage to Maryland, and for her being delivered to and remaining with such persons her Friends should recommend her to, upon her Landing on the Continent of America.

But your Majesties Petitioner receiving for answer, that She should have no such Companion during her Voyage and that She should be Sold as a Slave, and live in a State of Slavery for Seven Years, She now a second time most humbly approaches the Throne of Your most Gracious Majesty and Prays

That Your Majesty would grant such a Respite of her Sentence as to Your Majesty shall seem most meet and allow her Friends (upon their giving proper Security, and paying to the above Contractors such Sum of Money as shall be judged reasonable by any two Justices of the Peace residing within the City of London) the liberty of Transporting her, within a limited time, to some of Your Majesties Plantations or Colonies in America.

And Your Majestys Petitioner as in duty bound, shall ever pray &c

Elizabeth Canning

(We whose Names are Subscribed do humbly Certify and Attest that We have this day attended Elizabeth Canning in Newgate and found her Afflicted with a dangerous Fever and have prescribed for her a Blister and other Suitable Remedies And that We are of Opinion that She cannot at present be Removed without the manifest Hazard of her life

26th June 1754

J Eaton M.D.
David Carroll M.D.
and Members of the
Royal College of Physicians
London.

157

The two surviving specimens of Canning's signature, the evidence used to establish her literacy. Courtesy of the Public Record Office.

To the Kings most Excellent Majesty

The Petition of Elizabeth Canning Spinster

Most humbly Sheweth,

That Your Majesty's Petitioner submitting herself to your Majesty's Royal Pleasure, prepared to meet the Execution of the Sentence passed upon her, with the Patience and Resignation that become a Dutiful Subject.

That nevertheless your Majesty's Petitioner hoped she might enjoy all the Alleviations that common Humanity would indulge her with, and all the Liberty the Law can authorize

That therefore your Majesty's Petitioner applyed, by her Friends, to the Contractors for conveying the Convicts under Sentence of Transportation to your Majesty's Plantations for leave to be indulged with a Companion of her own Sex during her Voyage to Maryland and for ascertaining that freedom which the Laws do not take away upon her landing on the Continent of America.

But Your Majesty's Petitioner receiving for answer that she should have no such Companion during her Voyage, and that she should be sold as a Slave, and live in a State of Slavery for Seven Years, She now a Second time most humbly approaches the Throne of your most Gracious Majesty, and prays,

That Your Majesty would grant such a Respite of her Sentence as to your Majesty shall seem most meet, and allow her Friends upon their giving proper Securitys, the liberty of Transporting her within a limited Time, to some of your Majesty's Plantations in North America.

26th June 1754.

And Your Majesty's Petitioner (as in Duty bound) shall ever Pray &c. Elizabeth Canning

We whose names are subscribed do humbly certify and attest that we have this day attended Elizabeth Canning in Newgate and found her afflicted with a dangerous Fever and have prescribed for her a Blister and other suitable Remedies and that we are of opinion that she cannot at present be removed without the manifest hazard of her Life. H. Eaton M.D. } Members of the College
26th June 1754.   Daniel Cox M.D. } of Physicians

MARY SQUIRES, THE GIPSY OF THE TRAIL, CONTRASTED

Witnesses	Items of Evidence
Farnham (330)	"Very well dressed, as . . . now; . . . clean and fitty . . . not especially active."
Gladman (343)	"She said, No, she was no fortune-teller."
Wake (350)	Prescribed medicine for exciseman who had been exposed to the weather, got him "something hot," and made him buttered toast in the morning.
Wallace (355)	". . . asked me to dine with her."
John Hawkins (358)	"She told us she was no fortune-teller."
	No fortune-telling whatever except the single occasion reported by Aimer.
	Not one instance of offering to tell a fortune.
	Not one instance of seeking china to mend.
	Not one instance of begging.
	Not one instance of maliciousness.
	Not one instance of wandering around alone. (Her walk from Litton to Abbotsbury was in search of George.)
	Not one instance of entering private houses.
	No association with any horse.
	Selected inns rather than cow-houses or Wells-houses.
	No special peculiarities of carriage.
Summary:	AN ELDERLY WOMAN WHO WAS QUIET, CLEAN, ORDERLY, UNOBTRUSIVE, INOFFENSIVE, GOOD-HEARTED, NON-CHINA-MENDING, DISINCLINED TO TELL FORTUNES, AND GIVING TROUBLE TO NONE.

WITH SARAH SQUIRES, THE GIPSY OF ENFIELD

Witnesses	Items of Evidence
Story (542)	"She had a dirty clout or handkerchief over her head."
	"Dress so altered now I could not know them."
Dane (545)	"There was a great hole in the heel of her stocking."
Holding (563)	"She was dressed very poorly." (561) "China to mend."
Sherrard (578)	"Nasty and dirty."
D. Vass (552)	"Same person, but not the same clothes."
Dadwell (555)	". . . asked if we had any china to mend."
Wm. Headland (537)	". . . telling a young man his fortune."
Fenshaw (557)	". . . went up and down telling fortunes."
Basset (568)	Obtained a breakfast from Mrs. Basset and told her fortune.
Johnson (566)	Begged victuals from Mrs. Johnson and solicited china to mend.
Star (550)	Attempted to tell everyone's fortune at the Star home. Got rid of only by "a good piece of chittering."
Kellog (556)	Begged tobacco twice and attempted to tell Rowley his fortune.
S. Vass (564)	Begged tobacco and tea and tried to tell Mrs. Vass's fortune.
M. Gould (560)	"'. . . any china to mend?' I said, 'No.' She said directly, 'You will not live long.'"
Pratt (570)	Accused Pratt of having stolen her horse. Never seen outdoors in company with another. Several testified to the fact that she spoke of having owned a horse and lost him.
	Evidence in profusion of her habit of intruding in homes, begging, seeking china to mend, and attempting to tell fortunes.
Dane (546)	"She went crouching and cringing."
Summary:	A DIRTY, SLOVENLY, CROUCHING, CRINGING, CHINA-MENDING, FORTUNE-TELLING, BEGGARLY, IMPORTUNATE, SPITEFUL, MALICIOUS AND POTENTIALLY STAYS-RIPPING OLD GIPSY HAG.

Barrett Wellington's summary of the evidence leading to his two-gypsy theory in explanation of Squires's alibi. From Barrett R. Wellington, *The Mystery of Elizabeth Canning* (New York: J. Ray Peck, 1940). Reproduced by permission.

Survey of London, 1745. This section shows Canning's route from Salt Petre Bank to Aldermanbury Postern. Printed for the Guildhall Library, 1987.

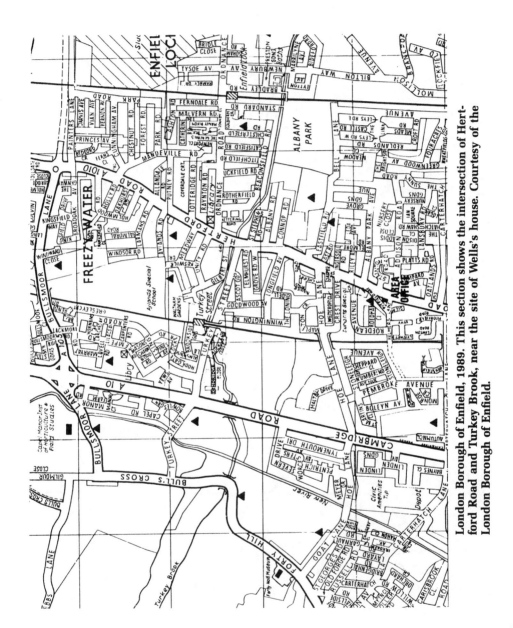

London Borough of Enfield, 1989. This section shows the intersection of Hertford Road and Turkey Brook, near the site of Wells's house. Courtesy of the London Borough of Enfield.

3

The Crime: Second Version

Sir Crisp Gascoyne and Mary Squires's Alibi

On 24 February 1753, between the verdict and the sentence at the trial of Squires and Wells, the Lord Mayor of London, Sir Crisp Gascoyne, directed the solicitor Thomas Ford, who was to act personally for him throughout the case in addition to serving as an officer of the court at the Old Bailey, to write to the minister of the parish church at Abbotsbury, Dorset, for confirmation or contradiction of Gibbons's and Clarke's evidence. As he wrote in his own defense, Gascoyne had found Canning's story unbeliev-able from the outset and the activity of her friends in tracking down the persons who had allegedly victimized her as "perfectly depriv[ing] . . . the poor creature"—Mary Squires specifically, as Gascoyne never manifested a comparable concern for Susannah Wells—"of the mercy of the law." Gascoyne "doubted the whole story, and was dissatisfied with the verdict," and he asserted that other members of the bench whom he could but did not name shared his suspicions (3). Ford accordingly summarized the is-sue and asked the minister, James Harris, to enquire in his parish "[w]here the perjury lies" (5).

Harris did not reply until 5 March, at which time he reported that only his having been away from home when Ford's letter arrived had delayed his response, given his "regard for the Pub-lic, and . . . respect for that great name"—Gascoyne's—invoked by Ford. He went on to provide the information wanted:

> I find that since your writing several of my neighbors have joined in an affidavit fully describing the person of Mary Squires, and proving her to be at Abbotsbury from the 1st of January to the 9th, etc. which affidavit I suppose you have before now. However, I have this morning sent for several of my parish who well know this woman and her companions, one particularly with whom they always lodged till this last time of their coming here. And he tells me, that he has known

this Mary Squires upwards of thirty years—That she, with others of
that name, and some of other names, have in that space of time often
come to his house, sometimes once or twice in a year, at other times
once in two or three years—That they (this Mary Squires and others)
were at his house about three years ago, which was the last time they
were at Abbotsbury till the 1st of January last. That he often saw
them at the house of John Gibbons between the 1st and 9th of
January—That they always went under the denomination of gypsies,
that they had goods (as handkerchiefs, aprons, gowns, etc.) to sell,
that they never wanted money, and always paid him very justly for
what they had. Their being here this last time could be proved by
most of the younger sort in my parish, for as it was Christmas-time
they had dancing almost every night at the house, and the son and
daughter of Squires danced constantly with the people of the town.—
As to the evidences I never knew anything by them but what was
honest, nor do I believe that they would by any means be induced
to give a false evidence. (5)

Harris had been Vicar of Abbotsbury since 1741 and also held
the living of Winterborne Monkton, an even smaller village than
Abbotsbury but considerably nearer Dorchester. His somewhat
disembodied awareness of his parishioners is not unusual for a
respectable eighteenth-century pluralist Anglican clergyman
and is compatible both with his own clerical integrity, a point
much stressed by Gascoyne, and with his being perhaps unfamiliar with much of the detail of everyday life in his spiritual do-
main. It is noteworthy that he names none of his own flock
besides Gibbons in his letter, and that all of his knowledge of
Squires and her family is by report. In a small village, with few
causes of excitement, which this spectacularly ugly woman visited fairly frequently, he had himself apparently never seen or
heard of her prior to Ford's enquiry.

　This is the only letter from Harris to Ford included in Gascoyne's *apologia* to his constituency, although he also printed a
short letter from Harris to Robert Willis, the under-sheriff of
Dorset, dated 27 February. Harris had been tracked down visiting
a friend at Piddletown and wrote to report that he had "reason
to believe from common Report that there were three persons,
who went under the Denomination of Gypsies, at the house of
John Gibbons within my parish, about the time mentioned . . .,
but their Names and persons I was an utter stranger to" (7). This
document adds no information to Harris's first letter to Ford, but
there is a second letter dated 11 March and included in the
bundle of state papers now lodged in the Public Record Office

which is considerably fuller and perhaps more fully revealing of the parish of Abbotsbury and its minister:

> It is the misfortune of my Parish that it consists chiefly of the lower class of People such as Sailors, Fishermen, and mean artificers. So that you will not be surpriz'd at the appearance of the two Evidences now sent up: Who tho' they know little of Mankind, have a just sense of Religion and a due Regard to Truth. . . . How to get these People up to Town was matter of no small Difficulty, for Money is really more than ordinary scarce here on Account of bad Fishing Seasons. And Nothing was to be done without advancing 5 guineas to bear their Expenses up to which Sum I must beg the Favour of you to return for me when you settle with them.

The witnesses had been sent on horseback to Salisbury and thence by post-chaise to satisfy Gascoyne's urgent desire for speed, and Harris hoped he would be pleased: "I believe myself much honoured by the Notice taken of me by so great a Personage as the Lord Mayor of London, and in Return beg you would be so good as to tender his Ld my most dutiful Respects" (State Papers Domestic, George II, Bundle 127).

Gascoyne would go on to make much of the evident impropriety of Canning's friends' public search for witnesses—"Advertisements for evidence (the parent of false evidence) were published in the daily papers, affidavits were taken, *privately taken*" (19)—but saw nothing comparable in his own funding of Squires's alibi witnesses or search for support for her cause. Ultimately thirty-seven witnesses would be brought from a distance to testify at Canning's trial, not counting the Enfield witnesses or the three London goldsmiths, Gawen Nash, John Hague, and Edward Aldridge, who had by that time changed allegiances from Canning to Squires—or Gascoyne, depending on how their altered opinions are interpreted. The expense on witnesses alone, given five guineas for three witnesses sent for only to give a deposition, not to remain in London for the duration of a trial lasting seven days, must have been considerable, certainly at least a hundred pounds. Not surprisingly no records survive to document it, no more than does an accounting of the funds spent on Canning's account.

What does still exist is some indication of the zeal with which Gascoyne pursued Squires's alibi. Having received the assurances of Harris and, from Willis, an affidavit from six Abbotsbury residents, and another from the Churchwardens and Overseers of the Poor in Abbotsbury, about the presence of the Squires family at the Old Ship on the relevant dates, Gascoyne noted that there had also been "laid before him" a certificate from the Churchwardens and other residents of the parish of Coombe Bisset supporting Greville's testimony (8). Gascoyne's first characterization of Canning's friends had been as "credulous, though perhaps good, men" (3); from the point at which all of this evidence was in his hands, his view of them becomes harsher:

> What effect, Gentlemen, would all of the foregoing letters and certificates have had with you? but the question is unnecessary, they had the same with me.
> However, as the girl's friends were pleased to doubt, . . . what was to be done?
> Was this Woman to be executed, or was her identity to be proved?
> If her identity was to be proved, how was this to be done? and at whose expense?
> The Woman and her Family were all utter strangers to me, pennyless and friendless; and it was evident, if I spared the expence, innocent as she appeared, she must suffer. (9)

Gascoyne's bearing of the expenses of Canning's prosecution can thus be assumed from quite early, although he did not mention it again in his own account. What did become a continuing point of reference there was the wilful malice, in his eyes, of Canning's friends: "the Girl's friends were pleased to doubt" (9); "the Girl's friends still doubted" (17); "it was too evident to me and to many others, that at the head of this faction were those, who believed the Girl an impostress, and yet continued to protect her, only in opposition to me" (18); and finally "what part should Canning's friends have taken? of that you will judge; I will only inform you of their actions. THEY STILL PROTECTED THE GIRL.—PROSECUTED THE THREE COUNTRY MEN, AND THIRSTED AFTER THE CONVICT'S BLOOD" (26). In other words, the support of Canning's neighbors and friends for the girl they had known and cared for from childhood and whose abused state on 29 January had horrified them into legal action was now increasingly seen and represented as an intransigeant political attack upon a public official of, in his own eyes at least, outstanding probity and concern for the public good. Gascoyne was clear in his own mind as to the impropriety involved and his duty to resent it:

> If I could submit to these reflections [on his conduct] so far as they regarded myself, yet it becomes me to vindicate your magistrate—It

is not proper that the Lord-Mayor of London should be condemned, where he is innocent.

Nor can I while a perfect justification of every step that I have taken is so easily in my power, suffer a blot to remain upon that year of the City's Administration—a City, amongst it's many other pre-eminent distinctions, at all times heretofore distinguished by the exemplary conduct of its Chief Magistrates. (1)

Gascoyne was something of a self-made man, having begun as a Houndsditch brewer, married the daughter of a wealthy physician, Dr. John Bamber, risen rapidy through the official ranks of the Brewers' Company, and served as alderman and sheriff prior to his term as Lord Mayor. He had been knighted ("on the occasion of presenting an address to the king") in November 1752 (*DNB* s.v. Gascoyne, Crisp), and had further political ambitions. He stood for Parliament in Southwark in April 1754, shortly before Canning's trial, but came in at the bottom of the poll. After the incumbent, William Belcher, who received 797 votes, and William Hammond, who received 597, Gascoyne received 523, a result at once respectable and completely unencouraging (*Gentleman's Magazine*, May 1754, 202). It is unlikely either that his support for Mary Squires and determination to brand Elizabeth Canning a perjuror were the only factors in his defeat or that they played no part in it at all; it is also quite unlikely that he himself saw their role as negligible—as I have already shown, Gascoyne saw the real motivation of Canning's friends as their political opposition to him: they "protected her, as the tool of their politics" (44).

Canning's friends, as might be expected, saw the relationship between their own cause and Gascoyne's differently. Responding directly to the last allegation, they wrote:

If he means that this affair was made *subservient* to disappoint him of his election . . . he is mistaken, for none, who supported the girl either with money or counsel, in *one single instance* took *this* opportunity of improving the liberty frequently taken at elections, or supported the girl that *others* might take it; but as his *popularity* or *unpopularity* did, indeed, in his opinion, *depend* upon the *issue* of this matter, *that* may account for his *inflexible perseverance*; and his *vexation* and *expence* might produce that *implacable resentment*, which would have *pursued* her even to the ship in which she was transported. (*A Refutation*, viii)

Gascoyne and Canning's friends saw different phenomena as

in need of explanation: for the friends, it was Gascoyne's persistence that seemed beyond reason. That he *was* persistent is undeniable. Elizabeth Edwards of Brentford, referred to in Squires's own version of her alibi, testified at Canning's trial that she could fix the date of Squires's stay in her house by the record of the christening of a neighbor's child: "This is a true copy of the register of the child when it was christened. Mr. Gascoyne went himself and took it out of the book" (*State Trials*, 19: 371). This joint evidence of Edwards and Gascoyne, incidentally, "fixed" the date of Mary Squires's stay in Brentford as 22 January, not the 6th as Squires herself had had it, but the discrepancy was not noted in Canning's trial, nor was Edwards asked about it when she was questioned about her role in Squires's alibi. It should be noted that the record of the christening, like other documentary references in the alibi defense, in fact fixes a date in the witness's memory and makes no overt reference to Squires.

While the Abbotsbury witnesses sent up to London by Harris were probably the first Gascoyne questioned, others soon followed: Fortune and Judith Natus, Ezra Whiffin, and Elizabeth Long on 12 March, Mary Landry, John Ford, Melchizedek Arnold, and Abraham Rondeau (testifying to the "very bad character" of John Iniser, whose testimony had placed Mary Squires in Enfield) on the 13th. On the back of Harris's 11 March letter there is a note in Thomas Ford's handwriting: "[Andrew] Wake must attend the Ld. Mayor in London on Monday Morning [probably 25 March] without Fail," (State Papers Domestic, George II, Bundle 127) and on Tuesday, 25 March, the man made his deposition. Wake was a former excise officer now in the army, having been dismissed from the excise for "stamping," which he acknowledged at Canning's trial meant "neglect of duty, writing at home instead of going abroad" (19: 351), but in January 1753 he swore that he had been at Abbotsbury, officiating for another officer who had been taken ill, and had met the Squires family there, lying in the same room with George and borrowing his greatcoat. Only three months had elapsed, but if Wake's memory had suffered he was told by Gascoyne to visit Mary Squires in Newgate—having already done so once, he obligingly went again. Even on the first visit, however, Squires recognized him and reminded him of how he had borrowed her son's coat. As Gascoyne recounted it in his *Address to the Liverymen of the City of London* and Wake, somewhat more haltingly, repeated the account at Canning's trial (23; *State Trials*, 19: 350–51), the story is yet another link in the highly satisfactory chain of evidence placing Mary Squires in the West of England until late in January.

Squires's alibi will naturally be referred to again, especially in the context of my discussion of Canning's trial, but it is worthwhile here to take an extended look at the question of why it carried such conviction for Gascoyne and why it had no such effect on the friends of Canning. In the general deficiency of forensic evidence common to eighteenth-century legal cases, much emphasis necessarily fell on the characters of the persons involved. As Douglas Hay observed some time ago, "Character witnesses were ... extremely important, and very frequently used," although "in character testimony too, the word of a man of property had the greatest weight. Judges respected the evidence of employers, farmers and neighboring gentlemen, not mere neighbors and friends" (42). Canning's friends had the fullest assurance possible to themselves, based on their own extensive personal experience, of her (and her mother's) character, and their belief in her was only reinforced by the notoriety of Susannah Wells and the general ill repute of gypsies, but they were not themselves generally men of wealth or distinguished social position.

Gascoyne, in high contrast, was not only not a neighbor of the Canning family but a leading member of another class altogether. He found Canning's pretensions, and those of her friends, inappropriate to their humble station—associated inextricably for him with a "popular voice" (2) which was by nature hopelessly irrational: "Besides the IMPROBABILITY of the story, many other things conspired to make me think a further inquiry necessary, amongst which were, the antecedent PREJUDICE in mens [sic] minds, the OUTRAGES of the mob . . ., and the CONTRADICTORY EVIDENCE" (4). He was impressed instead with the assurances of gentlemen and public functionaries such as Alderman Chitty, the Reverend Mr. Harris, and Under-Sheriff Willis of Dorset, "whose character for integrity and discernment is too well established to need further mention here" (7). Although he described Mary Squires as "an infirm old woman, a traveling pedler, and said to be one of the people called Gypsies" (2; my italics), he mentioned the even less presentable George Squires and Susannah Wells as infrequently as possible in his account. Compassion for the victim of injustice, Mary Squires, and outrage at the gross deception practiced by her accuser, Elizabeth Canning, are represented by Gascoyne as the parallel and sufficient motives of all of his own actions, and his own actions are presented as having an almost godlike simultaneity with his volitions, with little acknowledgment of the roles played by his instruments, notably Thomas Ford, and, somewhat surprisingly, George Squires.

George had already, after having been named by Virtue Hall as one of the men who had assaulted and robbed Canning, left London and gone to Dorset, whence he had sent Gibbons, Clarke, and, from Coombe in Wiltshire, Greville to provide an alibi for his mother (Gascoyne, 10). Although Gascoyne seems to have believed in the truth of this alibi, he apparently still thought it vulnerable to the threat presented by Canning's friends: "The repeated advertisements presented by her friends for evidence, the dangerous tendency of such invitations to perjury, the influence those temptations *already* had over the minds of the weak and wicked, and the prejudice which still prevailed in her favour, would not suffer me, in a matter of such general concern to public justice, and of such moment to myself, to rest the charge upon the evidence already disclosed." His response was to question George and Lucy Squires with a view to strengthening the alibi evidence, and he was evidently surprised when "they could not [tell the expected story], and I wondered at it, [that] they could only recollect the names of three or four places they had been"— although this interview occurred after George's trip to Abbotsbury and Coombe. Gascoyne turned from the disappointing George to one of those people whose credentials entitled them to more credit, Robert Willis, who "(happening to be in London) was so obliging as, upon his return into the country, to take George Squires with him, in order to ascertain the places he, his mother and sister had quartered at between Abbotsbury and London, and their last three stages before their arrival at Abbotsbury." Putting the best face upon his witness's failure of memory, Gascoyne took George's "readiness to accompany Mr. Willis to shew him the places he could not name" as "a most convincing proof of his innocence" (32).

George Squires would eventually retrace the steps of his mother's alibi "with Mr. Willis, and others, five times" (Davy, in State Trials, 19: 608), so that in his testimony at Canning's trial he was very sure of the sequence through South Parrott, Wynyard's Gap, Lytton, Abbotsbury, Portisham, Ridgeway, Dorchester, Chettle, Martin, Coombe, Salisbury, Basingstoke, Brentford, Page Green, and Enfield, all of which except the last, where there was no need for them, furnished supportive witnesses. Gascoyne's conclusion was simple: "'Tis too much to suppose, Gentlemen, that so many persons inhabiting so many different places, most of them strangers to one another—all of unimpeached character, and totally disinterested, should unite in such a falsehood" (33).

It was, as stated, certainly improbable. On the other hand, there were also problems with George Squires's story. While he could, at least with the aid of Robert Willis, remember the details of lodgings, meals, and companions at all the places named in the alibi, he could not remember how he and his mother and sister had come to South Parrott in the first place, when they had left their base at Newington Butts, in Southwark, how he had received a letter from his illiterate sister Mary summoning the family back to London (neither Mary nor the letter were produced in evidence), or what had been their route from Coombe to Basingstoke, a gap of three days and forty miles. He was at one point in John Morton's cross-examination reduced to the plaint, "I had not a thought of being called to such questions as these" (19: 337).

Lucy Squires, on Morton's insistence, had been sent out of court before George gave his testimony with the expectation that she would be called next to corroborate it. When George left the stand, however, Davy announced:

> We will not call Lucy the sister; she is rather more stupid than her brother, and has not been on the road since their coming to Enfield Wash; and so can give but a very imperfect account of times or places. But we will call Mr. Willis, who went with George Squires about the country since the commencement of this prosecution, in order to ascertain the particular places where Mary Squires and her family travelled through: and Mr. Willis will assign the reason of this man's remembering the times and places from the west with such exactness, when he can recollect so little of the journey of going down. (19: 342)

Willis was duly sworn, but Canning's counsel objected to his evidence as hearsay, as it had presumably originated with George—a position the prosecution would scarcely wish to dispute. Sir Crisp Gascoyne's son Bamber, prosecuting, did indeed argue in favor of hearing Willis's testimony on the grounds that he was "a person of reputation," but Morton insisted that the proper witness was Lucy: "You have shewn there was a person with them in court, (that is Lucy) and you refuse calling her, and now call this man to give an evidence of hearsay only, after a person has been examined an hour and a half, and told you of a person within your lordship's power to call, who he says has been with him on all the journey: will your lordship suffer a third person, that can only tell what this or that man told him upon his making enquiry? We are willing to risk the issue of this trial singly upon the evidence of George and Lucy, examined separately" (19: 342).

The prosecution were not so willing. George had been a problematic witness, and the fear that Lucy might be worse was evidently strong. The judges ruled Willis's testimony inadmissible, the prosecution again seated George and Lucy with their mother, and the procession of alibi witnesses resumed with John Fry, a Litton plasterer who said he had seen Mary Squires on 30 December 1752. In his closing argument Davy assured the jury that "the true and only reason of our not calling [Lucy Squires] is her gross stupidity: . . . we did not think it prudent to risk the credit of any part of our case upon the evidence of such a silly creature," particularly one who had not had the benefit of having her "memory . . . refreshed" as George's had been by going over the route again with the respectable Robert Willis (19: 608).

Gascoyne felt that the alibi evidence "removed all suspicion from the Gypsy," and that the almost equally large number of witnesses who placed her in Enfield, "invited by advertisements, and encouraged by faction," might some of them be "only mistaken" but must "several of them" be "guilty of perjury" (33–34), but in spite of his insistence on his own conclusion, not everyone found the alibi evidence equally impressive. Like George Squires's testimony, it had a tendency to alternate between brilliant illumination where the alibi itself was in question and blank darkness on its surrounding circumstances, as in the case of the "Witness[, probably John Hawkins, who] talked of a Dance he was at, at Gibbons's on the 7th of January, but though he knew well the Gipsey, her Son and Daughter, and saw them there, he neither knew his own Partner, nor any other Women of the Company" (*Copy of a Letter*, 2). The credibility of eyewitness testimony rested on the credibility of the witnesses themselves—on character, in other words, and to establish the character (or lack of it) of seventy-odd witnesses in court was, since it must logically lead to an infinite regress, beyond even Sir Crisp Gascoyne's resources. In any case, Gascoyne felt that Mary Squires's innocence had been quite conclusively vindicated by the evidence produced in her favor by depositions, and he accordingly presented the following memorial to the king, George II:

> May it please your majesty to permit your dutiful subject, the lord mayor of your faithful city of London, with the most profound humil-

ity and respect to represent to your majesty, that before the Trial of Mary Squires, for the robbery of Elizabeth Canning, and of Susannah Wells, as an accessary [sic], many unfair representations were printed and dispersed, which could not fail to excite public prejudice against them.

The fatal consequence whereof, in depriving those unhappy wretches of a material part of their evidence, engaged me, from the high station I have the honour to bear, to express my duty to your majesty, and the public, by making this inquiry.

In which the utmost caution has been observed.—All the witnesses have been strictly, separately, and publicly examined, and their credit well certified.

Many other informations, to the same effect, have been offered; but I declined troubling your majesty with further evidence, as humbly apprehending it totally unnecessary.

In the course of this inquiry, Virtue Hall, a principal witness, voluntarily and publicly retracted the whole of the evidence she gave upon the trial.

To this I presume, by your majesty's leave, to add, that amidst all the examinations I have taken, there has not appeared any variation or inconsistency, or the least circumstance or suspicion, that could lead me to doubt the innocence of those unhappy convicts. (Gascoyne, 26)

On 10 April 1753, Mary Squires's execution was put off for six weeks and the evidence on both sides (Canning's friends having now collected some, too) referred to the Attorney- and Solicitor-General. If Gascoyne was to be sure of his objective, however, he would need more than witnesses to Squires's alibi, however many of them might be amassed and thrown into the scales against Canning's witnesses. Instead, Squires's innocence seemed to require Canning's guilt.

One obvious possible explanation of the conflict between Canning's story and that told by the alibi witnesses, of course, was that Canning had certainly suffered all that she said she did but had unfortunately, because of the circumstances under which she had seen her attackers and her extreme physical debility at the time of her identification of them, fastened the crime on the wrong person, but this was an explanation that satisfied none of her contemporaries, and indeed did not even seem to give them pause. For Canning's friends, for Fielding, for the medical writers on the case, Canning's story was correct in every particular; for Gascoyne, Hill, Ramsay, and a number of unidentified anonymous pamphleteers, it was equally and obviously false. Gascoyne claimed in his defense that he had initially been "willing to think there might possibly be something in [Canning's] story, though aggravated to extravagance and folly in the relating," but at some point—not one very clear in his text but apparently a moment when the alibi evidence, the reluctance of Canning's friends to abandon her cause, and the clamor of "the tongue of insolence and falsehood" directed against himself fused for him into a single certainty—he became convinced that Canning's whole story "was a contrivance, a most wicked and cruel falsity," and that his own "duty and . . . station required" him to prosecute her for perjury. He would have felt himself "under an insuperable load of obloquy" if he had not (18–19).

Sir Crisp Gascoyne, Virtue Hall, and the Goldsmiths

Virtue Hall had been a reluctant witness from the first. Whether her status in Wells's house was lodger, prostitute, drudge, or a combination of the three, the words she uttered at Squires's and Wells's trial, "I was forced to do as they would have me" (State Trials, 19: 268) are almost certainly true. It is also true that when Squires and Wells were taken up she did not gain noticeably in independence. Instead, she and the equally marginal Judith Natus lingered on in Wells's house, and the next event in their lives was their apprehension to appear before Fielding.

Fielding prided himself upon his courtesy to witnesses, however negligible their social standing—"my Memory doth not charge me with having ever insulted the lowest Wretch that hath been brought before me" (A Clear State, 49–50)—but by his own account he did intimidate Hall when, his initial kindness eliciting only "Prevarications and Contradictions," he told her he would turn over her questioning to Salt and "commit her to Prison" (39). It was at this point that she produced the information Fielding found believable, the basis for her testimony at Squires's and Wells's trial, and from this point on that she was "supported [in the Gatehouse] by Canning's friends" (Gascoyne, 9; emphasis in original), a charity in their eyes but subornation of perjury in Gascoyne's and Dr. John Hill's. It was Hill who now, both later claimed, brought her whereabouts to the Lord Mayor's notice: "In the evening of the 6th of March, I received an account from Dr. Hill (whom I never saw before) that Virtue Hall, upon whose oath the robbery had been confirmed, a poor, illiterate, ignorant girl, . . .had the day before discovered to Justice Lediard great signs of uneasiness, and a willingness to declare the truth" (9). In his writings on the case, Hill constructed a dramatic struggle between Good and Evil, Innocence and Guilt, in which Virtue Hall's recantation played a pivotal role. She appears first as "a Person who had been awed by her Ignorance, and Fears, into swearing a Falshood." Then,

> we see her conscious that, by that Oath, she had procured a Sentence of Death against a Person whom she knew to be innocent. . . . Who is there lives, so abandoned, that he can say he never felt a Pang of Conscience? The Ideot, the Atheist would in vain attempt to persuade Men of it. Suppose what she had thus sworn to be false, as there are now a Multiplicity of Proofs that it all was false, what are we to imagine must be the Consequences? Unquestionably, Terror, Anguish, and Remorse; Wishes to speak, and Eagerness to do it. Where is the Wonder then that she should snatch at the first Opportunity; that she should be persuaded to do it, even by the most Uneloquent! Where the Wonder that she should thus go back into that Truth which she had late denied; and when she had confessed the Perjury, declare and testify, for she did much more than declare it, her Heart at Ease from that which had been a Burden and a Distress intolerable and insupportable? (*Story . . . Considered*, 34–35)

Hill's conversion, however, had apparently required some stage management. The *Gentleman's Magazine* for March 1753 had as its opening feature "A Summary of the Case of Elizabeth Canning, containing all the Facts as they have been affirmed, denied, or variously related, during the dispute, whether she is or is not an Impostor, and the Arguments on both sides the Question." This anonymous compilation noted that Fielding's and Hill's pamphlets "contain the substance of all that has yet been published, and . . . do not seem to agree about any single fact," and went on to give a more consecutive account, based on Hill's own writings in the *Daily Advertiser*, of the circumstances of Hall's recantation: "The Dr. says, that he thought her evidence improbable, and told her so.—That Mr. [Justice] Lediard expostulated with her, that she appeared to be in great confusion, in part went back from what she had declared at the tryal, and desired the night *to think upon what she should say further*" (109; emphasis in original).

This was the night of 6 March; while Hall, confronted yet again with persons more powerful than herself who wanted something from her, was thinking, or attempting to think, what to say, Hill was notifying the Lord Mayor that she was ready "to tell the truth." The *Gentleman's Magazine* writer quoted Hill as reporting that she had been "reasoned by [him] into an inclination to" do so. It is doubtful that Virtue Hall, possibly the wretchedest personage to figure in the Canning case, made a sharp distinction between reason and intimidation—Hill himself describes her as motivated by emotion, though he names the emotion remorse. Whatever power was at work, it brought her before the Lord Mayor that same night.

Gascoyne reported that he had not known prior to Hill's message where Hall was, so effectively had Canning's friends concealed her. Now she arrived before him accompanied by Canning's friends—Gascoyne had sent one of his "marshals men," Mr. White, to bring Hall to him, and White claimed that the friends had not been at the Gatehouse when he arrived there, leaving an unstated and undeveloped implication in Gascoyne's account that the friends had some improper source of information on Hall's movements.[1] According to Edward Rossiter, however, Gascoyne himself had, around noon or one o'clock on 6 February, sent to Francis Roberts, the treasurer of the informal group known as Canning's friends, and that Roberts had asked Rossiter and Thomas Myles to go along with him to the Mansion House, where they had been read affidavits Gascoyne had secured from Abbotsbury and the subject of a renewed interrogation of Virtue Hall had been discussed (Appendix 13, *A Refutation*, 11).

Against this background, Rossiter and Myles had gone to the Gatehouse later on the same day and discovered that Hall had already been sent for by the Lord Mayor a quarter of an hour before their arrival. They rushed back to the Mansion House in such haste that they actually arrived there before Hall—"in a coach, attended by two officers and a turnkey"—so that Rossiter, Myles, and Hall entered the room and encountered Sir Crisp Gascoyne together (Appendix 13, *A Refutation*, 12). Gascoyne's and Rossiter's accounts agree that none of Canning's friends were at the Gatehouse when she was collected, but according to Gascoyne White attested "upon his oath" that Hall was there given "the wicked instructions . . ., 'Be sure, Virtue, remember what you swore before, and stand to it'" (10). Who gave them? Gascoyne's agentless passive provides no clues, but his rhetorical echo, "But who to my great surprize came in with her?—Canning's friends! . . . but I was still more surprized to hear White attest . . ." (10), implies that Canning's friends, even if not actually present, were yet somehow responsible.

Canning's friends, however, denied that they had concealed Hall or otherwise practiced any deception. A note in *A Refutation of Sir Crisp Gascoyne's Address* (13) reports that Hall told one of the friends much later that it was a fellow inmate of the Gatehouse who had told her to stand to her oath, while also according to the friends Gascoyne had not asked where she was prior to 6 March. In any case, Rossiter had the day before told Thomas Ford, "clerk of the arraigns" and prime agent for Gascoyne, that Hall was in the Gatehouse and, still according to Rossiter, Ford acknowledged the fact to Gascoyne. As the *Gentleman's Magazine* had observed with reference to Fielding and Hill, Gascoyne and Canning's friends, here represented by Edward Rossiter's lengthy deposition printed as an appendix to the *Refutation*, "do not seem to agree on any one single fact," and the contradictions thicken perhaps most over the recantation of Virtue Hall.

According to Gascoyne, he examined Hall publicly "with all imaginable tenderness," but Hall gave only yes and no answers and those "with all the visible marks of terror and distress, without the least freedom or appearance of truth." At this impasse, "I asked her, if she was desirous to speak to me in another room; and she most readily assented." Cautiously, Gascoyne "desired Sir John Phillips, a gentleman, whose name is sufficient to sanctify what passed," to act as chaperone, and as soon as the three were alone together Hall "burst into a flood of tears, and *confessed that all she had sworn was false;* I asked her why she had not confessed this in the other room—her answer was—the *Friends of Canning were by.*" In no more than fifteen minutes Hall was again in the public room, declaring to all present that her earliest story was entirely false and furthermore that she now felt "great satisfaction . . . at the discharge of this heavy load from her mind" (10; emphasis in original).

Rossiter, as might be expected, recounts this scene quite differently. According to his version, Gascoyne told Hall "she was perjured, and that if she would tell him the truth no harm should come to her from what she said then." Hall "looked about her, and the said Sir Crisp Gascoyne bid her look at him, saying, 'tis I can protect you and not them, will you tell me the truth?" Hall was crying, and someone else suggested that she might speak more freely to Gascoyne if they were alone. Gascoyne then got up, took a candle, and asked both Hall and Phillips to come with him. After, in Rossiter's view, twenty or thirty minutes, Phillips returned to the public room and reported, "Why gentlemen, 'tis even so, this wench . . . has denied all she swore at the Old Bailey; *but there are some difficulties which his lordship cannot yet get over.*" In a few minutes more, Gascoyne and Hall returned, and Hall made her recantation, which no one took down in writing. Rossiter asked permission to question Hall himself and asked her why her previous story had agreed with Canning's. Gascoyne himself replied, "That is easily answered," but Hall said nothing, so William White intervened to report that she had overheard the story when Canning told it to Justice Tyshemaker.

It must by now have been very late. Sir Crisp Gascoyne "sent for the keeper of the Poultry Compter" and committed Virtue Hall to his custody (Appendix 13, *A Refutation*, 12–13; emphasis in original). Like the Gatehouse, the Poultry Compter was a prison, in this case one specially allocated to prisoners committed by the Lord Mayor of London, and although Gascoyne at first secured the promise of Canning's friends to continue to support her in it, the question soon arose for them of exactly what Virtue Hall was being maintained for. She had spoken on oath both in support of and against Canning's story, and her emotional demeanor, though attributed by both sides to the operations of a guilty conscience, can have reassured neither of her reliability as a possible future witness.

Canning's friends initially gave half a guinea a week on Hall's behalf but ceased the allowance when they learned that "particular persons only were permitted to see her." Apparently at the time of writing—late in 1754—the still indigent Hall was living in the Cheshunt Workhouse, for the authors of the *Refutation* report her as declaring to the mistress of that institution that "'she believed Sir Crisp allowed a guinea a week for her board, though she sometimes washed, and employed herself in other drudgery, to keep thoughts out of her head, and prevent her being uneasy'" (14). The "great satisfaction" reported by Gascoyne, if it ever existed, had given way to something less likely to impress a jury: "she did from that hour [6 March 1753], and does now appear terrified and confused; her looks are wild; she starts into sudden passions of rage and weeping, and is as lively a representation of a guilty conscience, as can possibly be conceived" (14). Barring the conclusion, this seems to me a plausible account of Virtue Hall's state as the focus of conflicting and irreconcilable demands from what must all have seemed to her intimidatingly powerful men. Terror and confusion, rage and weeping, may have signified the operations of a guilty conscience, but they may equally have been, and I think even more probably were, only what they were self-evidently, that is, the frustrated emotional expression of a bystander caught up in the irrational inexorabilities of a cause célèbre.

There was a further interrogation before the Lord Mayor on 7 March, reported with the same sort of difference of detail by Gascoyne and by Canning's friends—again it was Rossiter who took the lead in the questioning and recounted the event most fully, although "Counsellor Davy then objected to the asking her questions, which he called CROSS-EXAMINING her" (A Refutation, 14). The Lord Mayor had apparently already retained counsel with a view of Canning's future prosecution. Despite Davy's objection, however, Hall was questioned about her own previous conversations with Rossiter, in which she had reported both that Sarah Howit and Ezra Whiffin had attempted a forgery to prove that Whiffin had been in Wells's hayloft during January and that Mary Squires's daughter had worn an apron similar to the one taken from Canning after the robbery. Now Rossiter asked her how, if these stories were false, she had come to tell them, but Hall's replies seem to have been inconclusive—Gascoyne does not discuss them at all, or the questions that elicited them, while the writers of the Refutation say only that she could give no explanation. It would seem, in fact, that having both confessed to and denied almost everything with which she was confronted Hall was now more of a liability than an asset to both sides.

Gascoyne, indeed was able to make a somewhat theatrical use of her on 30 May 1753, when Mary Squires, having been pardoned by the king, was brought before him to be discharged:

[H]is Lordship sent for Virtue Hall, and in the Presence of a numerous Company, who were met at the Mansion-House on that Occasion, he spoke to Virtue Hall in Words, as near as can be remember'd by one who heard them, to this Effect: "Virtue Hall, you see this Woman Mary Squires, who, by your Evidence, and that of the Prosecutrix Canning, was convicted of a Robbery, and therefore receiv'd Sentence of Death, but has since obtain'd his Majesty's free Pardon; so that what you now say, either for or against her, can no ways affect her; neither have you any Thing to fear from me, or any other Person on Account of any Declaration you shall make at this Time; I desire you therefore to speak freely, and declare before all this Company, whether I ever took you into any private Room to examine you, or us'd any Arguments to persuade you to retract the Evidence you gave against Mary Squires at her Trial; and if the Confession you made before me was not free and voluntary, and without the least Compulsion or Persuasion." To which she made this Answer, "That his Lordship had not us'd any private or indirect Means to prevail with her to make that Confession she then did, which was the Truth, and that her Evidence against Squires on her Trial was False." (*The Controverted Hard Case*, 21–22)

It is difficult to see this exchange as more than a performance under highly controlled circumstances on the Lord Mayor's home ground of the Mansion House. Returning Hall to the stand in the Old Bailey would have been much more risky, and the prosecution at Canning's trial chose not to risk it, a point stressed by John Morton in opening the defense's case:

What, gentlemen, can the absence of this witness be imputed to, but that they were afraid (I do not mean the counsel were afraid, but the prudent management of their cause [i.e., Sir Crisp Gascoyne, always treated with great circumspection by Canning's counsel] was justly afraid) of another solemn and public examination of this witness. I think this observation a just one, or I would not have made it. The gentlemen have rather chose that I should make it, than risk another relapse from Virtue Hall. But, perhaps, whatever may be your verdict, her recantation will still serve for cases and newspapers. (19: 449)

The Recorder, consistently on the side of the prosecution during Canning's trial, interrupted Morton to assert that Hall, as she had "already discredited herself," could not be a witness, but Morton insisted on his point: "Courts of justice can take no notice of private recantations, or of discoveries supposed to be made to magistrates in private" (19: 449–50). Another of Canning's counsel, George Nares, emphasizing the importance of Hall's missing testimony to Canning's case, went beyond Morton to point out that "the methods that were used to bring about this recantation" ought also to be investigated under oath—"I am sure, by the knowledge I have of the worshipful magistrate, he could never intend to seduce her by rewards and promises: but this may be the case; the poor girl might weakly imagine, that, if she altered her evidence, she might have some rewards" (19: 455). Nares attempted later in the trial to call Justice Tyshemaker to show that Hall was not present when Canning swore her information before him, but Davy objected strongly—"With your lordship's leave, I will say, the jury are not to know that such a person ever existed as Virtue Hall"—and the judges ruled in favor of the prosecution on the grounds that "The perjury is assigned upon the evidence [Elizabeth Canning] gave at the Old-Bailey," and that therefore her deposition before Tyshemaker was "no way in issue in the case" (19: 590).

In his concluding statement for the prosecution, Davy said that Hall had in fact "attended the trial every day" and taunted the defense for failing to call her on their own account. He continued to assert that in his view Hall was not an admissible witness but that in any case he could not, "as an honest man," have exposed her to a charge of perjury for her earlier testimony, although it is unclear to me how altered testimony now would have made her more vulnerable than she already was. He added a third argument—who would believe Hall anyhow, whatever she said (19: 609–12)?

If Hall was indeed in court, these occasional references to herself must have seemed threatening. It was not possible for her to satisfy everyone, and it was all too obvious that even those whose demands she had temporarily appeased held her in suspicion and contempt. Our last glimpse of her is the report from the Cheshunt Workhouse, where we hear of her taking to laundry work in an effort to "keep thoughts out of her head" while her contradictory evidence went on to live a life of its own in "cases and newspapers." It was a fate not dissimilar to Canning's own, and a history very unlike that of the three goldsmiths, Nash, Hague, and Aldridge, who made by contrast with Hall a movement from Canning's side of the case to Gascoyne's, which apparently only enhanced their social standing and self-esteem.[2]

According to the three goldsmiths' testimony at Canning's trial, all of them had come to disbelieve her story on 1 February, the day of the visit to Enfield on which Squires and Wells were taken into custody and charged. Not only had they not expressed their disbelief to Justice Tyshemaker, however, they had also all three sat in court during Squires's and Wells's trial and heard them convicted on 21 February and sentenced on 26 February still without registering any opposition to what, by their own account, they believed to be a gross miscarriage of justice. It was not until 23 March, in fact, after Sir Crisp Gascoyne's resolve to reverse Mary Squires's conviction was well known, that they came to the Mansion House to swear a joint deposition on what they had allegedly concluded over seven weeks earlier. Gascoyne had already issued a warrant for Canning's arrest, but he made the most of the somewhat belated action of these "three worthy ciizens" as having been undertaken "voluntarily" and "[s]oon after the trial" (Gascoyne, 20).

Nash seems to have been the leading spirit among the three.

He, like the others, had not known Canning previously, but he was acquainted with her master, Edward Lyon, and went to see him to enquire about the story as soon as he heard it, in time to go along with the group who carried Canning before Alderman Chitty. It was Nash, in fact, who swore that Canning had described the room in which she was held as "a little square dark room" (19: 377), a description which does not appear in Chitty's version of Canning's information, and Nash, too, who swore that "she gave no account of any hay" being in the room (19: 382). Hague and Aldridge were enlisted by Nash, and all their information about the room prior to their own arrival at Wells's house came from him. Nevertheless, their information before the Lord Mayor concluded roundly:

> all these informants say, that although they had embarked in this affair at their own expense, as friends to public justice, and out of tenderness to a poor girl whom they believed was injured, yet from the satisfaction they received at the said Mrs. Wells's, from the appearance of things not at all answering the description that had been given, they concluded, that the story of the said Elizabeth Canning was impossible to be true, that they themselves had been imposed upon, and therefore they desisted to assist in the prosecution. (Gascoyne, 21)

The obvious question occurs, if the 23 March deposition is not in fact greatly informed by hindsight, why they had not in fact actively assisted in the defense of Squires and Wells, and at Canning's trial all of them were asked it. Gawen Nash said he had been in court during Canning's testimony but had left early to act as butler to "a very large feast at Goldsmith's Hall," where he had responsibility for "three or four thousand pounds worth of plate"—in any case, he had thought Canning's story so improbable that Squires would not be convicted. Asked, "How came you not to acquaint the Court, that you, of your own knowledge, knew [Canning] was guilty of perjury?" Nash replied, "I can give no reason for that." The examination continued: "What conduct did you pursue after the conviction of Squires, in order to atone for your not giving evidence for her?—Some time after that, I heard the old woman had a respite; I immediately waited on my lord mayor, and told him, I believed I could let him into the whole affair, as well as any man could" (19: 384–85). This does seem feeble, but if Nash did not change his mind as quickly as he later came to believe, his inaction makes more sense—he did nothing in Squires's defense because he still thought her guilty. On 10 February, in fact, a week and a half after the trip to Enfield, he wrote to Lyon, "I am informed by Mr. Aldridg, whoe has been at Enfield that if a person appointed their to recivvive contributions some money would be raised in that place for the unhapy poor girl. I wish you success, and am yours Gawen Nash" (*A Refutation*, 8; verbatim). Nash acknowledged the letter under oath when Morton produced it in court (19: 386).

Aldridge had a nephew (also named Edward Aldridge) living at Enfield Wash and also had some acquaintance with the Howards, Wells's near neighbors, who allowed the Wells household use of their pump. He acknowledged that he had returned to the neighborhood after 1 February and carried copies of the printed "Case of Elizabeth Canning" with him, but he did so reluctantly—"I only left the paper with him [his nephew]; I did not encourage the case either one way or the other." Asked how long after Squires's conviction—he, like Nash, had missed part of the trial in order to attend the Goldsmiths' dinner—it had been before he went to Gascoyne, he responded that "Mr. Nash and Mr. Hague had been there two or three times before I had been there, and they desired me to go with them." Had it not been "a matter of justice" for him to go? "It was no business of mine to trouble my head about it to go" (19: 394). By the time of Canning's trial, Aldridge was certainly dissociating himself from the case as completely as he credibly could, but it seems likely that, in reporting himself as inactive earlier, he was displacing his present feelings onto an earlier and more involved self. Both William Howard and his wife testified that he had come to Enfield twice after the first of February, that he not only brought a copy of the printed "Case" but "recommended a contribution on [Canning's] behalf." According to Howard, "He said, he thought the girl had been used ill, and he did believe she was there; but he was not quite clear in her description of the room" (19: 533). Nevertheless, according to Alice Howard, Aldridge was "as sure as he was alive" and urged her and her husband to solicit subscriptions from their neighbors, even going so far as to add that if they did not, "the gentlemen in London would not think we wanted to get rid of the bad company we had about us" (19: 534).

Of the three members of the Goldsmiths' Company, Hague was probably the most vehement in his assertions that he had disbelieved Canning from the first of February onward but he also gave the strangest explanation for his failure to speak for Squires in court:

Seeing such innocency in her [Canning] there [at Enfield], and when in court to hear her swearing such a thing that I thought to be as false as the gospel is true, I protest I had not power to speak: I believed she was perjured in all she said; that is the whole reason why I did not speak: but had I had spirits, I would have spoke.

After Squires was convicted, did you approve of your own conduct?—Upon my word, Sir, I was not easy upon my being silent. I went of my own free will before my lord-mayor, and gave an account of what I knew, the same as now. . . .

How long after the trial was it, that you went to my lord mayor?—It was about a fortnight or three weeks after. (19: 389)

Nevertheless, the date of Nash, Aldridge, and Hague's joint deposition is 23 March and even if Nash and Hague spoke to Gascoyne sooner, they certainly did not give any evidence through their actions either that they had come to disbelieve Canning's story as soon as they later claimed they had or that they in any way had acted to contradict her or to save Mary Squires. Certainly none of them mentioned fear of a mob as affecting their actions, even though Arthur Machen would later assert without qualification that "Hague and Nash were frightened out of their lives" (62). On the whole it was not at all surprising that when Edward Lyon saw Gawen Nash in court at Squires's trial, he assumed that Nash had come to "give evidence gainst the gypsey" (19: 473). For Sir Crisp Gascoyne, however, the sequence first of alibi evidence, then of Virtue Hall's recantation, and the supporting testimony of Nash and his colleagues was conclusive, so much so that he could no longer believe in the sincerity—or even the mere credulity—of Canning's supporters: "They were determined not to be convinced, *or not to appear so*"; they "*still affected to doubt*" (22–23; emphasis in original).

Canning's Supporters

Canning's friends had initially banded together for the purpose of prosecuting her attackers, not as the proprietors of a legal defense fund. There is nothing to indicate that the agitation in defense of Mary Squires after her conviction came as anything but a complete surprise to them, much less that they had in some way planned a prolonged case in order to raise more money, as some anti-Canning pamphleteers suggested. The anonymous author of *Canning's Magazine; or, A Review of the Whole Evidence that has been hitherto offered before or against Elizabeth*

Canning and Mary Squires gave Dr. John Hill's publicizing of the alibi evidence as the cause of "a Desertion of some Friends, a Wavering in others, and, what was of more *fatal Consequence,* a *Diminution of Subscriptions,*" and charged that the publication of Fielding's *A Clear State of the Case of Elizabeth Canning* was undertaken to counteract all of these problems (4–5).

Fielding, however, claimed to be writing in reluctant response to the "inflammatory Libels . . . in News Papers and Pamphlets" which had in his view attempted "to establish a kind of a Court of Appeal . . . in the Bookseller's Shop" (5). The reference is vague but is almost certainly aimed at Hill's initial Inspector essays on the case, which appeared in the *London Daily Advertiser.* The first of these was dated 9 March and met with such an eager public response that the paper sold out and had to reprint the piece on the following day. By the 12th the editors were prefacing Hill's regular column with an announcement that reprints of the controversial essay were available, and by the 14th, along with Hill's second essay on the case, they were providing a list of booksellers where it could be found. The presumably more fastidious Fielding commented, "[S]urely when such methods have been used to mislead the Public, . . . it can require little Apology to make use of the same Means to refute so iniquitous an Attempt" (5). *Canning's Magazine,* however, praised Hill's response to Fielding:

> [I]rresistible as [Fielding's] Arguments were then thought, Dr. Hill boldly dared to enter the lists with this redoubtable Writer, and fearless of Censure ventured to employ his Pen, that Pen, that has been so long and so eminently distinguished in the polite and literary world, in Vindication of a poor, abject, despicable old Gipsy! . . . Warm Passions, a quick Conception, and a ready Expression characterize most of the Doctor's Productions. He writes much because it is *necessary* he should, consequently Correctness and Regularity are less studied. (13)

Hill, indeed, may have produced *Canning's Magazine* himself, or had a hand in it. According to Isaac Disraeli's 1814 compilation of literary gossip, *The Calamities and Quarrels of Authors,* Hill "had written himself down to so low a degree, that whenever he had a work for publication, his employers stipulated, in their contracts, that the author should conceal his name" (374), but this must be to some degree an exaggeration. Hill did publish under his own name as well as anonymously, and on a remarkable range of subjects. In 1753, as well as *The Story of Elizabeth*

Canning Considered, he produced not only his daily Inspector columns and other works lumped together by his biographer G. S. Rousseau as "Grub Street" but also *The Conduct of Married Life* and *Observations on the Greek and Latin Classics* (Rousseau, xxix), although his area of actual expertise was—still loosely—the biological sciences.

Hill and Fielding did not differ only over their interpretations of the Canning case. In May 1752 Hill had been publicly assaulted at Ranelagh by a young Irishman named Mountefort Brown whom he had lampooned in the Inspector a few days earlier. According to Rousseau, Brown pulled off Hill's wig and kicked him, and Hill both told the story in the Inspector and "reported regularly on his health" (49). When the case came before Fielding, however, "Hill's physicians declared him healthy" and no verdict or damages were declared (49), thus making Fielding a partner with Brown in Hill's humiliation— the story can also be followed in Bertrand Goldgar's edition of *The Covent-Garden Journal*. Certainly the Canning affair provided Hill not only with an extremely popular topic but with an occasion for an attack on Fielding as well—at first simply as a magistrate concerned in the case but later as the author of the first commercial publication in Canning's defense, *A Clear State of the Case of Elizabeth Canning*, which appeared at some time shortly after 18 March 1753, when its concluding Postscript was dated, at a time when Hill's and Gascoyne's activities on behalf of Squires, most notably the securing of Virtue Hall's recantation, were already well under way and publicly known, primarily through Hill.

Fielding's discreetly general indictment of Squires's supporters, however, seems to be aimed as much at the Lord Mayor as at Hill: "Men who have applauded themselves, and have been applauded by others, for their great Penetration and Discernment, will struggle very hard before they give up their Title to such Commendation. Though they, perhaps, heard the Cause at first with the Impartiality of upright Judges, when they have once given their Opinion, they are too apt to become warm Advocates, and even interested Parties in Defence of that Opinion" (6–7). Gascoyne, of course, not Hill, was the one who had been a judge at Squires's trial and who had since become her advocate, with Hill's assistance and warm applause. Fielding now called for "the Government's authorising some very capable and very indifferent Persons, to examine into" both Canning's story and Squires's alibi (55–56), a proposal that moved Hill to fury as an aspersion upon the Lord Mayor's objectivity: "He is of no Side or Party; nor has (so I have often heard him say, and so I am convinced) the least Concern which way the Truth shall be determined. . . . Who, Sir, are you, that are thus dictating unto the Government? Retire into yourself, and know your Station! Who is more *capable*, or who more *indifferent* than this generous Magistrate?" (44–45). Gascoyne as "*Supreme Magistrate* of that Court in which the Cause was tried [was] the proper Person for this Examination," and indeed he had "already finished it" (45)—any further investigation would be an insult. "The Lord Mayor . . . [had been] convinced by Proof of what he first guessed by Reason," and he would, "as soon as that is proper, convince all the World" (50).

Hill's pamphlet appeared very shortly after Fielding's, around the end of March, and the case did indeed attract government attention, although not the sort of impartial investigation Fielding had called for. Evidently the Secretary of State, the Duke of Newcastle, asked Fielding for any affidavits in his possession, as Fielding is on record as replying on 14 April 1753, that although he had none himself he had sent his clerk to "the Attorney in the City"—probably John Myles—who he believed did. On 27 April, however, apparently after a second request from Newcastle, he was obliged to report that though he had sent for the affidavits repeatedly none so far had been forthcoming:

> but as I have no Compulsory Power over them [Canning's friends] I cannot answer for their Behaviour, which indeed I have long disliked and have therefore long declined giving them any advice, nor would I unless in Obedience to your Grace have anything to say to a set of the most obstinate fools I ever saw, and who seem to me rather to act from a Spleen against my Lord Mayor, than from any motive of Protecting Innocence, tho' that was certainly their motive at first. In Truth, if I am not deceived, I suspect that they desire that the gipsey should be pardoned, and then to convince the World that she was guilty in order to cast the greater Reflection on him who was principally instrumental in obtaining such Pardon. (Quoted in Lang, 30)

From this point indeed, Fielding seems to have dissociated himself completely from the case. His second letter to Newcastle strongly implies that although his belief in Canning was unaltered, her attorneys and managers were people he could not comfortably work with, particularly since he seems to have shared Gascoyne's view that political opposition to him had become as central to their case as support for Canning. Besides, Fielding's health was rapidly worsening. He was about to leave London in August 1753 for Bath, when he was requested by Newcastle to advise on a scheme for the suppression of robbers; he stayed through the winter and in the following year retired first to his country house at Ealing and then to Lisbon, where he died in October 1754. His name would continue to figure in accounts of the case and in the on-going arguments over it, but he would not participate personally in it again.

Hill, too, may have found the case and his own partisanship in it an embarrassment to his career. Sometime in 1753 he wrote to the Duke of Northumberland, from whose influence he hoped to gain a post at the newly created British Museum:

> Some have thought that I had reason to fear your Lordships Displeasure; on account of my publick address: nothing could be so far from my heart, as to have incurd it knowingly, but I have had the happyness to hear his Grace the archbishop of Canterbury say, that there is nothing in it improper or indecent. yet I hold it my Duty to declare to your Lordship, that if there be one word in it, which my worst Enemy could construe into an unbecoming Liberty, I thought not so when I wrote it; and I most earnestly request your Lordships pardon. (Rousseau, 57)

For whatever reasons, Hill's candidacy for a position in the Museum was not successful. He ceased for some time to write on the Canning case in the Inspector and published no more signed pamphlets, although the bookseller for whom he produced The Story of Elizabeth Canning Considered, M. Cooper, continued to produce anonymous anti-Canning works for months.[3]

Both Fielding and Hill referred to Wells's lodgers, Fortune and Judith Natus, as potential witnesses. Fielding had been sure that Judith Natus was lying and warned her against doing so in court (see above, chapter 2). He reinforced the point in his conclusion: "Why did not the Gipsy Woman and Wells produce the Evidence of Fortune Natus and his Wife in their Defense at their Tryal, since that Evidence, as they well knew, was so very strong in their Behalf, that had the Jury believed it, they must have been acquitted? For my own Part, I can give but one Answer to this, and that is too obvious to need to be here mentioned" (55). Hill, however, had another answer, not "conceal[ed]," as he described Fielding's, but "it shall stand openly. The Reason is a plain, and 'tis a dreadful one. They were subpoena'd, and they were ready at the Court; but the Mob without-doors had been so exasperated against all that should appear on the Part of the Accused, that they were prevented from getting in, and treated themselves like Criminals" (*The Story . . . Considered*, 40). The putative activities of the mob at (or outside of) the trial of Squires and Wells have been discussed in chapter 2, and I have already expressed my doubt that they were a significant factor in the presentation of the defense's witnesses—no mention is made of them before Hill's Inspector essay of 26 March. The Natuses, Ezra Whiffin, Elizabeth Long, and anyone else Long could muster, however, still remained possible witnesses, this time for the prosecution of Canning, and Canning's managers now began to investigate them with a view of impeaching their credibility: once again, the issue was character.

These four persons had all given depositions before Sir Crisp Gascoyne on 12 March, supplemented by an information from Mary Landry on the 13th. On 17 March another group of Enfield witnesses—Sarah Bass, Elizabeth Headland, Humphrey Holden, Joseph Gould, Mary Gould, Amy Hodge and Ann Gaylor, and Thomas Bennett—made their depositions before Justice Tyshemaker (State Papers Domestic). The documentation took time to assemble, but by July 1754, after Canning's trial, her friends were in possession of a deposition from the overseers of the poor in Ware, Hertfordshire, on how the Natuses had abandoned their five-year-old child in the churchyard there, and another on how Fortune Natus had once attempted to hang himself because of "the very great misbehaviour of his wife in getting drunk, and preventing his continuing in any place and employment to get his bread" (Appendices 21 and 22, *A Refutation*, 23). Character witnesses were produced both for and against the Natuses at Canning's trial, but there were more of the latter than of the former, and Davy's attempt to imply that the Ware bargemaster, Joseph Haines, was exaggerating the Natuses' defects met a response suggesting exaggeration was impossible, with Haines ending by congratulating the prosecuting attorney for grasping the venality of his own witnesses:

Do you think, if he was to come into a court of justice, and not to get a farthing by it, that [Fortune Natus] would perjure himself?—I think he would say any thing to get a shilling.
Suppose he could not get a shilling by it?—He would try for it.
Do you think he would rather swear false than truth, though he did not get a shilling by it?—I think he would, he hates truth. . . .
Do you know his wife? Is she a sad wretch too?—She is a sad body.

A drunken beast?—You have guessed right as any man in England.
You give a very good guess. (*State Trials*, 19: 588–89)

Ezra Whiffin was not such an unprepossessing witness as the
itinerant laborer and his alcoholic wife, but his evidence too
could be called into question. He was a "victualler," living at
the White Hart and Crown public house at Enfield Wash, although his business was apparently not thriving. Having had an
inn-sign he had bought earlier from Wells repainted, he allegedly
waited some weeks after 19 January 1753, when it was brought
to him, to put it up as he had no irons to hang it with and no
money to buy them. The sign painter, William Metcalf, testified
that "John Garret, a blacksmith, . . . told me, he would not do
them at all, till such time as Whiffin had paid what was due
already" (19: 590) and that he recommended Whiffin to see if he
could get some old hooks from Mrs. Wells, since she had kept a
public house in the past. According to Metcalf, this conversation
took place "ten or fourteen days" after delivery of the sign, meaning that Whiffin had not gone to Wells's house until very late in
January if not early in February, but Whiffin claimed at Canning's trial that he had gone there on 18 January, and, with Wells,
had extricated the sign irons from underneath Judith Natus's bed
in the hayloft with Judith Natus in it. Whiffin fixed the date of
the encounter through his having paid enough money on a debt
to stave off arrest.

The writers of *A Refutation of Sir Crisp Gascoyne's Address*,
however, believed that Whiffin's story had developed over time,
"as the general plan became more PERFECT. At first he declared,
that 'he went into a room to look at a sign iron, and found no
person in it.' Then he declared, that 'when he went into the room
to look at a sign-iron, Fortune Natus's wife was then in bed,
though he neither SAW her face not HEARD her speak: 'then he
was asked, how he knew it to be Fortune Natus's wife,' and he
could not tell: then this INCONSISTENCY in his account was objected to him, and he said, 'he WISHED he had never said anything
about the matter, but as it was out, it must go'" (*A Refutation*, 15).
By the time of Canning's trial, Whiffin described Judith Natus as
rousing up in bed and asking "What are you about?" (19:
416–17).

A bundle of depositions from Enfield residents, however, testified to the whole sequential evolution of Whiffin's testimony,
while outside of the scope of the trial itself further questions
about Whiffin's credibility were raised. Virtue Hall had told Ed-

ward Rossiter, prior to her recantation, that Whiffin had come to Wells's house on 7 February and conspired with Sarah Howit to produce "a note or writing, to make people believe the said Ezra Whiffin was in that room" in January, a subject about which Hall seemed to know little—Howit had sent her out of the room— but one on which Rossiter also knew too little to have prompted her (Appendix 13, *A Refutation*, 13). More impressively, though too late to make a difference at Canning's trial, the friends eventually collected three further depositions, all representing Whiffin as having debts he was unable to pay and putting off his creditors with the assurance that money was to be "raised for him by Mr. Alderman Gascoyne's brother and his friends," who had "desired him . . . to take pen and ink and write down an account of the debts which he the said Whiffin owed, and that the said Whiffin accordingly did so, and they amounted to between forty and fifty pounds; upon which one of the gentlemen said, it was but a trifle, and that they had done greater things for people in distress" (Appendix 24, *A Refutation*, 24). There is nothing to show that Whiffin's debts were actually paid, but it seems clear that he believed that they would be, and another deposition, this one from the attorney of one of Whiffin's creditors, quoted Thomas Ford as saying that while he had no obligation to pay Whiffin's debts "the man had been ill used; and . . . his friends (that is we) shall make a collection in his favour, and your client will have his debt paid . . ." (Appendix 27, *A Refutation*, 24). This may not amount to subornation of perjury, but it must at least suggest that the hopeful Whiffin would make a firm and loyal witness for the prosecution.

Like Fortune and Judith Natus and Ezra Whiffin, Sarah Howit, Mary and John Landry, Giles Knight, and Edward Allen were all called at Canning's trial to prove that the room in which Canning claimed to have been confined in January 1753 had in fact never held her before 1 February. Their specific story, apart from Howit's general assertion that she had been in the room almost daily and that so had Virtue Hall, was that on 8 January Giles Knight had been lopping the trees opposite the casement window of the loft while Edward Allen and John Landry hedged a nearby field, and that Sarah Howit and Virtue Hall in the loft and the young men outdoors had conversed through the open window, although neither they nor Howit could remember any of the actual conversation. Virtue Hall, of course, was not called to confirm this testimony, but Knight, Allen, and Landry all supported it, as did another public-house keeper, John Cantril, who also testified to selling gin to Judith Natus (19: 412–16).

There seems no reason to doubt that the trees were lopped as stated; the question raised by Canning's supporters was which window Howit and Hall had stood at—there was a gable window just above the one in the hayloft, and if the picture of the house printed at the time is to be believed, the trees behind it branch out closer to that one than to the window of the loft. Canning's friends took affidavits from Sarah Star, an Enfield farmer's wife who said that she had seen the women at the garret landing window, not at the one in the loft, and that although the men had borrowed a rope from her, they had in the end done very little actual tree-trimming, and from Thomas Edwards, a St. Giles soap-boiler, who said that Edward Allen had told him the upper window was the right one and that he had since heard in company at Enfield that Allen had "told other folks besides the same thing." One of those he told was Edward Aldridge, the Enfield wheelwright who was the nephew of the London goldsmith now on the other side of the case, who deposed not only that Allen had told him that the garret window was the one at which Howit and Hall had stood but that when he himself said to Allen that he believed Canning had been confined in the hayloft Allen said that so did he, "but added, that the said Edward Allen did not care, for he got money, booze and scram [OED: "a portion of food carried by a laborer into the field for a meal"]" (Appendices 62, 63, and 64, A Refutation, 50).

The efforts of Canning's friends to discredit the testimony of the Natuses, Whiffin, and Sarah Howit and the tree-lopping party came as a response to Gascoyne's determination to discredit Canning, as Fielding's and Hill's pamphlets represent an escalating response to each other's public positions. In defense of Canning herself, her supporters returned to the facts that had first made them her partisans, her physical suffering and shattered health. Thus the next significant documents to appear in the case were substantial pamphlets by two physicians, James Solas Dodd and Daniel Cox.[4]

Dodd's A Physical Account of the Case of Elizabeth Canning, With An Enquiry into the Probability of her subsisting in the Manner therein asserted, and her Ability to Escape after her suppos'd ill Usage appeared in April 1753 and explicitly based itself on the "firm Persuasion of the Gentlemen concerned in the Prosecution on her Behalf . . . of her Innocence and Injuries" (6). Dodd himself focuses on the injuries. The amount of water

Canning had available during January was in fact scarcely less than she was accustomed to drinking, "scarce half a Pint of Liquid in Twenty-four Hours" (13–14), and while the deprivation of food was by contrast more extreme, resulting in the loss of perhaps twenty pounds of the barely five-foot-tall Canning's body weight (which of course was not ever measured or recorded either before or after January 1753), such a loss in less than a month, though great, was not extraordinary—"Consumption[s, . . .] Fevers, Fluxes, and Acute Diseases" all produced equal or greater wastage. Canning's original state of health had been robust and had facilitated her recovery, although Dodd also reported his own observation at the time of writing that "the Lividness of her Skin [was] not totally gone off" (17). As he had observed in other cases, so it had been in Canning's: after a short time she had lost all appetite and eaten bits of her bread with no other "Spur to Eating, but Faintness and Desire of Preservation" (17). Canning's situation in captivity was "a mere enduring of life" (20), and a person "of a laxer Habit of Body" (29) might have died of it, as Canning indeed came close to doing; nevertheless, she did survive, and the timing of her escape, like her survival, made sense in Dodd's analysis of her condition:

Fear is a Passion which, till it rises to Despair, renders the Body cold, jellies the Blood, and numbs the vital Faculties. While the Mind was oppress'd with that Passion, the least Threat, the smallest Menace, is of surprising Force. It must be granted also that supposing a Girl robb'd, knock'd down, carried off, used with Threats, and confin'd, she must, except she had a greater mastery of Mind than could be supposed to fall to her Share, be sunk in Fear. . . . [W]here is the Difficulty to account for her not endeavouring her Escape while that Fear possessed her Mind. . . . [?] But though the Passion of Fear may last a long time, it cannot ever, but must arise to Extremes, and give place to Despair in the long Run, more especially when all Means of Life is taken away: Hence arises a sufficient Reason why she then used her Endeavour for Life. That Fear of Death is implanted in us for very strong Purposes; and it is no Paradox to say in this Case the Fear of Death prevailed over the Fear of Death: that is, when all the slender Support of Life was at an End, her Continuance there must be her Death, this raised her Fear to Despair, and she, who while any small Subsistance remain'd, sat fearfully inactive, when that was gone grew desperate, attempted and completed her Escape. (33–34)

It followed equally naturally that the extraordinary exertion of Canning's escape and flight was followed by physical collapse, with all the "sensible Effects" of "Weakness, Faintness of Voice, low Pulse, cold Sweats, great Consumption of Body, a livid Blackness of the Skin, the Body swell'd, the Head heavy, an obstinate Costiveness, and a want of other Evacuations" (37). Only starvation, in Dodd's view, could have produced all of these effects in combination; they could not have been produced, as some anti-Canningites had suggested, by a salivation—mercury treatment for venereal disease, which would have produced extreme pallor as well as characteristic lesions in the mouth.

Dodd went on to state the sheer unlikeliness of the girl he had come to know being the source of an elaborate deception—"I declare I never saw anything in her Countenance, Words, or Actions, that could indicate [a fear of the consequences of perjury]; so that if so, she must be an absolute Mistress of Dissimulation"—and gave a specific instance of her simplicity that would in fact evoke further ridicule: "She says all the Time she was there although there was Hay in the Room, she never lay upon it to sleep [because] she was terrified with a Thought which she could not put out of her Head, that a dead Man was hid under that Hay; . . . A very childish Reason, and not at all befitting her supposed Cunning" (48–49). Dodd tested Canning's veracity by asking her "many ensnaring Questions . . . on Purpose to find out if she was any ways influenc'd by either the Questions themselves [all apparently on the subject of her symptoms and their causes] or the Manner in which they were proposed" (50). Canning's answers were such that she must either possess a "thorough Knowledge" not only of the effects of starvation but of "many other Diseases," and this seemed to Dodd so completely unlikely that he could only conclude "I am morally certain that she spoke the very Truth" (51).

Dodd presumably wrote for an audience still trying to make up their minds, but all of the surviving written evidence suggests that works such as his must primarily have had the effect of reinforcing the certainties, on both sides, of those already convinced. The author of *Canning's Magazine* was thus not only unimpressed by any part of Dodd's argument but professed instead to find the whole of it simply ridiculous, of a piece with his earlier treatise, *An Essay towards the Natural History of the Herring*, which he represented as offering "this Chief of Fish" as "the Cure for all Diseases, and consequently rendering Man immortal" (22). Dodd's motive in writing about Canning was probably "that of rendering himself popular" (22), but his vindication of her was overall "very trifling" (26).

Dr. Cox, "an Author of greater importance . . ., whose Station in the World render[ed] him more distinguished" than the relatively youthful Dodd, presented more of a problem—his pamphlet, published in June, had been "very well received" and some of the public had thought his arguments "inexpugnable" (26). Cox himself acknowledged the polarization of opinion on Canning and the difficulty with which anyone who had already chosen a side would be persuaded to retreat from it. By the time he wrote, the King's pardon of Mary Squires had added weight to a popular belief that it would be positively "unbecoming" to argue Canning's case although "the truth of the facts" could not "depend upon his Majesty's determination concerning the life of the criminal"—for so Cox still thought Squires to be (6). If it had been legitimate to reopen the case after Squires was found guilty, it was equally legitimate to reopen it after she was pardoned, and Cox proposed to do so on a broad front. The title of his pamphlet, *An Appeal to the Public, in Behalf of Elizabeth Canning, In which the material Facts in her Story are fairly stated, and shown to be true, on the Foundations of Evidence,* asserts his emphasis unequivocally.

Cox began by recapitulating the very extensive and uncontradicted evidence of Canning's previous good character and his own corroborating experience of it—"Her understanding appears moderate; she has a remarkable simplicity in her answers to questions one puts to her, and appears to have no intention of guilt or deceit in any thing she speaks" (12)—and thus established the basis for his own investigation of the rumors and innuendoes that had been circulated to Canning's detriment and the particularity of his account of them.

Cox first met Canning on 30 March, at her current lodging in the family of a cheesemonger named Marshall in Fore Street, where presumably she had gone after her stay with Mrs. Woodward in Aldermanbury Postern, and interviewed her about her health—it was at this time that he learned about her irregular menstrual history (see chapter 2). On Monday 9 April, he visited the Marshall household again to inquire into the rumor that a midwife "had made information before the Lord Mayor that she had visited the mother of Elizabeth Canning a few days after the girl's return home, had seen her shift, and that it was too clean to have been wore so long as had been pretended" (16). Cox questioned both Mrs. Canning and Mrs. Woodward, separately and before witnesses, and heard from both of these "very decent, modest women" (18) that the midwife in question—Elizabeth

Mayle, who had delivered Canning and who would later testify at her trial both that she thought the shift had not been worn three weeks and that she could not tell how long it had been worn (19: 426)—had examined the shift and found no stains upon it suggesting sexual activity. The shift, however, which Mrs. Canning swore to as certainly her daughter's own, of a coarse fabric and bearing familiar patches, was "very dirty at the sleeves and neck, but cleaner in the body," compatible with having been worn the whole time of Canning's absence. Neither Mrs. Canning nor Mrs. Woodward believed that the midwife had any "doubts at that time about the girl's innocence" (18), nor did Mrs. Mayle express any at the trial—her primary concern in looking at the shift, like Mrs. Canning's, had been whether it provided any evidence of rape while Elizabeth had been insensible.

Cox visited Canning again on 9 May, when he looked into her mouth for the marks that would have been left by a salivation and failed to find them (like Dodd, he noted that the lividity of her skin, especially on her arms, had lingered for over two months), and returned on the 15th, bringing with him "Mrs. Frances Oakes, first midwife to the lying-in hospital in Brownlow-Street" to investigate the rumor that Canning had disappeared in January in order to give birth. Mrs. Oakes "first examined her alone by the several usual methods," presumably including vaginally, "and declared it to me as her positive judgment and opinion, that Elizabeth Canning ha[d] never had a child," and then asked Cox to examine her breasts and abdomen. In one of the very few instances in which a sentiment or emotion of any kind is attributed to Canning by the many men who wrote about her, Cox says that she submitted to this male investigation "with much reluctance." Cox, however, corroborated Oakes's judgment, and Mrs. Rossiter, Mrs. Woodward, and Canning's own mother were all asked to make "a full examination in the presence and under the instruction of Mrs. Oakes, and all declared their belief, that Elizabeth Canning never had a child" (23–24). Good as Cox's intentions undoubtedly were, these multiple explorations of her body can hardly have been comfortable for Canning, but we hear no more of her protests. If she made any, no one recorded them, and it seems unlikely that she persisted with them.

Cox went beyond the scope of his medical expertise to examine the evidences of Canning and Virtue Hall in relation to each other, noting particularly the elements in Hall's testimony—such as the identification of George Squires ("John" to Hall)—which could not have come from a prior knowledge of Canning's, and to report "the corroborating testimonies of several witnesses," some who reported Mary Squires's presence in Enfield from the middle of December 1752, others who had met Canning on her journey homewards, and still others who had heard both Wells and Squires on separate occasions acknowledge guilt in the affair, although neither at any time came close to making a formal confession. Cox refused to be drawn into accusations of perjury against any witnesses, but he argued that the Enfield witnesses were more likely to be right than those from Dorset "since the Gypsey woman they swear to is the very identical person that was taken at Mother Wells's on the 1st of February" (47).

Cox concluded his essay as he had begun it, with a plea that evidence should be preferred to notions of probability in weighing the truth of Canning's story:

People have been endeavouring to shew, that a fact *cannot* be true, because of some difficulties attending the relation, when they should be searching for *evidence* whether or not it *is* true. Where indeed such evidence cannot be had, reasoning about probabilities are [sic] proper, because we are furnished with no better principles to reason upon. But where evidence can be had, a very few substantial testimonies from people of character and credit, will outweigh a Volume of speculations without them. (49; emphasis in original)

The anonymous author of *Genuine and Impartial Memoirs of Elizabeth Canning*, however, found Cox's evidence unpersuasive, "for without derogating from Mrs. Oakes's obstetrical, or our Author's medical Abilities, there may be many, who will not think themselves sufficiently authorised to pin their Faith upon the *positive Opinion* of an old *Woman*, however experienced, nor much more upon the *uncertain Belief* of a Gentleman whose general Course of Practice does not often lead him into Enquiries of this Nature." Besides, these witnesses did "not pretend to certify, that they were of Opinion that Elizabeth Canning continued a Virgin, or that she had *never been pregnant*" (119–20); emphasis in original). *The Controverted Hard Case: or Mary Squires's Magazine of Facts Re-examin'd* carried the theme of sexual innuendo at Cox's (and Canning's) expense still further:

I shall not meddle with the Girl's foul Shift, which the Doctor handles with so much Judgment, and by the Rules of his Art, proves from the View of it, that it was impossible for the Owner of it to have any Commerce with Man while she had it on; neither shall I at all dispute the Exactness of his Skill in ascertaining her Innocence by feeling her Belly and Breasts. These are so peculiarly the Prerogatives of a Physician that it would be an unpardonable Presumption in one, who is not of the Faculty, to offer his Opinion in so nice and delicate a Point. Leaving him therefore in full Possession of the dirty Smock, and every Use he can make of it, I shall proceed to other Matters. (23)

Despite Cox's hopes, evidence—his "few substantial testimonies from people of credit"—could not be disentangled from probability. Instead, the credit of witnesses, himself included, became a casualty, with no one—Canning, her friends, Sir Crisp Gascoyne, Fielding—emerging unaspersed. *The Controverted Hard Case* insisted on the priority of probability in determining the truth:

> It is sufficient in the Eye of the Law, and for the Satisfaction of every reasonable Man, that [Canning's] Case is attended with the highest Improbabilities, and that it is next to an Impossibility that it should have happen'd in the Manner it had been set forth. Now, tho' there should not be Proofs in hand to shew, that she was in any other Place ... yet there will be no Impeachment of the Evidence against her, because that lies wholly in her own Knowledge and that of her Accomplices, who, for their own Sakes, it's presum'd, will never divulge the Secret. (24)

Behind the scenes, every effort was of course being made to find evidence of Canning's presence anywhere other than Wells's house in January, and the argument that such evidence would be supererogatory was in effect a stopgap, but it never became possible to abandon it because no such evidence was ever found. Probability thus never ceased to be an issue, or, with it, the character of those figures whose probable or improbable actions and motives were so vividly discussed. Cox's pamphlet appeared in June 1753, *The Controverted Hard Case* in July. Canning's trial did not take place until late April and early May 1754. For almost a year, then, the hunt for evidence and the speculation continued, while the partisanship of both sides only increased.

Legal Maneuverings

John Myles, who replaced Salt at some fairly early stage in the case though perhaps not until after the trial of Mary Squires and Susannah Wells, at about the time the investigations of Sir Crisp

Gascoyne became known, seems to have been one of those people with whom Fielding was at pains to dissociate himself with the Duke of Newcastle. The most recent writer on the case, John Treherne, characterizes him as "the unscrupulous John Myles . . .[, a] wily and resourceful lawyer [who] missed no opportunity to defend his client's position—by pamphlet, rumor, and advertisement" (48). I can find no evidence that Myles was responsible for any Canningite pamphlet—Fielding, Dodd, and Cox, her principal defenders in print during 1753, were none of them anonymous hirelings—and rumor is difficult to reanimate, but Myles certainly used advertisements, at least some of which were later conveniently collected among the appendices to the hostile *Canning's Magazine*.

The earliest notice reprinted there (for which no source is cited) is dated 28 February and briefly tells the story of a poor street-seller of sticks who was knocked down, beaten, and robbed by gypsies—"a further Instance of their Barbarity to our Subjects, and shews the immediate Necessity of rooting these Villians out of their Dens" (80), and this was followed up on 2 March by another pointing out the discrepancy between Mary Squires's own version of her alibi and that given by her witnesses, a contradiction that ought to "awake the public Attention, to bring the Rest of those Miscreants (and all such Persons, who, in Defiance of all Laws, human and divine, shall dare to become Partakers of their Crimes by Perjury . . .)" to trial (80).

Both of these pieces may in fact have been written by the editors of the unnamed journals in which they appeared rather than by Myles, but a 19 March notice from the *Public Advertiser*, coming after such reverses as Virtue Hall's recantation, is certainly a product of Canning's partisans: "Notwithstanding the many Puffs on the other Side of the Question, the Friends of Elizabeth Canning flatter themselves, her Case will not be attended with that Intricacy as is insinuated; and the World in due Time will be acquainted with a true State of her Case, attested by Persons of undoubted Probity, Fortune, and Reputation [probably a reference to Fielding's forthcoming pamphlet]; and they will likewise be informed who the King of the Gipsies is" (81). The final promise would never be fulfilled, but the deviant character of gypsies was kept insistently before the public eye with a long notice in the *Gazetteer* for 3 April summarizing existing law on the subject and concluding threateningly: "Look to it Espousers and Upholders of Gipsies, Fortune-tellers, Impostors, Bawds, Whores, Thieves, Robbers, Smugglers, Murderers, and

Plunderers at Shipwrecks, if you credit those the World will question yours" (81). This was followed by an undated notice signed by John Myles:

> Whereas there are various scandalous and malicious Falshoods raised and reported of Elizabeth Canning by several Persons, particularly by Mr. Hill and his *Associates* (for whom this is done, or to answer what Purpose, it is not easy for Persons, Strangers to the secret Springs of their Hearts, to guess at) thereby imposing on the Publick, and to the great Injury of Canning; I do hereby take upon me to declare, that several Persons, for the Sake of Justice only, are daily informing me of several material Circumstances, still corroborating her unhappy Case, and proving her Innocence, in Spite of her Enemies. And as it is apprehended there are Numbers of other Persons that have not yet been heard of by Canning, or her Friends, who know of Matters material and relative to her Case, the Favour will be greatly acknowledged, if *such Persons* will give *Information* thereof to
>
> John Myles
Attorney, in Brickin-Lane (82)

This notice is evidently the one so strongly objected to later (in the plural, as "advertisements") by Sir Crisp Gascoyne (19). The friends of Canning themselves, having ended their association with Myles some months before Canning's trial, denied its efficacy—"There was not a single affidavit or information taken in *consequence* of advertisements" (*A Refutation*, iv). Nevertheless, Myles retained his ascendancy at least through spring and summer 1753. He signed a 24 April announcement that an Enfield man named John Lee had been set upon and beaten as an associate of John Iniver (*sic*; "Iniser" in *Trials*), who had testified against Squires at the latter's trial, and another of 11 May that, on 22 and 23 April the neighbors of Susannah Wells in Enfield had been threatened with arson if their testimony should lead to Squires's execution, and offered a ten guinea reward for the discovery of any of the utterers of these threats. A 16 May notice in the *Gazetteer* added that since the truth of this story had been doubted Myles was prepared to show affidavits on the events to anyone enquiring.

Myles's energy, if nothing else, is unquestionable, but it is doubtful whether any of his activities actually helped Canning's cause. Before her trial her friends were obliged "to make new enquiries, to take new informations, and to do again all that had been done before" since "all the papers by which she could make her defence [were] still in the custody of Mr. Myles" (*A Refutation*, 21), while in the midst of the trial itself the friends were "served with copies of writs for the balance of Mr. Myles's bill, amounting to a very large sum" (25).

It was probably Myles's idea to pursue the three witnesses who had testified unavailingly on behalf of Squires's alibi with a formal accusation of perjury. Gascoyne had already, if his rather lightly dated account is read as chronological, issued a warrant for Canning's arrest on the same charge and taken bail from her friends before Myles's advertisement for evidence, which he treats along with the indictment of "the three innocent countrymen" as a part of the "extraordinary" response of Canning's friends to his own action (20)—"for it will appear the prosecutors themselves THEN *knew them to be innocent*" (21). In support of this charge, Gascoyne included in his account a correspondence with John Cooper of Salisbury, who had written to him on 31 March to inform him that John Myles had made inquiries in the neighborhood about Thomas Greville's character and to pass on to him the same testimonies supportive of Greville and Squires that he had sent to Myles. Like all other testimony of the same purport, this appeared to Gascoyne so conclusive as to leave no room for a defense of Canning, but the defense continued its charges against Gibbons, Clarke, and Greville regardless, reinforcing Gascoyne's disbelief in the sincerity of Canning's friends.

The Lord Mayor was also "credibly assured, that Mr. Arbuthnot of Weymouth near Abbotsbury, a gentleman of fortune," had sent Fielding more than sixty affidavits testifying to the truth of Squires's alibi and added, "I wish Mr. Fielding, who had before published so much on this subject, had now obliged the world with the publication of those certificates" (23–24). Fielding had in fact published only the one pamphlet on the case, although it may have seemed "much" to Gascoyne. The date of his *Address to the Liverymen*, however, is 8 July 1754, by which time Fielding was on his way to Lisbon, where he would die three months later. According to the anonymous author of *A Liveryman's Reply to Sir Crisp Gascoyne's Address*, this was "a circumstance . . . that should have made him sacred from all slander" (27), but Gascoyne was at least no more slanderous than some of his predecessors in print, Hill among them. The anonymous *The Case of Elizabeth Canning Fairly Stated*, available from the same M. Cooper who was the publisher of Hill's *The Story of Elizabeth Can-*

ning *Considered*, implied that Virtue Hall had charged Fielding with coercing her information before him, although

> we are not at Liberty to explain ourselves any further on this Head. . . . However, if the Report which is current should prove true, that a certain M[agistra]te and his C[ler]k divided eighteen Pounds of the Money which was collected for the Girl for Services they did her, the Reader will not be much at a Loss to guess at the Reasons for the extraordinary Management in this Affair. . . . What a Wretch then must that Person be, especially if he bears the King's Commission to do Justice, if he perverted his Authority to such vile Purposes, and for any private or sinister Ends, has worked upon the Passions or Credulity of a poor weak, ignorant Woman, so as to drive her to commit the most enormous Crimes! (22–24)

Fielding did not reply to any of this, and Mr. Arbuthnot's certificates, if they existed in anything but rumor, never appeared. It had become for both sides standard practice to attack everyone associated with the opposition, and it was in that spirit that the opposed factions presented cross bills of perjury against Canning on the one side and Gibbons, Clarke, and Greville on the other to the grand jury, which threw out both of them—"For though the evidence is directly opposite, yet that on both sides is so well supported that neither can with sufficient reason be declared false" ("Historical Chronicle," May 1753, *Gentleman's Magazine*, 23: 245). It was an opportunity for honor to be declared satisfied by both sides in the legal duel, but this was not what happened. *The Controverted Hard Case of Mary Squires* begins with a six-page prologue labeled "The Dispute between Mr. Ford and Mr. Myles, argued, Pro and Con," which in the format of a rather stilted dialogue between Gascoyne's and Canning's attorneys summarizes the on-going legal jockeying.

Myles, the first speaker, claims that after the grand jury's action "it was generally thought all farther Prosecutions would have dropt; but just before the following Sessions in June, Canning's Friends were informed, another Bill would be preferred against her at that Sessions, as it was." They had—still in Myles's view—no choice but to re-present their own bills against Gibbons, Clarke, and Greville, and this time, on 9 June, the grand jury returned both bills as true (3). The *Gentleman's Magazine* interrupted its "Historical Chronicle" to comment: "More mystery and opposition!" (23: 293). Ford's response to Myles in *The Converted Hard Case* states that this renewed indictment of Squires's witnesses proved an indifference to the cause of justice, since the friends and their attorney would have been "very well satisfied to let a Perjury of the blackest Dye (on one Side or the other) escape unpunished" until they heard that Canning was to be indicted again (4).

Myles next reports that he and Ford had come to an agreement that all of the indictments, with appropriate bail for the defendants, should be removed from the Old Bailey into the court of King's Bench, but that Ford had backed out at the last moment— "which greatly surprized Mr. Myles" (5). Ford responds that since there was, "for Reasons which I am not at Liberty to mention," no possibility of a hearing in the King's Bench in the current term, it would be better to try all of the indictments in the Old Bailey, for which the alibi witnesses gave bail for their appearance on 26 June. (It was Gascoyne who had the power to consent to the removal of Canning's trial to the court of King's Bench; according to her friends, he refused two applications to do so [A Refutation, iv].) Ford claims still to have offered "to consent to the Removal of the Indictments upon Condition that the Girl's Friends would undertake to produce her," but that they had "declined" (Controverted Hard Case, 5–6).

The next argument attributed to Myles is that Ford's proceedings had been "intended only to amuse and gain Advantage," and that Canning's friends were obliged to resist any action which would bring her to trial in the Old Bailey while Sir Crisp Gascoyne remained Lord Mayor, a position utterly rejected by Ford on the familiar grounds that the Lord Mayor had no power to "unduly influence a Jury by means of his Authority, and pervert the Course of Justice." Not only was it true that "any Danger of an unfair Trial at the Old Bailey, no Body in his right Wits, who knows any Thing of that Court, ever feared it," but also the Lord Mayor had already "openly declared his Intention not to sit upon the Bench nor so much as appear in Court, during the Trials of any of the Parties accused" (6–8).

Assertions about the unquestionable fairness of trials in the Old Bailey are about as frequent in eighteenth-century writings on the case as are allegations that Squires's trial was unfair because the Canningite mob prevented her witnesses (or some of them) from testifying, but they are never put into relation to each other. The fairness of such trials may be posited strictly on the formal proceedings of the court, excluding not only what went on outside the courtroom but much of what happened inside it as well. In the event, Canning did not come to trial until 1754, several months after Thomas Rawlinson was sworn in as Sir

Crisp Gascoyne's successor on 4 December 1753, and her antago-
nist thus did not preside directly over her case. He did not, however, avoid the court altogether—his son was one of the
prosecuting counsel and Gascoyne himself, according to *A Refutation of Sir Crisp Gascoyne's Address to the Liverymen*, "was
present; sometimes at the bottom of the court, among the crowd,
and sometimes in his seat, exclaiming that *it was a plain case,
a plain case*" (v).

The legal maneuvering between Ford and Myles gained some
advantages for both sides but probably more for the former—
Myles got Canning's trial delayed but only at the expense of a
move that added fuel to her opponents' attacks on her character.
To avoid her appearance before Sir Crisp Gascoyne at the Old
Bailey, Canning's friends concealed her whereabouts—"the only
remaining expedient, as they believed, to prevent her being transported or pilloried, for having been robbed and famished" (*A
Refutation*, 19). Meanwhile the dates set for the perjury trials
of Gibbons, Clarke, and Greville were fast approaching, and the
friends had great hopes that if they were found guilty any prosecution of Canning would be moot, but here they encountered
the first of their financial problems with John Myles. Myles was
entangled in expenses pursuant to a prosecution by Gascoyne
over his treatment of William Clarke, whom he had kept in his
house for two days because of a verbal anomaly in his warrant
that prevented his giving bail (Gascoyne, 27; *A Refutation*, 18),
and although Gascoyne's charge was later dismissed, Myles now
refused both to proceed himself or to deliver his papers to anyone else until the friends paid him. Anticipating no quick solution, he left the city with all of the relevant documents in his
possession, and the friends were obliged to turn to another—
unnamed—attorney, who, having no time to prepare the case,
secured writs of certiorari which, if accepted, would delay the
trials till the prosecution could be prepared without reference
to John Myles.

According to Gascoyne, these writs were obtained by a mixture
of trickery and impropriety. Having already been refused a removal into the King's Bench, the friends were deceptive in their
attempts to secure that end once more. Their even darker purpose was to provide "an excuse (such as it was) for producing
no witnesses . . ., and thereby robbing [the defendants] of the
opportunity of manifesting to the world their innocence by evidence." Fifty witnesses, "who attended at a great expense," were
waiting to provide it (31).

According to the friends, the writs were sent to court with such an expectation that they would be routinely accepted that the attorney himself did not attend, and when the agent who brought them was unable to explain the process by which they had been obtained, they were handed back to him and "the countrymen were called to the bar, and acquitted without any prosecution" (*A Refutation*, 20). The writs had been authorized by Lord Chief Justice Sir William Lee, who died on 8 April 1754, before the issue of their appropriateness could be resolved: the friends asserted that their belief in the writs' vaidity was proved "by a motion which they made the next term to enforce a return of them," while Sir Crisp Gascoyne asserted that "there are those of unquestioned credit, who had the honour of frequently being near his person, who have heard his Lordship often declare, he would not, *knowingly*, have signed these *fiats*" (*A Refutation*, 20; Gascoyne, 31).

The factuality of these accounts is thoroughly entangled with mixed motives and interpretations after the fact, and their tone on both sides is defensive.The trial records add the information that William Davy was the counsel for the defense who blocked acceptance of the writs, and the transcript consists merely of the lengthy indictment, the summary nonappearance of all witnesses except, oddly, Mary Woodward, who said she "knew nothing of the matter," and, apparently subsequent to the actual acquittal of Gibbons, Clarke, and Greville, a lengthy concluding address by Davy asserting the readiness of the three men to prove their veracity, the presence of "witnesses, more in number than perhaps ever appeared in any one cause, collected together at a vast expence, and from different remote places," and the probity and disinterestedness of Sir Crisp Gascoyne (presumaby the provider of most of the money laid out for the defense) in pursuing Mary Squires's vindication and Elizabeth Canning's conviction in spite of "all the reproaches which malice could suggest to little, dark designing men" (*State Trials*, 19: 281–82).

The trials of the three aibi witnesses were in fact held separately on 6, 7, and 8 September, and their formal discharge took place on 10 September, a sequential proceeding not followed in detail by any of the available accounts including that in *A Complete Collection of State Trials*. Probably nothing very significant is concealed by the narrative decision to represent three virtually identical proceedings as one (if someone had gained an advantage by it the climate of the case suggests that someone else would have been quick to point it out), but it can serve as a useful reminder that what we are looking at is representations, not unmediated actualities, and that even contemporaries shared that circumstance with us.

In general, Sir Crisp Gascoyne, whether because his cause was just or because his resources were greater, was now scoring more points than Canning's friends and their perhaps ill-chosen attorneys, although he continued to express and presumably feel considerable grief and annoyance at their persistent defiance and the disbelief manifested by some segments of the public in his motives and the rightness of his conclusions. On 21 May, Mary Squires had received the king's pardon, allowing him to stage the dramatic tableau of 30 May (see chapter 2), an event he does not himself recount, preferring to emphasize the inexplicable obstinacy of Canning's friends, but which is given with lavish detail in *Genuine and Impartial Memoirs of Elizabeth Canning*:

> The old Woman, well worn with Years, and more so by her late Hardships, her Son and two Daughters, the Moment they entered the Room, fell on their Knees, and, with all the Warmth of real Gratitude, expressed their Sense of their Obligations to his Lordship in the most humble and affecting Manner. Tears were almost their only Language for some Time. . . . At the Request of some of the Spectators Virtue Hall was sent for; whose visible Confusion at so unexpected an Interview, was of itself a sufficient Evidence of her former Falsehood.—The old Woman, far from reproaching her, endeavoured to comfort her, in Terms superior to what might have been expected from one in her low Station of Life; she told her, that *she heartily forgave her, and hoped God would also forgive her.* (105–6)

The friends, as might be expected, had their own version of the circumstances of Squires's pardon:

> They had . . . taken some affidavits to prove, that the Gipsey was at Enfield when the robbery was committed; and the duke of Newcastle having acquainted them, that his Majesty had referred the consideration of the evidence on both sides to his Attorney and Sollicitor General, they took many other affidavits to prove the same fact; but when these affidavits were presented to the Attorney and Sollicitor General, they rejected them, because they were not at liberty to examine any evidence that was taken after the day of reference. It necessarily followed, therefore, that the weight of evidence was in the convict's favour; and so it was reported: the Gipsey, therefore, . . . received her pardon in consequence of this report. Upon this view of the case, however, it does not become in any degree more PROBABLE, that she was innocent. (*A Refutation*, 18)

In justice to the Duke of Newcastle, it is to be remembered that he had twice applied to Fielding for these affidavits and that Fielding had not been able to get them from Myles, who seems less and less to be an asset to Canning's case, but there is another marginal figure whose situation was considerably worse than Newcastle's and that is Susannah Wells.

If Mary Squires was no longer held to have committed a robbery, Susannah Wells could not logically have been her accomplice. She could not be unbranded, but she could certainly have been released from Newgate at the same time as Squires, and it would seem ought to have been. In fact she served out her six-month sentence in full and was released, noted only by the *Gentleman's Magazine* in its "Historical Chronicle" and ignored by all the other writers on the case, on 21 August 1753 (23: 390). Very curiously, a "Warrant for discharging Susannah Wells out of custody" appears first as item 195, under the date 31 December 1753, which is crossed out, and then as item 226, of a later but unspecified date, in the Public Record Office's Catalogue of State Papers Domestic, 1751–1760 (34–35). The draft itself, complete except for the date and the King's signature but very beautifully written out, is addressed "To our Trusty and Wellbeloved William Moreton, Esq., Recorder of Our City of London" and annotated in the same formal hand, "Susannah Wells. Imprisonment Remitted." However, not a day of Wells's sentence was remitted, and the appearance of this draft well after her scheduled release is difficult to explain. It may be a copy of an earlier document, but if so, why is it undated and why did it have no effect in shortening Wells's imprisonment? If it was actually written in December 1753, or January 1754, was this because someone believed her to be still in prison? Or was it produced as a late gesture in the vindication of Mary Squires, in recognition of the logical connection between the two defendants?

Certainly Sir Crisp Gascoyne had acted consistently throughout the whole sequence of events first to exonerate Mary Squires, then to convict Elizabeth Canning, never mentioning Susannah Wells except as the householder on whose premises Squires had *not*, in his view, robbed Canning and as the corroborator of Virtue Hall's recantation—Gascoyne had her summoned from prison for the purpose and seemed to think nothing of her returning there after she had served it (Gascoyne, 12). He may have initially pursued a pardon only for Squires because her conviction was capital; once the pardon was secured he may have ignored the anomaly presented by Wells's continued imprisonment because of her notorious bad character: what is certain is that he said nothing about her and did nothing for her. I see two further possible reasons for this. The first is that while alibi witnesses for Squires were "a great expense," they were procurable, while witnesses for Wells, though apparently closer to hand, were less so—Wells's neighbors had little good to say of her. The second is that Gascoyne had some reason for defending Squires which did not extend to Wells.

According to Thomas Myles, a distiller and John Myles's brother who had been one of the friends of Canning from an early date and who may have introduced his brother into the case, on the occasion when he, Edward Rossiter, and Francis Roberts were sent for by Sir Crisp Gascoyne on 6 March 1753 to hear the earliest alibi evidence Gascoyne had collected from Abbotsbury, a dispute had arisen over the discrepant dates in Squires's own version of where she had been in early January. Gascoyne first attributed her inconsistency with her witnesses to "confusion and terror," and when Myles and the others pointed out that she had persisted in the story after the trial, he suggested that she must have been reckoning by the Old Style, as "gypsies always" did. When the friends pointed out that this still left Squires's dates inconsistent, Gascoyne "broke off the conversation with some expressions of anger, and as the result of all, told the persons present that 'one Squires, a horse-dealer in the borough, was determined to save the gipsey, and had applied to him for that purpose.'" Francis Roberts corroborated Myles's testimony (Appendix 50, A Refutation, 41). Why the horse-dealer's request should have received such a full response as Gascoyne gave it is at best a speculative question. Rumors evidently circulated, embittering his public career for months to come, but there is nothing in the Canningite pamphlets to support them. An 1820 account claimed that "one of the gipsy's sons had been many years in his service; and, it was reported, was privy to some secret offence his master had been guilty of, the fear of divulging which, compelled him to preserving the life of the mother" (Caulfield, 148), but over a period of nearly seventy years this story may well have altered considerably from whatever it was in 1753, when in turn it may have borne only the slightest relation to any demonstrable facts.

A consideration of Wells's continued imprisonment in relation to Gascoyne's alleged special interest on behalf of Squires is suggestive but far from decisive. What is certain is that Squires's pardon, like the failure of the prosecutions against Gibbons,

Clarke, and Greville, only further stimulated his zeal to punish Canning, whose friends still concealed her:

> All this time the indictment was pending, writs upon writs, and warrants upon warrants, were made out to apprehend her, but she was not to be found; at length every necessary step, even to the exigent and proclamation, was taken to outlaw her.
>
> She was publicly proclaimed at her Parish Church, upon the Hustings at Guildhall, and at the Quarter Sessions, and her outlawry almost perfected; and then in the February Session, but not before, she appeared, pleaded, and gave bail to take her trial at the ensuing Session. (Gascoyne, 32)

Outlawry comprised a set of serious legal disadvantages including the loss of all legal rights and the forfeit of all property to the Crown, and it was thus arrived at only through a lengthy sequence of writs and proclamations allowing the potential outlaw every opportunity to become aware of his/her danger and to return from whatever refuge he/she had found and appear to answer the prosecutor's charges—hence Gascoyne's reference to Canning's outlawry being "almost perfected," as if it were some complex alchemical work frustrated just short of accomplishment. As both the penalties and the pronouns suggest, it was an extraordinarily draconian procedure to direct at a nineteen-year-old maidservant accused of perjury, however wilful and corrupt.

Canning's friends were painfully aware that to say the least her cause had not fared well in their keeping, but they made the best of the circumstance:

> But tho' the girl suffered extremely in the opinion of the public by the fate of the certioraries, and her cause by the differences among her friends; yet these circumstances afford a fresh testimony, that they were engaged in no UNLAWFUL COMBINATION to establish false facts by false attestations; for when the association was once broken, the SECRET, had there been any, would certainly have escaped. From this time neither of the attornies who had acted in Canning's affairs proceeded any farther; but others who heard of her distresses, and were desirous that she should either be delivered from persecution, or punished for her guilt, undertook to bring her cause to a trial. (A Refutation, 21)

It was not an ideal situation: Sir Crisp Gascoyne was no longer chief magistrate but still had a seat on the bench, and Thomas

Ford, his solicitor, was still an officer of the court, but Canning and her friends had run out of alternatives.

The Trial of Elizabeth Canning: Prosecution

Elizabeth Canning's trial began on Monday, 29 April, and, unlike the typical eighteenth-century jury trial, continued on Wednesday, 1 May, Friday the 3rd, Saturday the 4th, Monday the 6th, Tuesday the 7th, and Wednesday the 8th. The 30th of April and 2 May, although they were weekdays, were not trial days as several of the aldermen were engaged in an election that week which effectively took precedence of the trial, and the jury were "permitted to go at large" when they were not in court, prompting one of a series of questions which Canning's friends presented to Sollom Emlyn, a distinguished legal scholar, directly after the verdict went against her:

> Is it agreeable to law, that a jury, once charged with the evidence, may be permitted to go at large, before they have delivered in their verdict?—A. I am of opinion, that though a jury once charged may, by consent of parties, be discharged wholly from trying the cause; yet I do not apprehend that the law will allow them to go at large, in a criminal case, while the trial is depending: for though in a long trial such a confinement may be inconvenient, yet I cannot find that the law has provided any remedy for it; it being in the eye of the law a less inconvenience, than exposing the jury to be tampered with before they have brought in their verdict. (*State Trials*, 19: 670–72)[5]

The length of the trial was so extraordinary for its time that the failure to sequester the jury may be attributed simply to inexperience. Both sides did give unusual attention to the jury's selection, although the three challenges of potential jurors made by Canning's defense fall far short of the seventeen made by the Crown (19: 284), according to Canning's friends without any stated cause. The friends themselves received a message warning them to challenge the soon-to-be foreman on the grounds that he had already publicly called Canning "a LYING B—H, a CHEAT, or an IMPOSTOR, or . . . words equally gross" (*A Refutation*, 25), but the man was sworn before Canning's solicitor arrived in court, a lapse which initiated a pattern that over the course of the trial worked cumulatively to her detriment.

Canning's case was being handled at this point by three attorneys, George Nares, John Morton (not to be confused with the

Recorder, William Moreton), and a Mr. Williams, not further identified, while the Crown's case was in the hands of Bamber Gascoyne, Edward Willes—the son of Sir John Willes, who had presided over the truncated trials of Gibbons, Clarke, and Greville, and who was himself to become Solicitor General in 1766 and judge of Common Pleas in 1767—and William Davy. Nares was a man of thirty-eight who had been admitted to the bar in 1741 and apparently practiced primarily in the criminal courts, while Morton would become Chief Justice of Chester in 1763. In Davy the prosecution had paid for the services of a lawyer well known for his effectiveness at cross-examination and not at all impeded by gentlemanly reticence. He was reported to have been either a grocer or a druggist in Exeter who first became interested in the law when a business failure led to his imprisonment for debt. He had become serjeant-at-law in February 1754, and had a reputation for a forthright wit, as when, in response to a charge that he had "disgrac[ed] the profession by taking silver, he replied, 'I took silver because I could not get gold, but I took every farthing that fellow had in the world, and hope you don't call that disgracing the profession'" (*DNB*, s.v. Davy). His colleague Bamber Gascoyne was still under thirty, but his relationship to Sir Crisp Gascoyne at the very least assured his interest in the trial's outcome. Canning's attorneys, though they seem to have done their best, were neither personally involved nor, apparently, in the process of establishing courtroom reputations; in fact, as Morton acknowledged at the opening of the session of 7 May, they had not even maintained a consistent presence there:

> It has been among the many misfortunes of the defendant, that it has been impossible for any one of her counsel to have attended through this whole trial. Mr. Williams, whose proper province it was to have replied [to Davy's closing statement], has necessarily been absent during great part of the evidence; therefore it is impossible for him to discharge his duty in that.
>
> It has likewise been my misfortune to be absent, and it has also been Mr. Nares's misfortune to be absent, so that we could not attend upon that part of the evidence. I mention this, that I may lay in my claim with your lordship [the Recorder, William Moreton], who has been so very acute and attentive, that whatever observations are proper to be made, the jury may carry the facts along with them, as well as the prosecutor's charge; and that your lordship will be so kind as to supply what we have been obliged to omit. (19: 592)

The misfortune here seems to have been primarily Canning's.

The final address to the jury which ought to have been made by her attorneys was to come instead from the Recorder, whose summary of the evidence is consistently slanted in favor of the prosecution. Moreton's statement runs through thirty-seven columns of the *State Trials* text (19: 633–69) and was the last thing the jury heard before its post-midnight withdrawal to consider its verdict. Moreton tended to summarize each prosecution witness's testimony as if it were simple fact—e.g., "George Towil, *who saw them* there on the 14th of January at Mrs. Greville's" (19: 642; my emphasis)—and to overstate their actual testimony—"John Howit . . . was at the Old Bailey at the time of that trial, but was very near being killed there by the mob" (19: 651)—while constantly denigrating the defense witnesses' testimony—e.g., Robert Beals "says the gown the woman then wore was white, though he says there was no moon that night" (19: 660), and Elizabeth Arnott "thinks her husband sold a load of pease that day, and that there was a note given on that account; but that note has not been produced" (19:662). Overall, a careful reading of the record provides considerable reason to doubt the judgment of the trial made by James Fitzjames Stephen and thereafter widely accepted on his authority that it was "remarkable . . . because it is the first specimen to be found of those elaborately conducted criminal trials in which no time or expense is spared on either side, and in which all the characteristics of English criminal law are seen at their best" (Stephens, 1: 424).[6]

Canning's trial began, after the impaneling of the jury, with the reading of the indictment by the Clerk of Arraigns, Thomas Ford, who had probably also drawn the document up in his alternate role as Sir Crisp Gascoyne's solicitor. Despite the numbing legalese in which it is couched, the indictment is not a simple *pro forma* document. It takes up twelve columns of the *State Trials* text (19: 285–97) and repeatedly reports every aspect of Canning's testimony in the trial of Squires and Wells in the following terms:

> not having the fear of God before her eyes, but being moved and seduced by the instigation of the devil, and having no regard for the laws and statutes of this realm, nor fearing the punishments therein contained, and unlawfully, wickedly, maliciously, and deliberately advising, contriving, and intending to pervert the due course of law and justice, and to cause and procure the said Mary Squires untruly to be convicted of the felony and robbery charged upon her . . . ,

[and] did falsely, wickedly, and voluntarily, and corruptly, by her own proper act and consent, and of her own most wicked and corrupt mind, upon her said oath, ... say, depose, swear, and give in evidence. (19: 287)

Every clause of her earlier testimony is now weighted with the adverbs "wickedly" and "corruptly." This indictment was followed by opening statements by all of the prosecution counsel, beginning with Bamber Gascoyne, who merely reiterated briefly that Canning's story was false as "the prisoner at the bar was never taken or carried to the house of Susannah Wells, and ... Mary Squires was at that time in Abbotsbury, in the county of Dorset" (19: 298). As all of Sir Crisp Gascoyne's evidence-gathering had attempted to prove, not only did Mary Squires have a well-supported alibi—unimpeachable, as Bamber Gascoyne presented it—but Canning herself had no credibility at all: she had, for whatever reason, invented her whole story, probably as part of an as yet undiscovered conspiracy. A charge of perjury, after all, could not be supported on the basis of an error, however careless, but had to be proven "wilful and corrupt." Gascoyne's decision to prosecute may in fact have arisen from his belief that Canning was such a perjuror; once taken, it legally behoved him to pursue her as nothing less.

Davy spoke next, at considerably greater length. He expressed a regret that perjury as aggravated as Canning's was not a capital offense and attacked head-on the prosecution's own most glaring weakness, that in over a year no amount of investigation or expenditure had been able to discover any evidence that Canning had been anywhere other than Wells's house for the period of her disappearance or that her character was any less excellent than her neighbors and employers swore it to be:

> What could tempt one so young to such accumulated wickedness, though the prosecution is not concerned to account for it, may be easily conceived upon recollecting what had happened. ... To preserve her character, it became necessary to frame an excuse for her absence from her master's service. ... To what such absence was really owing, I am not inclined to suggest, lest I should wrong her. But her flight was sudden, unexpected, and alarming. (19: 298–99)

Davy posited an initial lie designed only to save Canning's reputation, its elaboration by "unexpected inquiries," and a final persistence determined by the prospect of enrichment—"And having by this time subdued all remains of virtue, she preferred the offer of money, though she must wade through innocent blood to attain it" (19: 299).

Having read her information given before Fielding to the jury, Davy characterized it as "a story . . . intirely destitute of all human probability" (19: 301) and asked, "Does there need much evidence to contradict this? Does not common sense, and the observation of all mankind upon the course of nature, refute it in every instance? Yet such arts have been practised to engage men to believe it, that there are, at this day, thousands who embrace it as zealously, as an article of religious faith" (19: 302). These are very much the arguments of the pamphleteers, particularly Hill and Ramsay, rather than legal arguments, and Davy used them to create a climate in which the introduction of Mary Squires's alibi evidence would be offered to the jury as a sort of additional support for a conclusion they could perfectly well reach without it.

According to Davy, Mary Squires, "with her son and daughter Lucy, travelled on foot into the west of England with smuggled goods, such as they meet with in sea-port towns, and sell again to people in the country" (19: 303). Smuggling and the sale of smuggled goods never became a central issue in the case, but it is arguable that they ought to have. The alibi witnesses at Squires's trial had said she was selling goods, but this feature of her activities was considerably less stressed in Canning's trial, where holiday-making seems to be the main purpose of the Squireses' alleged visit to Abbotsbury. It is difficult to explain why smuggled goods would be carried for sale to a village itself notorious for smuggling, located only a mile from the coast and graced with the presence of an exciseman who would later be dismissed for falsification of his records, or why peddlers would spend nine days in a small and remote community whose clergyman considered it "more than ordinary scarce" of money. None of these considerations simply overthrows Mary Squires's alibi, but they do tend to cast doubt on the good character of many of Squires's witnesses, and it is characteristic of Davy that he named smuggling in the case before the defense could.

Having named it, he went on to another aspect of the alibi evidence that was new since Squires's trial, a romantic attachment between William Clarke, one of Squires's original defense witnesses in February 1753, and Lucy Squires. At that time Clarke had testified to seeing the family at Gibbons's inn when he went there for his evening "pot of liquor" and "going about the town . . . to sell things"; he had accompanied them on their departure because he was carrying goods the same way. He described George Squires's appearance in some detail and added of Lucy, "the girl was in a camblet gown." Although he had previously said in a presumably rather fiery way, having just admitted that he could give no account of Old Style and New, "[I]f I was to die for the woman, I'd speak the truth," this seems clearly to be related to his swearing to specific dates than to romantic passion, which is never mentioned—"the woman" on whose behalf Clarke was testifying was Mary Squires, not Lucy (19: 273). By the time of Canning's trial, however, the romance of Lucy Squires and William Clarke had become an important part of the prosecution's case.

I am inclined to doubt the reality of this romance and to doubt as well whether Davy himself believed in it. In taking yet another prosecution witness, George Clements, through his portion of the alibi evidence late on the long first day of the trial, Davy had to ask the by now routine questions who Clarke had danced with—Lucy—and who had accompanied the Squires family from Abbotsbury—Clarke. Clements added helpfully, "[H]e and Lucy went together." Davy interjected, not as a question and perhaps in a flash of irritated boredom, "I hope they are married by this time," and Clements dutifully answered, "The Lord knows, I don't know that" (19: 352).

The importance of the romance between Lucy Squires and William Clarke, however, was not the addition of a touch of sentiment to the case but the provision of the only piece of documentary evidence directly supporting Squires's alibi. According to Davy,

Lucy Squires had promised her sweetheart, William Clarke, to send him a letter on the road. It was at [Basingstoke] she performed her promise. But being an illiterate girl, she was obliged to have recourse to the lady of the inn to write for her. The letter is dated from Basingstoke, the 18th of January 1753. The landlady, Mrs. Morris, will tell you it was wrote by her at the time it bears date. It will appear with the Basingstoke post-mark upon it. There being no direct post from Basingstoke to Dorchester, the letter was put into the London bag; and therefore the London post-mark is also upon it, by which it will appear, that it came into the general-post office on the 19th of January. It happens that this letter (which will be read to you in the course of the evidence) refers to the circumstance of Clarke's travelling with them from Abbotsbury. (19: 304–5)

It is worth wondering what purpose the letter could have

served other than as documentation of Mary Squires's alibi. Addressed "To the post-house in Dorchester, to be directed to Abbotsbury for Mr. William Clarke, cordwainer. This with care," it apparently never reached Clarke in spite of this clear direction but went to another man of the same name at Charlster, a William Clarke who was not called in evidence but allegedly returned the letter to the post office, according to the brief testimony of under-sheriff Willis of Dorset. The Abbotsbury Clarke may be held not to have missed much, particularly when one considers that the charge for the person receiving the letter was seven pence. Dated "Basingstoke, Jan 18, 175–," the last digit of the year being torn off although the corner on which it appeared was folded into the center of the letter, it reads as follows:

> Sir; this with my kind love and service to you, and all your family, hoping you are all in good health, as I be at present. This is to acquaint you that I am very uneasy for your troublesome journey, hoping you received no illness from your journey; so no more at present from your most obedient and humble servant, Lucy Squires.
> I desire to hear from you as soon as possible. Direct for Lucy Squires at Brentford, near London. George and Mother give their compliments to you and all your family. (19: 369)

In spite of Davy's preliminary statement about the letter, it is neither dated 1753 nor is Clarke's "journey" clearly identified as the very short and not particularly troublesome one he supposedly took with the Squireses on 9 January from Abbotsbury to Portisham—two miles—and on the next day to Ridgway Foot—another four miles (19: 346). Davy questioned Thomas Ravenhill, the "assistant-clerk to the western road" of the London post office to establish that the "very imperfect" postmark was probably 19 January. Morton established on cross-examination that a postal stamp lasted only a day or less, its boxwood surface becoming "so defaced and clogged" that the marks were illegible and that used marks were "thrown into a drawer, where they remain five or six months, and then we burn them," but he pressed this no further, although he also established that Ravenhill did not know whether Basingstoke had its own stamp or not or what the name of the place (two lines long, which generally meant a town with a long name) was in the illegible mark under discussion (19: 370–71).

In introducing the case for the defense, Morton recurred to the letter. If it did in fact originate in Basingstoke on 18 January, it went far to weaken the bad impression created by George

Squires's inability to tell where he had been between Coombe and Basingstoke by fixing him definitely at the end of the hiatus just where he had said he was. But the damaged date and the prosecution's failure to produce "this wrong Mr. Clarke . . ., who could not, I am sure have perused so unexpected a letter without some degree of attention . . . [a]nd from [whom] we might possibly have known how the date appeared, when delivered to him" (19: 445) were certainly flaws in the prosecution's evidence.

Ravenhill was recalled to the stand on 7 May to testify that the Basingstoke bag came into the London post office on Mondays, Wednesdays, and Fridays, and Davy produced an almanac to prove that 19 January had not occurred on one of those days between 1749 and 1753. Morton objected that the letter had never been proved to be in the Basingstoke post office at all (19: 593), but Davy in his summation insisted that the letter was now conclusive evidence, along, indeed, with all of the rest of the prosecution's case.

After Squires's alibi evidence, Davy moved on to Canning's "account of the room she pretended to have been confined in" as the second major aspect of the case against her—it was in his view as "unapplicable" to Wells's hayloft as to St. Paul's Cathedral. Davy went through the sequence of events from Canning's return home on 29 January to her appearance before Alderman Chitty on the 31st to the visit to Enfield Wash on 1 February, all from the point of view of the hostile witnesses whom he would call to make the prosecution's case—Alderman Chitty, Gawen Nash, Ezra Whiffin, the tree-lopping party—and concluded with one final allegation, that on the occasion when Canning was present on 7 February 1753 to hear the formal recantation of Virtue Hall's testimony,

> the bed-gown which she pretended to have taken out of the workshop, as also the pitcher, were both produced. She was very desirous of taking them with her, which my lord mayor objected to, and proposed that they should be deposited in some public place to be seen by any body, because they might possibly lead to a discovery. What induced the defendant to be so extremely anxious for the possession of the tattered bed-gown, and broken pitcher, is hard to say, but she was so much bent upon it, that she unwarily claimed a property in the bed-gown, and said, It was her mother's. If it was her mother's bed-gown, how did it get to Mrs. Wells's? (19: 311)

This story was supported in the trial, where it occurred as the last item in the prosecution's case, by the testimony of Mr. Deputy Molineux and Samuel Reed, and the defense barely cross-examined them. Davy assured the court that the prosecution had several character witnesses ready to support its witnesses, but the court advised him, "Stay till they are attacked" (19: 431), and in the event the defense did nothing to attack this part of the prosecution's case, although they certainly possessed the materials to do so. The bed-gown had been in the possession of the Cannings since Elizabeth's return home on 29 January and the pitcher since the end of Squires's and Wells's trial, so that when Sir Crisp Gascoyne reported that they "were produced" (11) for the occasion of Hall's recantation, his use of the agentless passive construction conceals the somewhat awkward fact that they were produced by the compliance of the two Elizabeth Cannings, mother and daughter. Both Edward Rossiter and Thomas Myles, neither of whom were called at Canning's trial, nevertheless deposed that Canning had said "she was going to take [the bedgown and pitcher] to her mother's" (Rossiter, Appendix 13, *A Refutation*, 13; see also Myles, Appendix 50, 43), and that if she had said otherwise they would have heard her. Based only on an overheard fragment of speech, the story of Canning and the bedgown was of marginal probative value anyhow, and the defense had other evidence from which it hoped for more.

There remained only Willes's opening statement to be made before witnesses could begin to be called. It was shorter than Davy's and concentrated on the discrepancies in Canning's various accounts of her story—important since "Truth is always constant, but falshood and fiction must be judged by another criterion" (19: 314). Willes's own credibility is questionable, since he compared Canning's statement to Alderman Chitty (written down by Chitty sometime later and never endorsed by Canning) with what she told Justice Tyshemaker, information never taken down in writing at all and never produced in court in any form, as well as with the signed information given before Fielding. Willes's main objective, presented with the "certain flippancy of manner" attributed to him by Foss's *Biographical Dictionary of the Judges of England* (739), was to present the jury with an initial picture of Canning that would contrast strikingly with the plain and silent young woman in the dock, something he accomplished by the use of periphrastic expressions in place of her name—"this wonderful girl," "this mirror of modern virtue," "this romantic girl," "this extraordinary girl" (19: 316–18).

According to the trial record, "It was agreed upon by the counsel on both sides, that the witnesses should be examined apart, and, when examined, not to return to the others" (19: 323), although as I have already related it was necessary to insist that Lucy Squires be removed from court before her brother's testimony when it was expected that she would corroborate it, and that although Lucy was not called after all, the entire Squires family thereafter sat in court, in close proximity to all subsequent witnesses. The friends of Canning later maintained as well that although "[t]he court had ordered, that the unexamined witnesses should have no communication with those who knew what was given in evidence; yet a clerk of Mr. Ford's, and several witnesses who had been examined, were found among them" (*A Refutation*, 25), and I find this plausible: keeping close to a hundred witnesses separate from each other was clearly beyond the court's resources, and even if it had been feasible, it would have been too late to make a great deal of difference to the evidence. The alibi witnesses especially had been repeatedly consulted by Sir Crisp Gascoyne's agents for a period of more than a year, and many of them knew each other even before the investigation started. Canning's friends made the most of the minor discrepancies in their testimony—"That Mary Squires had a BLACK colour under her chin, which black colour was RED: that she was of the different ages of FIFTY SIXTY and SEVENTY years: that she was IN-FIRM and STOUTISH: . . . that she waded THROUGH a brook, over which her son George CARRIED her upon his back" (*A Refutation*, 26)—but overall Sir Crisp Gascoyne was correct in his statement that the prosecution witnesses gave their testimony with "clearness, certainty, and consistency" (33). The question for the jury, however, would be whether those qualities produced conviction as to their truth.

Certainly quantity of evidence was present on both sides. Even on the opening day of the trial, when much time was taken up by the indictment and opening statements for the prosecution, thirty-nine witnesses (exclusive of George Squires himself and the prosecution's frustrated attempt to question the under-sheriff of Dorset) were questioned and cross-examined, most of them briefly, to establish Mary Squires's alibi from South Parrott, Dorset on 29 December 1752 (19: 329) to Page Green, Tottenham, four miles from London, on 23 January 1753 (19: 372–73). For what it was worth, what George Squires could remember was fully supported; what he could not had no witnesses.

Prosecution counsel confined their questioning of these witnesses to the alibi, ignoring any discussion of the Squires fam-

ily's reasons for their journey. Defense attorney Williams asked
William Clarke on cross-examination if George had sold anything
at Abbotsbury, and Clarke said, "Yes, he sold an apron to the
landlady at the Old Ship, and another to the servant" (19: 347),
but this seems a small amount of commercial activity to justify
a long journey by three people in the middle of the winter. Morton asked John Hawkins, "What had the old woman used to deal
in?" and Hawkins replied, "I never saw her deal in any thing;
I have heard people talk she sold things." Morton had earlier
attempted to get Hawkins to acknowledge that George Clements,
with whom the Squires family had stayed on earlier visits and
whom Hawkins characterized as of "no trade, but a fisherman,"
was engaged in smuggling, asking, "Does he never catch such a
thing as a handkerchief, such as is round your neck, at sea?" but
Hawkins had replied, "No, not as I know of" (19: 358). None of
the witnesses asked—not all of them were—seemed to know
anything of the Squires family's business. David Wallace, asked
why they had come to Abbotsbury, replied, "That I don't know;
they have at different times sold things" (19: 355), and Francis
Bewley of Ridgway said, "Upon my word, I cannot tell" what
trade they had carried on (19: 361).

At last the lateness of the hour persuaded the court to adjourn.
The next phase in the prosecution's case was to be the evidence
relating to Canning's deposition before Alderman Chitty, which
would clearly take a good deal of time, and it was not begun
until the morning of 1 May. Meanwhile, on the evening of the
first day of the trial, "[a]bout seven o'Clock in the Evening, at
the Close of the Examination of the Witnesses, Mr. Alderman
Gascoyne was advised by his Friends to retire, to avoid the Danger of a formidable and threatening Mob, who openly avow'd his
Destruction" (Truth Triumphant, 29). According to the account
given by the writer of Genuine and Impartial Memoirs of Elizabeth Canning, always more elaborate if not more reliable than
earlier versions, the time was nearer ten, and the mob that first
cheered Canning also "had the Audacity to assault [Gascoyne]
with Dirt, Stones, or any other offensive Material that fell in their
Way" until he was forced to take shelter in "a neighboring Tav-
ern" (161). This episode was not, to the memoirist, merely unfortunate: "Mobs . . . may be easily collected . . .: But still they must
have some Directors; they must be taught to believe themselves
or their Friends injured" (160–61). Denying that he is accusing
Canning's friends of this, the writer goes on to do so: "By their
unwearied Assiduity in advertising and dispersing their Publications, some of which conspicuously decorated the walls of

Alehouses, and Posts on the Highway, the Multitude were inspired to look upon Canning's Purity and Virtue with a sort of Reverence, and to consider her Innocence as a Matter that ought not to be disputed" (162); they were equally "industriously instructed to believe Sir Crisp Gascoyne the *cruel Oppressor*" (162–63).

The first business of the court on 1 May was thus not the examination of Alderman Chitty, as it appears in *State Trials*, but a reaction to "the riotous Transactions of the Monday Night preceding, and particularly of the Danger to which Sir Crisp Gascoyne had been exposed." A guard was appointed to attend both him and the jury, and "[t]he Recorder very pathetically represented the ill Consequences of suffering the Insolence of a Mob to escape with Impunity," adding that he, too, "had not been exempt from Abuse" (165). Once more, the Canning camp was thrown on the defensive. One of Canning's counsel (it is not stated which) went so far as to "apologize for his Client," although he hoped the jury would not be prejudiced by this external circumstance. A newspaper paragraph in the *London Daily Advertiser*, unsigned but probably the work of the indefatigable Hill, had appeared that morning claiming that a "Mob (as it may be reasonably believed) hired for the Purpose" had attempted the "Destruction" of anti-Canning witnesses. "Must it not appear an extraordinary instance of the Girl's Innocence," the writer of the *Genuine and Impartial Memoirs* asked rhetorically, "that those who have so long endeavoured to elude the Course of Justice by a continued Train of Artifice, now seek to impede it by Violence and Outrage?" (165).

Although the memoirist claimed that the newspaper paragraph was "so far from being designed to prejudice the Girl, was intended for her Service; by showing what Construction her Opponents might put upon these Disturbances," the court here concurred with Canning's counsel that the publication of such a paragraph while the trial was in progress was "cruel, unjust, and illegal" and grounds for a charge against the printer (166).

By that afternoon, Canning's friends had in print a notice headed "To the Persons assembled about the Sessions House in the Old Bailey." At least as "pathetically" as the Recorder can have done, they beseeched the crowd, "If you have any regard for public justice, for this poor injured girl, or for yourselves—by all that is dear to you, be persuaded to peace, and without the least murmur or insult to any, to wait the event of this business—God and her innocence have hitherto supported her, in the opinions of many, thro' unexampled distresses: leave it to God and her innocence only to carry her through this, and all will be well" (Appendix 55, *A Refutation*, 45). *Genuine and Impartial Memoirs* reprints this document with the phrases "poor injured girl" and "unexampled distresses" italicized, and argues that the actual intent of the notice was inflammatory, "for surely nothing could be more likely to incense them further than *appealing to themselves*" (167). For whatever reason, the mob was again outside the courtroom when Wednesday's session adjourned, and Thomas Rawlinson, the current Lord Mayor, was obliged to read the Riot Act while Alderman (now Sheriff) Chitty (who would be Lord Mayor in turn in 1760) "thought it no more than necessary" to escort Sir Crisp Gascoyne as far as the Royal Exchange with "a Body of Constables" (187–88).

The jury had presumably had a good deal of opportunity to observe both the actions of the mob and the discussion of them on the following Wednesday morning; they seem not only to have "gone at large" but to have heard all arguments between counsel and the court over what was and was not admissible evidence and to have had no restraint placed on their reading of pamphlets and newspapers discussing the case. It is impossible from the bare list of their names to guess what sympathies of class or even of neighborhood might have moved them, but class was certainly an issue both outside and within the courtroom. Was it appropriate to criticize a man of Gascoyne's standing, or to appeal to a mob to have regard for themselves and consider "all that is dear to you"? Certainly the bias of the system was in favor of authority and the holders of official positions. When Alderman Chitty was not immediately available to testify on the morning of 1 May, Gawen Nash was put on the stand, but as soon as Chitty arrived Nash, who "had been for some Time before extremely ill of a Fever, and was not perfectly recovered at the Time of his Examination, which took up near two Hours," was "bid to stand down," not resuming his evidence until Chitty's was completed (167–68). The printed version of the trial smooths out the interruption of Nash's evidence by simply printing Chitty's first; perhaps the jury was expected to perform a similar feat.

I have discussed Alderman Chitty's evidence and his version of Canning's statement in chapter 2, and the evidence of Gawen Nash, John Hague, and Edward Aldridge both there and earlier in this chapter. They were followed on the stand by a group of witnesses "who, at various times, during the month of January, 1753, were in the very room in which the defendant swore she was confined" (19: 397). This was Davy's rubric for Fortune and Judith Natus and a further selection of witnesses who were not to be heard until Friday, 3 May—Mary Landry, Sarah Howit, John Landry, Edward Allen, John Cantril, Ezra Whiffin, Alexander Livingstone, John Whiffin (Ezra's son), Elizabeth Long, John Howit, and Robert White. These in turn would be followed by what might be termed the odds and ends of the prosecution's case— John Donoval, who had built the model of Wells's hayloft; George Talmash, who had helped Elizabeth Long to get subpoenas for her mother's trial but not to do anything with them; Elizabeth Mayle, who had examined Canning's shift, Fielding's clerk, Joshua Brogden, who swore to the information Canning had given before Fielding; and Mr. Deputy Molineux and Samuel Reed, who told the story of Canning and the bed-gown.

If Gawen Nash's evidence, which fills nine columns of the *Select Trials* text, took two hours, then a rough equation of four and a half columns per hour suggests that the proceedings of 1 May lasted just over seven hours, although this is certainly an underestimate, omitting not only all breaks and interruptions, but the whole preliminary discussion of events outside the courtroom. The same calculation, however, yields the result of a twenty-hour courtroom session on 29 April, an impossibility if the proceedings began at 9:00 A.M. and ended in the vicinity of 10:00 P.M. The point of these operations, though, is not really to establish the duration of the court's proceedings but the impossibility of recovering them with more than the most approximate accuracy.

I have discussed most of the evidence in the case as it developed, drawing upon but not confining myself to the trial record, in an attempt not only to come somewhat closer to the sequence of events as contemporaries experienced it but also to de-valorize the status of the trial itself as both a specially accurate form of representation and as an official record of truth. Thus I have emphasized not the usual "courtroom drama" of question and answer, examination and cross-examination, but the rhetorical representations constructed both in long opening statements and in occasional remarks by both prosecution and defense counsel, who, however imperfectly, framed, elicited, and mediated the evidence presented to the jury, and I will continue to do so in discussing the second half of Canning's trial, the defense.

The Trial of Elizabeth Canning: Defense

Although the heading of Canning's trial in *A Complete Collection of State Trials* gives the dates as including both Friday, 3

May, and Saturday, 4 May, the text of the trial itself does not mark
the proceedings of the two days as separate. The 3rd of May runs
from column 405 onto 532—by the four and a half column per
hour rule of thumb, for over twenty hours. Even if the session of
3 May lasted past midnight, it is unlikely to have continued until
six o'clock in the morning, and in fact it did not. According to
Elizabeth de la Torre's account of the trial, an adjournment took
place on what would be column 478 of the text of the trial, after
the testimony of Canning's aunt and uncle (193), but although
de la Torre was thoroughly familiar with the documents in the
case, having even compiled the standard bibliography of it,[7] she
gives no documentation in her dramatized account.

The record of the adjournment can be traced to *Genuine and
Impartial Memoirs*, which notes rather sourly that "Three Persons, who had been committed for Misbehaviour, were, upon
making a proper Submission, discharged; and the Court ad-
jurned [sic] till the next morning. A numerous Mob were assembled, who escorted the Defendant from the Session-House; but
were not guilty of any particular outrages" (198).[8] De la Torre's
claim for her pseudonymous *"Elizabeth is Missing," Or, Truth
Triumphant: An Eighteenth Century Mystery* is "This is the way
it happened in 1753. These are the very words people spoke.
Nothing has been invented, nothing has been added" (Foreword,
unpaged), but representation and interpretation have nevertheless been at work, as in de la Torre's habitual scene-painting: "It
was a bad time to open the defence, on a Friday afternoon after
dinner. The jury was torpid, the judges were bored. Mr. Nares
and Mr. Morton were eloquent. Mr. Williams was not so eloquent
as wise. Here is his speech verbatim: 'We shall lay our evidence
before you, and begin first with Mr. Lyon, the master of the girl'"
(192). The adjournment de la Torre reports comes from a contemporary source, but the torpor, boredom, eloquence, and wisdom
she reports with equal confidence are supplied from her own
imagination.

In my view of the framing of Canning's case, however, the "eloquence" of Morton and Nares plays a critical role, and my account therefore reverses de la Torre's decision to dismiss it. I
would be disingenuous if I denied that I think my method "better" than de la Torre's, but the difference nevertheless springs
from our different rhetorical purposes. Neither of us is or can be
telling the complete truth, no more than could the documents
we depend on—in this particular instance of the adjournment
on the evening of 3 May, the very tendentious *Genuine and Impartial Memoirs*.

Morton's opening statement began by emphasizing the great misfortune by which Canning now stood before the jury, "brought to answer for a most foul offence in herself, merely for having done her duty in prosecuting others for the most unheard-of violation of her own person and property, and the laws of her country" (*State Trials*, 19: 431). He alluded, without naming Alderman Chitty, to "short minutes [which had] swelled to no less than six or seven sheets," complimenting the jury, over whose selection the prosecution, he observed, had exercised "unparalleled" care, for its patience and attention, and he justified Canning's efforts to avoid prosecution before Sir Crisp Gascoyne, also unnamed (19: 431–34). He addressed himself in considerable detail to the improbabilities Davy had alleged in Canning's story, expressing his own doubt that street robbers should be expected to be "humane, . . . deliberate . . ., [and] wary" (19: 436), and went on to offer a similar argument in Canning's favor—that she "would not have ventured to mention any one circumstance she did" (19: 437) if her object had been to tell a story that could not be checked.

The problem with this sort of argument, Morton acknowledged, was that it could never come to a conclusion. Even if the prosecution's claim that Canning's story must be "forged" was accepted, "could a weak, illiterate woman (however supported) have either invented, or, when invented, be uniform in the proof of it?" (19: 438). This was an argument whose force the prosecution had, in fact, felt, and Sir Crisp Gascoyne in part responded to it by raising a doubt whether Canning was properly called illiterate at all, alleging that she had signed her information before Fielding with her mark in order to further a deception already well underway: "She could write much better than most persons in her station. Why then did she sign her mark, unless it was to appear illiterate? Will it be said that she who could take so long a journey on the 1st of February, continued unable from thence to the 7th to write her name?" (Gascoyne, 41). It is not easily evident to me why a very minimal level of literacy should have been of any great help to Canning as the perpetrator of an essentially oral fraud, assuming that she was one, but certainly the prosecution found meat for its case in the supposition with Davy subjecting her mother to a fairly lengthy cross-examination on the subject:

Can your daughter write?—She can a little; it is a sad hand.
Can she write a letter well enough for you to find out the meaning of it?—She can hardly write at all.

Can she write her name?—I believe she can; I have seen her write it.

How long was she at a writing-school?—About a quarter of a year.

When did you see any of her hand-writing?—I do not know that I have seen any of her hand-writing these six years.

Look at this paper (it was a notice of trial with her name to it, the name wrote by her:) Is this name her hand-writing?—I believe it is her scribbling like.

Do you think, when your daughter could write, she would only make her mark?—I do not know for that.

Mr. Davy. I ask this, my lord, because in her information before Justice Fielding, there she only makes her mark, and by the paper I see she writes an exceeding good hand. (19: 487)

Two specimens of Canning's signature exist to my knowledge, on two copies of a petition of 26 June 1754 for an amelioration of her conditions of transportation (State Papers Domestic, George II, Bundle 127). Both "scribbling" and "an exceeding good hand" seem wide of the mark, but "a sad hand" seems punningly appropriate. Canning's mature signature (like the notice of trial, these documents came late in her case, well after she can be assumed to have recovered her physical health) is painstakingly neat, the memorized signature of a child to whom writing is an alien act, out of scale and alignment with the document to which it is attached, aslant and wavering. On one of two otherwise identical documents she has omitted the second "e" from her own first name. It would have taken her a long time, I believe, to write a letter, but Davy recurred to the question of Canning's literacy in his concluding statement with ferocious innuendo:

I should have added to the observations upon the evidence of the mother, who proved the defendant's hand-writing to some papers now before you, that the innocence of the defendant having been most cogently inferred from her supposed simplicity, and she having been represented as a poor, silly, illiterate creature, incapable of inventing such a story, to furnish her advocates with so excellent an argument, she set her mark to her information before Mr. Fielding, as if unable to write her name. . . . I dare say, it was not then imagined that this marks-woman had received so good an education. Who would have thought, upon reading the pamphlet, which that good magistrate was pleased to oblige the world with, containing the information at large, with such ingenious remarks upon her stupidity;—who would have dreamt, that this "child in years, more so in understanding" was able to write a fair, legible hand?

And this may serve as a specimen to shew what mean artifices have been made use of to deceive mankind. (19: 631)

Fielding had not, of course, characterized Canning as either silly or stupid, merely as innocent and unassertive, but for Davy's purposes the only guarantor of innocence in a case like Canning's was imbecility, which her signature was sufficient to disprove.[9]

Morton's opening statement, presumably a part of the structure of "mean artifice" denounced by Davy, continued, reminding the jury that if Canning had succeeded in concealing herself during January 1753 for some discreditable reason, she had managed something "that money, art, and friends have scarce ever effected" (19: 439). He made the inference from the prosecution's emphasis on "suppositions and arguments of improbability" that there existed "a diffidence in their proof of facts" (19: 440) and turned next to that aspect of the case:

Abbotsbury was to be the great scene of contradiction: there all the witnesses, whether united by a long course of smuggling, or only occasionally there, are express and positive: other circumstances, surely not altogether common in the course of a gypsey's life, are reserved only for their residence at Abbotsbury. In all other places Squires is attempted to be shown properly as a vagrant,—fortune-telling,—staying a night only in a place, and lodged in barns.

But when once brought to Abbotsbury, without any cause opened or proved, they are at once to halt, not as gypsies, but became, in an instant, remarkable guests; live in the new part of the house, instead of lying in a barn; instead of being gypsies, that every one avoids, except such as want to deal in fortune-telling and smuggled goods, they are now companions of those of the best rank in the place, and at two balls in one week. (19: 441)

The Abbotsbury evidence was much linked to the calendar change, a piece of legislation Morton said he had opposed as a source of "falsehood and confusion . . . likely to be productive of mistakes in evidence," and of no visible "use . . . to the public," and even more to the credibility of George Squires, who "hardly supported himself." Davy had assigned his refusal to call Lucy, after George had gone to pieces under cross-examination, to her stupidity, but this reason, "like many others, [was] the effect of a quick invention, unsupported by proof. Both these witnesses were, at once, made almost ideots," Morton observed, but they had not been so represented before George's debacle.

George himself, in fact, had been a good witness so long as his questioning was in friendly hands: "Where did there appear any defect of understanding, during his examination on behalf of the prosecution? He was clear, quick, and minute, both as to times, names and places, that were within the route to be proved. Of other places, certainly as remarkable, certainly as natural objects of memory, not a tittle was to be remembered, for to have remembered any thing, would have given a clue" (19: 442). The Squires family had, according to George's evidence, returned to London because of a letter informing them that their second sister was ill, but neither the sister nor the letter had been produced in evidence, and George could not tell where or how the letter had been received. Further, "the nearer he arrived to his own home, the less [George Squires was] capable of remembering things and places himself,—the less [he was] able to produce persons to remember him and his mother and his sister" (19: 444).

From the alibi evidence—about which, in my opinion, Morton did raise some pertinent questions—the defense attorney proceeded to that relating to Wells's hayloft and Canning's descriptions of it. Here, he asserted, the prosecution had really been wasting the jury's time: "For what doth it all amount to more than this, that a general fact, compounded of a variety of things done and said, when related on particular occasions, and at different times, has not always been minutely and exactly related the same way?" These sorts of arguments from "seeming contradiction [had] been the only materials which the printed trash of quacks, inspectors, and justices" had resorted to, but they were not, in Morton's view, credible in the context of a trial (19: 447). Morton cited the goldsmiths' evidence alongside their tardiness in coming forward with it as proof that apparent contradictions did not in practice carry the profound conviction that the prosecution argued that they should and went on to question the omission of Virtue Hall from the prosecution's witnesses, incurring the opposition of the Recorder.

Morton's summary of the defense case to follow was the briefest part of his statement: it would depend on "absolute fact, not [on] refined observations on them," many of them, "such as the absence of Canning, her return, her account of herself, her real condition" already proved by the prosecution, and it would concentrate on the contradictions of Squires's alibi, calling "many witnesses, who have lived in or about Enfield-Wash, from fifteen to thirty years, people of known and established credit." The prosecution had had the list for several days, and the adjourn-ments of the trial had afforded them the opportunity to look into their characters. None of them were known to Canning—unlike the Squires family and the alibi witnesses, particularly the Abbotsbury ones—and they would not produce the same sort of "exact . . . diary" of the Squireses' movements that those witnesses did: "Whether the want of such particular exactness in the relation of facts in themselves, at the time performed, entirely indifferent, will diminish the credit of an account or not, I shall leave it to your own observation" (19: 450). The implication was clear enough that the Enfield witnesses, unlike those supporting Squires's alibi, were independent both of Canning and of each other. If the virtues of the alibi witnesses, in Sir Crisp Gascoyne's view, had been clarity, certainty, and consistency, then the contrasting virtues of the Enfield witnesses would be detachment, disinterestedness, and spontaneity. It would be the jury's task to determine "the weight and credit of the evidence" but even more to give "facts expressly sworn" precedence over "arguments and observations" (19: 451).

George Nares's opening speech supported Morton's. Nares emphasized the societal disadvantages inherent in any common practice of indicting for perjury witnesses who had initially been believed—such prosecutions "must serve to intimidate and prevent numbers of people from commencing prosecutions to endeavor to bring the guilty to punishment, lest, by some strange alteration of affairs, they themselves may, in their turn, be prosecuted" (19: 453). He reiterated the frustration of the defense at the prosecution's failure to call Virtue Hall, who ought to have been examined not only about the events of January 1753, but about how she had come to change her story—not that "the worshipful magistrate . . . could [have] intend[ed] to seduce her by rewards or promises: but . . . the poor girl might weakly imagine, that, if she altered her evidence, she might have some rewards" (19: 455)—and at their similar failure to call both of Mary Squires's daughters about the letter that had supposedly recalled the family to London and the route they had taken there. Nares described the alibi witnesses as a group of people who "had been half a year conferring together on that point only" (19: 459), while the Enfield witnesses all lived within ten miles of London and had long been known to the prosecutor—if their characters were impeachable, there had been ample opportunity to do so, just as there had been to inquire into Canning's story, without any evidence surfacing that in any way contradicted it.

Sir Crisp Gascoyne would later assert that the Enfield witnesses were as a group either incompetent or corrupt, but although he was sure that "several of them"—he did not specify which—"were guilty of perjury, and may easily be proved so, even from their own acknowledgments," he himself, "if . . . not called upon, for the sake of public justice, to maintain this assertion," would not do so: "'tis time for me to be at rest" (34). It is not easy to see how such a case might have been made, but the point is moot; Gascoyne had, by his own account, prosecuted Canning for perjury because of the promptings of his conscience. By the time he wrote his *Address to the Liverymen*, these were apparently satisfied by the publication of his conclusions:

> Some [of the Enfield witnesses] pretended to remember the times by written evidence, *but without producing any*, and in one instance, where the written evidence referred to, was said to be in the hands of Mr. Smithram, a man of character at Endfield, I ordered it to be sent for—Mr. Smithram himself produced it, and it proved the very *contrary* of what the witness had attested—she swore she saw the Gypsey at Endfield on the 18th of January, the written evidence proved it to be the 25th—some pretended to have seen her cursorily, and some at great distances—whilst others spoke positively as to the time, yet could not tell whether Christmas happened in June or December; and I don't remember that any two of them spoke to their seeing her at the same time.
>
> Some of these witnesses might be only mistaken; and I wish my charity could plead thus favourably for the rest. (33)

As the writers of *A Refutation of Sir Crisp Gascoyne's Address* noted, only one of the Enfield witnesses, a farmboy, had failed the test of knowing in which month Christmas fell, and "he might well know the market days of Waltham and Epping, by which, and not by the months, he fixed the time of seeing Mary Squires." At least one of the written evidences that might have supported a witness's evidence had been detained by John Myles, while others had been, surely rather naively, "neglected to the injury of Canning," although they had "been since examined, and found to correspond" (v). In the main body of their text they set forth all of the Enfield witnesses' testimony in chart form, with the witnesses' names and residences, the times when and places where they had seen Mary Squires, and "their reasons for fixing particular times of seeing her" in parallel columns (22–25). The dates range from 1 December 1752 through 30 January 1753 and are, I think it fair to say, as compatible with the idea that Squires was then a casual resident of the neighborhood of Enfield Wash as the testimony of her own alibi witnesses is with her being then on a journey from South Parrott, Dorset, to London—the point is both crucial and indeterminable.

After devoting most of the latter part of Friday's court session to Morton's and Nares's opening statements for the defense, the trial spent all day Saturday on witnesses to Canning's homecoming, her evidence before Justice Chitty, and the trip to Enfield, holding over the Enfield witnesses themselves until Monday. Since I cannot see that weighing the Enfield witnesses against the West Country ones can produce anything approaching certainty, a detailed examination of both is likely to lead only to frustration. However, a look at just one of the contested points is worthwhile to show the extreme difficulty of assessing this evidence conclusively.

Gascoyne had referred triumphantly to Anne Johnson's testimony as being overthrown by Mr. Smitheram's—this being how his name is spelled in the *State Trials* text. Johnson was the widow of a fishmonger, who had lived at Enfield for twenty-seven years and who earned her living by spinning. She took wool home from her employers and returned it to them spun, and she had taken wool home from Mr. Smitheram, she said, on 16 January—it was the first work she had taken home all year, and it fixed the date for her when she saw Mary Squires at her door two days later, asking if she had any china to mend (19: 566). On Tuesday the prosecution called Thomas Smitheram to show the book in which he recorded that wool had been "delivered out" to Anne Johnson on the 16th and "brought home" on the 23rd. As I read Johnson's and Smitheram's evidence, the only "contradiction" I see—although I think the word is too strong—is that each uses the expression "bringing work home" to refer to his/her own home, but neither was asked the simple question which might have cleared up the discrepancy.

John Morton, showing signs of fatigue, spoke only briefly at the end of the evidence on Tuesday. He had already consigned the defense's case to the hands of the Recorder and his only comment on the Johnson-Smitheram issue was that Johnson was "a poor old woman" who would never have referred to Smitheram's book unless she believed in the truth of her own evidence: "It is only a mistake" (19: 596). Such mistakes, however, and the unasked and unanswered questions that leave them unresolved on the surface of the account, form the unsearchable and tangled underside of the trial of Elizabeth Canning.

If Canning's defense counsel may be said to have effectively abandoned her at the end of her trial, the prosecution showed no such weakness. Instead, they entrusted the entire closing argument to their most effective pleader, Davy, who solemnly apologized to the jury for holding them so long over a case of great "intricacy and difficulty," one whose problems arose "not so much from the nature of the question, as from the clouds of darkness in which it was inveloped by those, who, merely in opposition to the prosecutor, adopted the crime of perjury and formed a faction to support it." Officially, Elizabeth Canning was on trial, but her whole defense was caught up in a political contest that enabled the prosecution to question its integrity even as it pretended not to—"The insolence of the mobs about this court" sprang from a "design . . . easily discovered, yet it would be very hard that such misbehaviour, however, occasioned, should affect the unhappy person at the bar" (19: 597).

This "unhappy person" was merely, in Davy's account, the perpetrator of "the most impious and detestable [crime] the human heart can conceive"—perjury—"by all the arts of hypocrisy . . . insinuat[ing] herself into the compassion of others . . . [being] the peculiar sin of this person, not yet twenty years of age" (19: 598). If Davy went beyond his evidence in representing Canning as a moral monster—later in the same speech he would express himself "willing this young woman . . . should be considered (exclusive of the present charge) as a modest, virtuous, honest, creditable girl . . . [b]ut there is a time, gentlemen, when people begin to be wicked" (19: 614)—he also allowed himself considerable license in recapitulating for the jury what they had themselves heard over the past week. I have already given his revision of Alderman Chitty's testimony (chapter 2); he went on to operate similarly on the testimony of defense witnesses as well. Canning's mother, the apprentice James Lord, Robert Scarrat, and more came in for the same sort of treatment as Thomas Bennett and his story of seeing Canning after her escape and relating that she was afraid of the tanner's dog (see chapter 2). Mrs. Canning "has said enough to create a jealousy, at least, that neither her daughter's perjury, nor the motives to it, are unknown to her" (19: 615), while Scarrat was charged with a long-standing hostility to Susannah Wells only compounded by his denial that "he ever vowed revenge against her" (19: 619), a motive for his support for Canning's story for which the prosecution had produced no evidence at all.

Davy gave Canning's friends the dubious credit of having so

far been "so faithful to her" that her secret was still safe with them, but he held out the hope that if Scarrat was in on the truth, self-interest would soon lead him to discover it. "[I]n all likelihood, the time is not far off for an ample discovery," for if all else failed once Canning was convicted and found that "those people can no longer protect her; when she shall seriously reflect upon the distress to which her guilt has reduced her; conscience, perhaps may prompt her to atone in some measure for the mischiefs she has occasioned, and she may, at the same time, hope to obtain some remission of punishment, by the gratification of an universal curiosity" (19: 608). The jury's vote for conviction, in other words, would itself produce the much desired and delayed revelation of the hitherto hidden truth.

Davy's argument was followed by yet another squabble over the availability or not of Virtue Hall as a witness, with the prosecution counsel and judges once more agreeing against George Nares that she was not a proper witness—the jury might call her, Davy said, probably fairly confident that at this late stage in the proceedings they were unlikely to do so, but neither the prosecution nor the defense could (19: 633).

The final address to the jury was the summation of—supposedly—the defense's case by the Recorder, William Morton, a windfall to the prosecution not only because of Moreton's very obvious bias but perhaps equally because of the lulling colorlessness of his presentation and its apparent judicial objectivity. I give a section of his conclusion as a sample:

When you have laid this evidence together, and weighed it with proper attention, you will then take her defence into your consideration, and determine whether she has answered the crime with which she is charged to your satisfaction. In the first place, you will consider, whether the evidence she gave against Mary Squires, can possibly be true; and in the next place, whether you think it probable. As to the first, there is no evidence even to assist you in determining whether it is possible for human nature to subsist for twenty-nine days together upon no more than a quartern-loaf, and a pitcher of water of the size you have seen. If you should think this possible, you will then take the probability of her defence into consideration. Her master Lyon tells you, that he differed from the rest of his companions who went with him to Enfield, and that, for his part, he had no doubt of the truth of what she had sworn. (19: 669)

And so on, until, with a final compliment, the jury were at last sent out to consider the evidence and arrive at a verdict.

Verdicts and Aftermaths

According to the version incorporated in *State Trials:*

> The Jury withdrew at twenty minutes after twelve o'clock in the morning to consider of their verdict, and returned at fifteen minutes after two, and brought in their verdict, Guilty of perjury, but not wilful and corrupt.
>
> Upon which the Recorder told them, "That he could not receive their verdict, because it was partial; and they must either find her guilty of the whole indictment, or else acquit her."
>
> Upon which they were sent out again at twenty-five minutes after two, and returned at forty-one minutes after two; and brought in their verdict Guilty of Wilful and Corrupt Perjury.
>
> Upon which she was committed by the Court to the custody of the keeper of Newgate. (19: 669)

After the heavy exposure to the prosecution's view of the case with which the trial ended, it may seem remarkable that the jury took as long as it did or expressed its initial—and unaccept-able—discomfort with the terms of the indictment, but this would in fact be giving them too little credit. Despite the Re-corder's invitation to judge the case on their own ideas of prob-ability before weighing the evidence, the jurymen settled down with the notes they had evidently been permitted to take as well as with the various written documents in the case and began to review in sequence the testimony of the various witnesses.

After they had looked at the first twelve or fourteen witnesses' testimony, however—while they were still, in other words, re-viewing the prosecution evidence from the first day of the trial— "an officer . . . came (as he said) from the court, to know whether the jury were agreed in their verdict." This information comes from one of the jurymen, Joseph Russell, who was sufficiently dissatisfied with the proceedings in which he had taken part to give a long deposition about them a month later, on 10 June 1754. Russell went on to report that another member of the jury, William Parsons, asked, "How can they think we can agree on a verdict in so short a time?" but other members of the jury—not named—replied, "You will find the court is impatient, there is a perjury in the two informations [the signed information given before Fielding and the unsigned one generally referred to as Alderman Chitty's minutes] that lie on the table." Some of the jury objected that they had not yet arrived at these in their sequential review of the evidence, but others—and here Russell specified the foreman, William Manning, whom the friends had been warned of but failed to challenge before the trial began—said, "If you can make these two informations one thing, there is no perjury; but as one mentions all the water to be drank up on one day, and the other mentions its being made an end of on a different day, there is a perjury." There was at least a discrepancy between the two accounts, but several of the jury could not consider it wilful and corrupt. At this point—it is unclear whether the officer of the court had remained in the room, but the request for a verdict certainly added a pressure for haste—the jury decided on a compromise: "Without further examination of the evidence in evidence in behalf of the prosecution, or any examination of the evidence in behalf of the defendant, or once reading of the indictment, or any mention being made of the criminal import thereof[, the jury] unanimously agreed to bring in the defendant guilty of perjury, but not wilful and corrupt." Russell felt enough distrust of Manning to ask to see what he had written down before it was read in court (Appendix 54, *A Refutation*, 44).

None of Canning's counsel were present when the compromise verdict was announced, and it was thus left to her friends, after the Recorder had secured the final courtroom verdict he wanted, to question Sollom Emlyn on the legality of the proceedings. Was it not necessary upon an indictment for perjury to prove not only that the fact sworn to was false but also that the defendant knew it to be so? Emlyn's reply was unequivocal: "I think it to be very clear, that a mere mistaken false oath, without wilful and corrupt design, is not perjury within the meaning of the indictment. . . . Nor did I ever know, hear or read of any one convicted of perjury, without evidence to prove a corrupt design, plot or confederacy, or else that the party must needs know it to be false; as in this case, if it were proved that Elizabeth Canning was elsewhere at the time she pretended to be at Enfield . . .," something the prosecution had had no evidence to suggest and had therefore held during the trial to be irrelevant.

Further, did the law require a general verdict of either guilty or not guilty? It did not, as by "a general verdict [the jury might] find the defendant guilty of more than they believe or intended to find him." And finally, did not a finding of "not guilty of wilful perjury amount to an acquittal?" Indeed it did: "If the jury really believed the party innocent of wilful forswearing, this is in effect a general verdict of an acquittal, for this is the only criminal part of the indictment." There was, however, one final question whose answer effectively rendered the foregoing discussion moot: "Suppose the jury, through surprize, inadvertency, or mistake, find such a verdict, is there any remedy to prevent judgment in such case?—A. This is extremely difficult, unless some error can be shewn upon the face of the record, which may be cause for arresting judgment. Perhaps the suffering the jury to go at large in the midst of the trial may be such a cause, as being a mistrial" (19: 671–72).

Sent out of the courtroom by William Moreton to produce a general verdict, the jury seems to have been confused and demoralized. According again to Russell, "several of them were for bringing in the defendant E. Canning not guilty . . ., but the foreman of the jury declaring they could not bring in the said E. Canning not guilty, because they had already found her guilty; it was upon that account, and for that reason, and no other, as this deponent believes, agreed by the said jury, by their said second verdict, to bring in the defendant E. Canning guilty of a perjury" (Appendix 54, A Refutation, 44). Russell deposed that no other argument was used to secure the jury's agreement to a general guilty verdict, and that he would himself not have agreed if he had "known or considered" that perjury is a volitional act going beyond "an undesigned mistake," e.g., that the day when Canning drank the last of the water "could have no tendency to prove the said M. Squires guilty, or if she was guilty, could not aggravate or lessen her guilt." Perhaps uncomfortable with their conclusion and the speed with which they had reached it, the jury added a unanimous recommendation of mercy and returned to the courtroom in fifteen minutes.

In an earlier affidavit on 13 May, five days after their verdict was given, Russell had been joined by another juryman, Richard Froome, in deposing that they had been led to believe "that the words wilful and corrupt were mere matter of form, and . . . that they [were] very uneasy in their minds, and dissatisfied in their consciences, by finding that the verdict delivered by them" was in fact being taken as meaning that Canning had knowingly and maliciously lied (Appendix 53, A Refutation, 44). Russell and, according to him, William Parsons also, although Parsons had been advised by a friend not to make any affidavit on the subject, did believe "that Mary Squires was at the house of mother Wells, at Enfield-Wash, and that the said defendant E. Canning was wronged at Enfield-Wash" (Appendix 54, *A Refutation*, 44).

Parsons may have been grateful for his friend's advice. Russell and Froome were described by the writer of *Genuine and Impartial Memoirs* as "not distinguished for a remarkable Depth of Discernment" and claimed by him to be the only two Canning sympathizers on a jury that otherwise "perfectly concurred, in opinion, of the girl's having sworn falsely." The other ten jurors had agreed to the first verdict only because they knew it "could not be received," stipulating that if it was not (as in this version they knew it would not be), Russell and Froome would go along with the second, and Russell and Froome had duly fallen into the trap. The recommendation to mercy, the writer reported, was due either to "the popular Clamours" or to something "that was said in Court" but not, presumably, to any real sympathy with Canning on the part of the jury. He gave as a source for his version of events that it "ha[d] been related" to him, but he did not indicate by whom (269–70).

If Russell's signed account was right, however, then Elizabeth Canning was now in the process of being wronged again at the Old Bailey. Some at least of her counsel were now in court, and opposed her committal to Newgate, but the court was adamant, conceding only that "she should be indulged with having a Friend or two always with her" and that she should "not be intruded on by strangers without her consent."[10] Sir Crisp Gascoyne was not present to witness his victory; his friends had advised him to slip away early to avoid the "outrageous [and] threatening" mob, and he had done so at about 7:00 P.M. (*Genuine and Impartial Memoirs*, 233). By the time the court adjourned, it was close to three in the morning; it had been sitting for eighteen hours.

When the court reconvened for sentencing on 13 May, Canning's counsel read the affidavit of Froome and Russell and the court sent for William Manning, the foreman, to comment. Manning's version is unlike either Russell's or that of the *Genuine and Impartial Memoirs*. According to him, Froome and Russell had supported Canning because they believed that, though guilty of the fact, she had been the tool of someone else and added "in short, they all believed so" and had thus given their first verdict. He did not mention either the discrepancy in Canning's alleged and signed accounts of when she had finished the water or any knowledge on his part that the first verdict would be unacceptable as factors, and represented the recommendation to mercy as a trade-off to Russell and Froome in exchange for their support for the second verdict. According to the *Genuine and Impartial Memoirs*, nine other members of the jury were present and "every one of them separately declared his Satisfaction in their last Verdict" (270–71), although this corroboration does not appear elsewhere, certainly not in the *State Trials* record.

The extent of the confusion over the jury's deliberations does seem to me sufficient to warrant the defense's request for a new trial, but since it had to be addressed to the same court which had just asked for and received a verdict that, however arrived at, was the one it explicitly wanted, it is not surprising that the request was denied. The Recorder expressed his regret that the case had "so much become a party affair" and on that basis put the request off until the next sessions, "that it may be argued before the same judges that tried her." As before, when the effort to get out of the Old Bailey and into the King's Bench had failed, Canning was in a sort of judicial version of *No Exit*: the judge who ruled against her argument for a new trial was Lord Chief Justice Willes, who had presided at the trials of Gibbons, Clarke, and Greville the previous September and who was the father of the prosecuting attorney whose opening speech had ridiculed her. Willes Senior now argued that since the jury's verdict had been general, "and they all abide by it, but two, who are but weak men, first to consent and give in their verdict according to their oath, and then to recant," the motion for a new trial was overruled (19: 673).

There was seemingly nothing now between Canning and sentencing, but at this point Sir John Barnard got up and, speaking on behalf of seven other aldermen as well as himself, recommended mercy. Like the jury, if we accept Manning's account, "he believed she was not guilty alone" (19: 673). Barnard was what all of the prominent men involved in the case seem to have aspired to be, a man widely and genuinely respected not only for his social standing—he was a wealthy merchant who had been a member of Parliament since 1722 as well as Lord Mayor in 1737—but for his personal integrity and public beneficence. His intervention in the Canning case brought a swift reply from Willes, who argued that since "he had observed that collections had been made for her amounting to considerable amounts of money . . . if her sentence was only to remain in Newgate, there would be such sums collected, and such assemblies of an evening, as would render her sentence a diversion rather than a punishment" (19: 673), but Barnard's otherwise ineffective action was another blow to the effect of conclusiveness that Canning's prosecution was attempting to convey along with her conviction. The final vote in favor of a month's imprisonment followed by seven years' transportation passed by a bare majority of nine to eight, the eight being headed by Barnard. As the writer of *Genuine and Impartial Memoirs* put it: "A Gentleman, whose Services to the Community, have done great Honour to himself, was pleased to think a small Five or Six Months Imprisonment sufficient; the Reasons he gave were grounded upon the two Verdicts; which, he observed, implied a Sort of Doubt of her Guilt; the same Argument had been made use of by her Council, and would have been plausible, had not the jury so fully explained their Sentiments." The writer could hardly impugn Barnard's "Depth of Discernment." Instead he went as far as he could in implying that some sort of major error, not necessarily caused in this case either by folly or venality but which charity compelled him not to spell out, had occurred: "My Respect to those Gentlemen who were for the milder Punishment obliges me to conceal their Names" (272).

Sentenced, accordingly, to transportation, Canning was now permitted to address the court, which she did, if the *State Trials* is accurate in its representation, briefly, and "with a low voice.— 'That she hoped they would be favourable to her; that she had no intent of swearing the gypsey's life away; and that what had been done, was only defending herself; and desired to be considered unfortunate'" (673). Even if this is a paraphrase, as the third-person pronouns suggest, rather than Canning's exact words, it seems to fit better before the judges' vote rather than after it, where the *Trials* text places it. Whenever it occurred, however, it seems to have been ineffectual. The Recorder's final address to the convicted prisoner treats her guilt as unequivocal and unmitigated:

> Elizabeth Canning, you now stand convicted (upon the clearest proof) of wilful and corrupt perjury; a crime attended with the most fatal and dangerous consequences to the community, though (as yet) it is not punished with death. . . . [T]here is not one unprejudiced person, of the great number who have attended [this trial], but must be convinced of the justice and impartiality of the jury in the verdict they have given.
>
> It is with horror that I look back, and think of the evidence you gave at the trial of Mary Squires, whom you knew to be destitute and friendless, and therefore fixed upon her as a proper object to make a sacrifice of, at the dreadful expence of a false oath; this you pre-

ferred to the making a plain discovery to those who had a right to
know where you really were those twenty-eight days of your pretended confinement at Wells's; and in this you were encouraged to
persist, as well by that misapplied charity, which was bountifully
given you in compassion to your supposed suffering, as by the advice
of your mistaken friends, whom you had deluded and deceived into
a belief of the truth of what you had falsely sworn.

This audacious attempt, and that calm and deliberate assurance
with which you formed a scheme to take away the life of one (though
the most abject) of the human species, together with your youth, and
the character you then had, as well as your seeming inexperience,
imposed upon many, and gained you a credit which must have exceeded your highest expectations; and being thus abandoned, and
thus encouraged, you not only wickedly persevered, but even tri-
umphed over those who would not suffer their judgments to be misled by so gross an imposition.

The best result that Moreton could hope from Canning's case
was that it would teach the general public "not to suffer their
credulity to get the better of their reason," although the Recorder
himself, like his friend and colleague Sir Crisp Gascoyne, had
"always thought your evidence false, and that the witnesses produced in your defense were most grossly mistaken." Because
perjury did not carry the death penalty, the court could only
impose a "sentence . . . in no degree adequate to the greatness
of [Canning's] offence": "That you shall be imprisoned in the
gaol of Newgate for one month; and after the expiration of your
imprisonment, you shall be transported to some of his majesty's
colonies or plantations in America for the term of seven years;
and if within that term you return, and are found at large in any
of his majesty's dominions of Great Britain or Ireland, you shall
suffer death as a felon without benefit of clergy" (19: 673–75).

This, as it were, officially climactic moment in practice marked
no change in the public interest in Canning or in the division of
opinion over her guilt or innocence. Given the dissensions
among both the jury and the judges, the trial verdict itself only
reinforced the faith of those who, like Gascoyne and Moreton,
already thought Canning guilty; it did little or nothing to convince anyone else—if by this time any significant part of the
public was still open to argument at all.

The weak point in the anti-Canning case remained, of course,
the failure of a well-financed and powerful prosecution to gener-
ate any evidence at all that Canning had been elsewhere than
Wells's house in January 1753. Thomas Ford himself, according

to *Genuine and Impartial Memoirs,* had "often and publicly repeated that *he knew where she was* during that Time, and that
he would prove *where she had been Day by Day,*" but his failure
to do so had become an embarrassment: "He may have said so,
and therein may have asserted a Falsehood, by pretending to
know more than he really did or could know: And what then?
Does Mr. Ford's Vanity in the least extenuate Canning's Guilt, or
his having told an Untruth, render her more Innocent?" (275). Sir
Crisp Gascoyne did not mention Ford's name in his discussion of
the problem of Canning's whereabouts, but instead makes his
own failure to discover them a part of her guilt. He had sought
"to trace, if possible, where, or under whose direction Canning
was" not because the information was necessary but "for general
satisfaction" (40), and he claimed to have proven to his own
satisfaction that some sort of conspiracy, presumably for gain, by
Canning's mother and some, at least, of her friends—Gascoyne
is more than vague here—was behind her disappearance. The
elements in the case which he educes as evidence in support of
this conclusion are his suspicions about Canning's literacy, the
relative cleanliness of her shift, some similar references in Alderman Chitty's minutes and Mrs. Canning's advertisements, and
the visit of the latter to the Cunning Man:

> Under whose directions Canning was, upon what occasion, *and to
> whom the* BED-GOWN BELONGS, every person will now form his own
> conjecture.
> Far from triumphing at the Girl's Conviction, wicked as she is, I
> wish her discovery had been the means of intitling her to mercy, and
> of bringing those more guilty to justice: but this could not be ex-
> pected; the curtain, behind which the secret lay, was too closely
> drawn; and none but her own friends permitted to see her.—And
> those who before protected her, as the tool of their politicks, in oppo-
> sition to me, must not *now* desert her. (44)

In spite of its framing assertions, however, this assemblage of
conjecture and coincidence is evidence of nothing at all, and
Canning's friends treated it with contempt in their *Refutation.*
Notwithstanding Gascoyne's "repeated declarations" that he
could prove Canning had not been at Wells's house, he had found
the task "IMPOSSIBLE" (vii). The prosecutors, however, still held
to the hope uttered by Davy in his closing argument that conviction and sentencing would bring Canning herself to a confession,
and now that the trial was over the scene of conflict shifted to
her cell at Newgate.

Canning had been sentenced and returned to prison on 30 May. On 1 June a paragraph appeared in the *Whitehall Evening Post* claiming that one Elizabeth Knot, alleged to have been a witness for Canning, had been convicted of theft at the Old Bailey. On the 2nd Dr. John Hill retold the story more pointedly in the *London Daily Advertiser and Inspector:* "Thursday last Elizabeth Knott, one of the evidences in behalf of the virtuous Mrs. Elizabeth Canning at her late trial for perjury at the Old-Bailey, was at the same place found guilty of feloniously stealing two gowns from a female acquaintance: 'tis hoped, however, that means will be found to prove this poor injured Mrs. Knot innocent of the fact, as the public have been so well and so often assured, that none but persons of reputation and character were engaged in support of that famous modern story-teller" (Appendix 56, *A Refutation*, 45). It was an absolute misstatement, however, that Knot had appeared at Canning's trial or even been subpoenaed for it, and this phase of the propaganda war had to be conceded to the Canningites:

Elizabeth Knot had, indeed, some time since, given to one of Elizabeth Canning's friends a circumstantial detail of such incidents related to her by Vertue Hall in the gatehouse, before and after the boasted Recantation, as might have been urged to prove that this Recantation was made under such circumstances as rendered it of little weight, when opposed to a testimony upon oath; but her character prevented her being subpoenaed or called, or intended to be subpoenaed or called, for Elizabeth Canning. (*Gazeteer*, 4 June 1754, rpt. as Appendix 56, *A Refutation*, 46)

Later, the writer of the *Genuine and Impartial Memoirs* would claim that Knot's name had appeared in the list of witnesses provided to the defense, and that "on the Evening when the Defence was opened, she was confin'd in the same Room with the rest of the Witnesses, though they thought fit to dismiss her the next Day," and would exclaim, "How trifling is the Evasion!" (284). But Knot's name was no longer useful to Hill, and he now dropped it for another angle.

Since Hill almost certainly knew the Elizabeth Knot story was false when he printed it, he may have expected that the outcome of the trial had left the defense too demoralized to respond. In-

deed from this point forward Canning's attorneys disappeared
from the story, but the friends continued their voluntary efforts
on her behalf, as their rapid response in this case demonstrates,
although it was not sufficient to ward off similar attacks. Thus
on Friday, 7 June, Hill published another Inspector essay de-
nouncing the friends for controlling access to Canning in prison,
thereby preventing visitors to whom she might confess from
seeing her. Three such gentlemen, two of them magistrates, had
indeed made their way to Canning's cell and there discovered

> the girl surrounded by a circle of enthusiasts . . . Upon the table were
> bottles full and empty, to support the weakness of the flesh; and in
> her hand a book, which was, as the enthusiasts said, the next in value
> to the Scriptures: If I were to repeat the title it would not be known.
> Is this . . . a conduct to obtain confession? Is it probable that a young
> and ignorant creature, inflamed, perhaps, with wine, and made
> drunk with enthusiasm, should ever be brought to a sense of her
> condition? Certainly a moderate allowance, retirement, and the ex-
> hortations of a disinterested clergyman, would give the ground of a
> more reasonable expectation.

Hill went on to relate that one of the visiting gentlemen spoke
to Canning, suggesting that she might want to tell him something
weighing upon her mind, and that Canning "changed countenance . . ., rose from her seat and came toward him, with all the
apearance [sic] of beginning an instant and a full confession"—
whereupon her friends "intercepted, and prevented her from
speaking" (rpt. as Appendix 57, A Refutation, 46). On 8 June
Canning's friends invited Hill through the Gazetteer to "declare,
at what time those incidents happened, who were the persons
concerned, and upon what authority his assertions were
grounded, after which he may be thought worthy of a reply." In
the meantime, they supplied a statement from an actual disinterested clergyman, William Reyner, rector of St. Mary Magdalen,
Old Fish Street, and canon of St. Paul's Cathedral:

> The many falsities daily propagated in relation to the story of
> Elizabeth Canning, oblige me to acquaint the public, that soon after
> the commitment of that unhappy girl to Newgate, I was requested by
> one of her friends to visit her as a clergyman. I have visited her
> often, without giving notice of my coming; and always found the
> appearance of order, decency, and sobriety, both in the prisoner and
> her few attendants. I have conversed with her alone, and in the pres-

ence of her friends, on the crime for which she was indicted: I have read to, and prayed with her and them; and as she professed herself a member of the Church of England, she always joined cordially and earnestly in the devotional offices of the liturgy; nor have I been able to discover any thing that could give occasion to a charge of enthusiasm. On the contrary, the appearance, the conversation, and the behaviour of Elizabeth Canning have, to the best of my observation, been always such, as indicated a mind not unsettled in the principles of religion, or conscious of flagrant guilt. (Appendix 58, *A Refutation*, 47; Reyner's statement is also reprinted in *State Trials*, 19: 679.)

The friends now awaited Hill's response, but when none was forthcoming, they went on to publish the affidavit of one Thomas Butts in the *Gazetteer* on 13 June. Butts told the story of how on 11 May he and four other persons, including Canning's uncle Thomas Colley and one William Kemp, were in her cell when the keeper of the prison, Richard Akerman, introduced three more visitors—two of their names were Smith and Lediard; the third Butts did not remember. Justice Lediard asked Akerman to remove Butts and Kemp from the room, but Akerman said he had no authority to do so and instead left himself. Lediard, who had had a hand in the recantation of Virtue Hall, then addressed Canning, declaring he felt great pity and friendship for her and wanted to ask her some questions. Smith reinforced this approach by averring that Lediard was Canning's "good friend," and had "the power to serve her." At this point the suspicious Butts intervened, saying he did not know if they were friends or enemies and adding with considerable confidence—he himself had known Canning for only three weeks, and Kemp had met her just half an hour ago—"I believe, Betty, you don't chuse to answer any questions—Do you?" Still according to Butts, Canning stood up, said, "No, Sir, I don't chuse to answer any," and sat down again.

There followed a good deal of rude badinage between Butts and Kemp on the one hand, Lediard and Smith on the other, all given in dialogue form by Butts, while Canning, presumably, sat quietly by. Smith accused Canning's friends of "spiriting her up," and Butts admitted it as far from being a fault: "I tell her she has cause to be chearful, from a consciousness of her own innocence; and I advise her to trust in the living God, who has hitherto supported her, and I doubt not will to the end: (*here was a general sneer.*) I am sorry, Gentlemen, that advising a person to trust in God should give offence to justices of the peace." Lediard assured him that it did not, but Smith detected the influence of "Whitfieldites," occasioning another dialogue between Butts and Canning:

> *Butts:* Betty, do you know Mr. Whitfield?
> *E. Canning:* No, Sir.
> *Butts:* Do you know any of his followers?
> *E. Canning:* No, Sir.
> *Butts:* Do you know me to be one of his followers?
> *E. Canning:* No, Sir.

Butts had Canning show Lediard the book in her hand, which was *The Christian's Pattern, or a Treatise of the Imitation of Jesus Christ, Written in Latin by Thomas a Kempis, and rendered into English by George Stanhope, D. D. Dean of Canterbury.* Lediard was obliged to agree that it was "a very good book."[11] Nevertheless, he made one further attempt to question Canning, but according to Butts she replied, "No, Sir, I have said the whole truth in court, and nothing but the truth: and I don't chuse to answer any question, unless it be in court again."

Butts went on to say that there were no bottles, full or empty, on the table, and that while he and William Kemp had each a glass of wine after the rout of Lediard and Smith, Canning did not join them; he had never seen her drink anything but tea, with the single exception of a glass of wine and water on the evening after she was sentenced. He also said that he had visited Canning frequently, at all hours of the day, and sometimes more than once in a day, and it is difficult to refrain from the suspicion that such visits may not have been an unmitigated pleasure to their object (Appendix 59, *A Refutation,* 47–49). As with Dr. Cox's medical examination, however, Canning was obliged to submit for her own good. It was all part of the price she paid, whether for prosecuting the people who had robbed and starved her or for committing perjury.

To be fair to Canning's friends, they remained loyal to her even if, or perhaps in part because, their personal advocacy could be oppressive and embarrassing and their legal defense of her had thus far served her badly—it would certainly have been awkward to abandon her gracefully. Thus, on 5 June 1754, the vicar of Canning's parish church, St. Giles Cripplegate, Dr. William Nicholls, wrote in rather a hopeless tone to the Duke of Newcastle:

> I take the Liberty of giving your Grace this trouble at the earnest request of many of my Parishioners, who have a good Opinion of the

unfortunate Elizabeth Canning, and desire I would do that Justice to her general character among us, as to assure your Grace that her Parents were honest, sober, industrious Persons, who gave her a good Education as their Circumstances would admit of; that her Behaviour while she continued at home with them in my Parish was (as all the neighbours inform me) modest, sober, and vertuous; and that the masters with whom she has since lived in service, whom I know to be men of worth and probity, give her an unblemished character. I could not well refuse stating these Facts to your Grace, and hope you will excuse this Freedom. (State Papers Domestic)

An initial petition from Canning for an alleviation in the conditions of her transportation was also ineffective, prompting a second one (the surviving document on which her signature appears) acknowledging the failure of her first request for "a Companion of her own Sex during the Voyage to Maryland" and asking that her friends now be granted "the Liberty of Transporting her, within a limited Time, to some of her Majesty's Plantations in North America." This petition was subscribed on 26 June by both Daniel Cox and John Eaton of the College of Physicians with an attestation that Canning was suffering from "a dangerous Fever ... and that ... she cannot at present be removed without the manifest hazard of her life" and annotated, by whom it is not clear, "From the Archbishop of Canterbury" (State Papers Domestic). No response to it appears to exist.

Agitation meanwhile continued for a new trial, including a petition from thirty-four "near neighbors" on the grounds that "they have Personally known Elizabeth Canning from her Infancy [and] that she has always been remarkable for her Veracity, Dutifulness, Industry, Honesty and Modesty, and that they do not think her capable of the Crime for which she has been sentenced." The signers included such consistent supporters as Canning's two employers, the apothecary Sutherton Backler, Edward Rossiter, and Edward Woodward, and they were supported first by a further six pages of signatures from people basing their subscription on "the general Relation of her good moral Character, a Belief of her Innocence, and a Concern by her present Condition" and second by an additional sixty-five signatures from Enfield, including the vicar and churchwardens, several other clergy, both Church of England and dissenting, and the younger Edward Aldridge. In addition, a highly respected lawyer, Henry Gould, who perhaps not coincidentally was Henry Fielding's cousin and friend, had petitioned for the king's permission to act legally on Canning's behalf (State Papers Domestic).

In spite of the prosecution's claims to finality, which would be most firmly expressed in Sir Crisp Gascoyne's *An Address to the Liverymen of the City of London*, to appear under the date of 8 July 1754 and now therefore being either written or prepared for the press, the trial had by no means satisfied public opinion, and Canning's enemies—a term certainly used by her friends and I think not an overstatement for figures like Hill who pursued her with unabated zeal even after she had been sentenced to transportation and committed to Newgate—now evidently turned to the device of oral rumor-mongering in a last attempt to discredit her. Thus on 27 June a notice appeared in the newspapers signed by Canning herself. It was reprinted both among the appendices to *A Refutation of Sir Crisp Gascoyne's Address* and in *State Trials* but not by Gascoyne or the writer of *Genuine and Impartial Memoirs*, neither of whom even alluded to it.

After being forced, by the most confident assertions, to summon a physician and midwife upon my trial, to clear my character from the foulest aspersions, whose examination was made unnecessary by the testimony called on the part of the prosecution [Elizabeth Mayle]; after being prevented examining the far greater number of the cloud of witnesses ready to appear to my character, by the express declaration of counsel retained against me, that they had nothing to alledge to my prejudice but the single crime for which I was indicted; after the public has been assured that Elizabeth Knott, who was convicted of [a] single felony, was a principal witness to prove my return from Enfield, when she was not subpoenaed or examined, or intended to be subpoenaed or examined, to that or any other fact; after having been represented by the Inspector, as a person inflamed with wine, and made drunk with enthusiasm, and as rising from my seat, and coming towards a justice of the peace, with all the appearance of beginning an instant and full confession; assertions that have been publicly proved to be false: after these things, there seemed some room to hope, that the torrent of abuse against me would have stopped of itself. But being informed that a report has been diligently propagated and prevailed, that I had squeaked, and declared I would confess or reveal the whole, upon condition I was pardoned, and permitted to conceal names, if I expected any mercy, I must name names; I am compelled to declare, and do in the most serious manner, and with the strictest regard to truth, hereby declare, that I remain at this instant of time fully persuaded, and well assured, that Mary Squires was the person who robbed me, that the house of Susannah Wells was the place in which I was confined twenty-eight days; and that I did not in my several informations or examinations before the different magistrates, or in my evidence on the trial of the said Mary Squires and Susannah Wells, knowingly, in any material or even in the most minute circumstance, deviate from the truth. (Rpt. in *State Trials*, 19: 679–80)

Such a rumor, if believed, would certainly have served the purpose of undermining Canning's story without providing any new information to contradict it, and it was thus essential that it be contradicted, though I doubt whether Elizabeth Canning, despite her now long exposure to legal language, composed the actual document. At the time of its composition, both Cox and Eaton testified that she was gravely ill, a condition that might have sprung equally from the notorious unhealthiness of her prison and from anxiety about her immediate future. She had been ordered transported to Maryland on a merchant ship, the *Tryal*, commended by Isaac Johns, and the ship was now at anchor at Blackwall, where some at least of the seamen were vocally anticipating her arrival. According to Robert Pladger, the boatswain, "one of the crew . . . swore, that if the said Elizabeth Canning was put on board the said ship he would lye with her; and some others of them also swore they would lye with her." Pladger, whose sympathies had been enlisted on Canning's behalf by a friend of his who was Reverend Nicholls's footman, declared to the sailors that he would permit no one to "use her ill," but the captain intervened, telling Pladger that he was to do for Canning only what he would for any other transport, "lock her down every night,"—a situation in which rape would apparently be nothing extraordinary. Pladger was given overnight to give up his knight errantry, but when he continued adamant, the captain discharged him from the ship, "in derision, call[ing] the deponent Mr. Canning" (Appendix 61, *A Refutation*, 49–50).

This was a story which, however far from being their immediate responsibility, could do the anti-Canningites no good. It was in circulation before either Sir Crisp Gascoyne's *Address* or the *Genuine and Impartial Memoirs* appeared, but neither mentioned it, unless it ambiguously underlies the latter's account, dated 30 July, of the one indulgence granted to Canning out of all her petitions: "She has been indulged with the liberty of being transported in a private Ship: How this Indulgence was obtained I choose to forget; may there never be any Occasion to remember it" (289). The implication seems on the surface to be that Canning's friends had managed some impropriety on her behalf—bribery, perhaps—but it is at least as likely that the public threat of rape was more than either Canning's enemies or the authorities in charge of her fate (in practice two overlapping groups) were prepared to include in the punishment for perjury, and that they therefore did not oppose the proposal to send Canning to America in a different ship. The *Tryal* sailed without her; she traveled instead to New England, not Maryland, aboard the *Myrtilla*, embarking on 7 August (Pearson, 205; de la Torre, 223).

After Canning's actual physical departure from England, publication on her case rapidly diminished—so much so, in fact, that tracking the later history of the principals is difficult or, often, impossible. Prominent men such as Gascoyne, Hill, and Fielding present no problem, of course—Fielding's death the same year has already been noted, while Gascoyne and Hill survived until 1761 and 1775 respectively. Gascoyne had reached the apogee of his career at the time of the Canning case, although it is unclear whether his advocacy of Squires's innocence was responsible for its failure to progress thereafter. He had been born in 1700 and seems to have seen himself at the time of his mayoralty, not without some reason, as only in the middle stages of a triumphant public career, but the end came comparatively soon, and without further honors. Hill, a younger man (born in 1714), lived until 1775, controversial and prolific to the end. In the last year of his life he was awarded a Swedish honor, the Order of Vasa, and thereafter called himself Sir John Hill. He figures briefly in Boswell's *Life of Johnson*, in which Johnson is represented as telling George III that Hill was "an ingenious man, but had no veracity," a judgment in which most of his contemporaries concurred and with which I see no reason to differ (Boswell, 2: 38).

Beneath this level of prominence, the Canning case abounds in obscure lives. None of the respectable tradesmen who took on the role of "Canning's friends" were the sort of people whose histories are recorded in the *Dictionary of National Biography*, and the principals in the case were the sort of people actually expected to live out their lives without coming to public notice— part of the hostility Canning's story generated seems to have come from its having been in some sense forced on the attention of her betters. Thus the last glimpse we have of Virtue Hall is in the Cheshunt workhouse, confiding her hopeless anxieties to its mistress, and the beleaguered Mrs. Canning and her four younger children make their last public appearance at her daughter's trial. The nineteenth-century legal writer, John Paget, found the record of Susannah Wells's death in the Enfield parish register for 5 October 1763 (590) while a correspondent in *Notes and Queries* reported in 1879 that "Squires was buried with gipsy pomp at Farnham in Surrey, on February 26, 1762" ("I. P." 12: 30). But these dates tell us nothing of the lives preceding them, although the date of Squires's death does suggest that she was probably neither so old nor so frail as some accounts make her—a woman perhaps in her fifties in 1753 rather than her eighties. An unsigned note in an unknown hand bound into the back of the copy of the Dublin edition of Gascoyne's *Address* now in the Guildhall Library gives a different date for Wells's death—16 February 1767—and describes her as having "detained the celebrated Elizabeth Canning in her house." It also reports that "pursuant to her dying request" her bearers were provided with "a pennyworth of beer at each public house on the way—nearly 2 miles."

Elizabeth Canning also survived, though not to a great age. She became a domestic servant in Wethersfield, Connecticut, in the household of the Reverend Elisha Williams, and in November 1756 she married a man named John Treat. The report that she worked as a schoolmistress seems to me quite unlikely to be true, given her apparent level of literacy, nor is there any evidence that her husband was, as was also sometimes reported, "an opulent Quaker" (Caulfield, 148). A surviving letter from her mistress, Elizabeth Williams, speaks of Canning's learning "to become mistress of spinning" for what are clearly domestic purposes (Stiles, 1: 689–90), while according to Edmund Pearson, whose research on the American life of Elizabeth Canning seems the most reliable I have seen, Treat was "a 'scatter-brain young fellow of good family.'" The couple had three sons and a daughter, the eldest of whom, Joseph Canning Treat—evidently named for his mother's brother—served as a soldier in the American Revolution.

Elizabeth Canning herself died in June 1773 at the age of thirty-eight, and was buried in Wethersfield (Pearson, 205–6). Rumor credited her with large sums of money contributed by a gullible public but never reported any remarkable expenditures by her or on her behalf, and the friends' problems with their legal bills have already been noted. I am thus inclined to doubt the otherwise unsupported report in the *Annual Register* for 1761 that Canning had come to England on the expiration of her sentence of transportation to collect a five hundred-pound legacy (de la Torre, 227; see also chapter 4). The *Gentleman's Magazine* notice of her death suggests that her residence in New England was unbroken and concludes either pertinently or perversely, depending on the reader's disbelief or belief, "Notwithstanding the many strange circumstances of her story, none is so strange as that it should not be discovered in so many years, where she had concealed herself during the time she had invariably declared she was at the house of Mrs. Wells" (43: 413).

4

Writing Canning's Story

Contemporaries

I have already drawn heavily on several contemporary accounts in constructing my version of the Canning case. Lillian Bueno McCue lists forty-three separate items with eighteenth-century dates in her bibliography, and that includes a lumping together of all the references in the *Gentleman's Magazine* under a single number. Many of these publications, however, are extremely repetitive of each other, incorporating material already published under one title under a new one, or filling a generous proportion of their pages with extensive quotation from earlier texts.

As the reprinting of Hill's earliest Inspector essays demonstrated, publications with the name of Canning somewhere in the title seem to have met a fairly indiscriminate demand, and a good many of the surviving documents apparently came into existence primarily to cash in on the phenomenon. Titles like "The Truth's Found Out at Last," "The Inspector Detected," "The Inspector Inspected," and "Truth Triumphant" exploit both the controversial reality and the public craving for a solution to the mystery. The rapidity with which one title succeeded another, never priced at more than a shilling and usually offered for sixpence or less, particularly during the periods March–July 1753 and May–August 1754 provides paradoxical evidence that none gave either the revelations or the assurances all professed to offer.

A methodical evaluation of all of these publications in sequence would, in my opinion, yield more redundancy than enlightenment. Instead, I wish to concentrate on three exceptionally carefully produced—and expensively priced—accounts: *An Address to the Liverymen of the City of London from Sir Crisp Gascoyne, Knt., Late Lord-Mayor, Relative to His Conduct in the Case of Elizabeth Canning and Mary Squires*, published by James Hodges in July 1754, for two shillings; *A Refutation of*

176

Sir Crisp Gascoyne's Address to the Liverymen of London: By a Clear State of the Case of Elizabeth Canning, in a Narrative of Facts, Ranged in a Regular Series, and Supported by the Informations and Affidavits of Near Eighty Witnesses of Good Credit, published by John Payne in November 1754, for two shillings and sixpence; and *Genuine and Impartial Memoirs of Elizabeth Canning, Containing a Complete History of that Unfortunate Girl, from her Birth to the Present Time, and particularly every remarkably Occurrence from the Day of her Absence, January 1, 1753, to the Day of her receiving Sentence, May 30, 1754[;] In which is included, The whole Tenor of the Evidence given against, and for her, on her late extraordinary Trial[;] With some Observations on the Behaviour of the Court, and the Conduct of the Jury[;] Also Free and Candid Remarks on Sir Crisp Gascoyne's Address,* published by G. Woodfall in August 1754, for three shillings. Each of these works proposes itself, by varying strategies, as a definitive, final, and truthful account, and while an analysis and comparison of them cannot, in my opinion, yield anything of the sort, they can at least tell us a good deal about the ideals of credibility to which each addresses itself—about, that is, what counted as truth for their writers and their projected audiences.

Sir Crisp Gascoyne's *Address to the Liverymen of London* is cast in the form of an open letter, beginning "Gentlemen" (1) and closing with conventional compliments: "I am / Gentlemen, / With the most profound Respect, / Your most faithful Servant, / Crisp Gascoyne," with the information "London, / July 8, 1754" set off to the right (45). The audience is evoked repeatedly throughout the text: "Give me leave, Gentlemen . . ." (1); "This, Gentlemen, is the sense I have of my present Condition . . ." (2); "I have thus, Gentlemen, given You the occasion of my doubts . . ." (4); "What effect, Gentlemen, would all the foregoing letters and certificates have had with You?" (9); and so forth until the conclusion: "What I did, as a man, my heart tells me was right; but as a magistrate, I readily submit to Your judgment" (45). "Gentlemen" and "You" are consistently capitalized, but the general practice of the text is to capitalize only conventionally for proper nouns and exceptionally for emphasis: thus, "a perfect justification of every step I have taken" occurs in the same sentence as "that Year of the City's Administration" (1). The effect is of a constant directing of the reader's attention to what is not so much simply important as to what is worthy of formal and public respect, or, as in the repeated capitalization of "Girl," of exceptional scrutiny. If the reader happens not to be one of the specific group addressed, he or she may feel either flattered by the association or distanced by the exclusion; for the liverymen themselves, the emphasis is presumably both flattering—they, not the mob, are the only group with a right to judge Gascoyne's conduct—and subtly argumentative—he is, after all, one of them.

The first two pages of Gascoyne's text are thus devoted solely to establishing the relationship between himself and his audience—his high sense of the importance of the office of Lord Mayor and its distinguished history, his modest assessment of his own worth, made up for by the "care, attention, and integrity" he brought to the position, his experience of "censure" from "the popular voice" and his "duty . . . to vindicate himself" against it, delayed only by his recognition that prior to the resolution of Canning's trial "the weight of [his] justification" would unfairly damage her, and his consequent self-denying resolution "to dispense with the injuries my silence countenanced, rather than persue a remedy at her expence" (2). In establishing his sense of his obligation to the liverymen, Gascoyne also established his authorial persona: his characteristics as a narrator will be modesty, candor, integrity, and forebearance. Only after all of this is clear can the actual narrative commence.

Gascoyne very briefly recapitulates Canning's story, which he says "could not be more contrary to reason," and describes the eagerness with which "some credulous, though perhaps good, men . . . persued uncommon means to raise toward her the pity of others." This activity led to Mary Squires at her trial—Wells is not mentioned—being "perfectly deprived of the mercy of the law" and to his own immediate reaction: "I doubted the whole story, and was dissatisfied with the verdict" (3). The merely natural consequence of this doubt was the investigation of Squires's alibi, and Gascoyne now turns to documentary evidence to support his account of his actions: Thomas Ford's letter to Mr. Harris, Harris's letter to Ford, a letter from under-sheriff Willis of Dorset, a deposition from the Abbotsbury churchwardens, a further letter from Harris to Willis, depositions from citizens of Abbotsbury and Coombe, follow in rapid succession (5–8), interspersed with references to the known good character of the correspondents and the information that Canning's friends, apprised of all of this material, still "were pleased to doubt" (9).

The defense of Gascoyne's actions overtly merges here with the attack on the modesty, candor, integrity, and forebearance of

Canning's friends, and, though shielded by them, of Canning herself. The same constellation of qualities Gascoyne assumes in his role as narrator are the ones he denounces the lack of in his opponents, making his defense of his actions as a magistrate also a personal contest between his own beleaguered public virtue and the thrusting private vice of a group of men—small tradesmen and artificers who were not for the most part liverymen—supporting a dishonest and discreditable maidservant and supported by a faceless, indistinguishable, contemptible, but dangerous mob. From this point on, his basically narrative presentation consistently includes both the colorless narrative markers necessary to intelligibility—"I thereupon directed Mr. White . . .," "In less than two hours White returned . . ."—with something rather more overt than a subtext impeaching the motives and credibility of those opposed to him—"But who to my great surprize came in with [Virtue Hall]?—Canning's friends!" (9).

This contrapuntal presentation is kept up consistently through the narrative of Virtue Hall's recantation, the examinations of Wells, the Natuses, Ezra Whiffin, and Mary Landry, the arrival of the Abbotsbury witnesses, the reconsidered opinions of the three goldsmiths, and finally through the petition for Squires's pardon. All are supported by the incorporation of signed documents within the text and punctuated by addresses to the liverymen—"Now, Gentlemen, let me appeal to You" (12); "I do most readily, Gentlemen, submit to Your opinion" (18)—and animadversions on the integrity of Canning's friends—"Yet Canning's friends were still pleased to doubt" (15); "Though the Convict's innocence appeared to a demonstration, the Girl's friends still doubted" (17). All three dimensions of Gascoyne's narrative in this phase lay the groundwork for the real object of his justification—his decision not merely to vindicate Mary Squires but to indict Elizabeth Canning: "After all these proofs were taken" (and "these proofs," given the structural components of Gascoyne's narrative, must be understood to include the impertinent arguments of Canning's friends as well as such things as Mr. Harris's letters), "there was no room to retain the least favourable thought—humanity itself could no longer plead for her—'twas plain the whole was a contrivance, a most wicked and cruel falsity" (18).

It is therefore on a firm basis of moral justification that Gascoyne proceeds, even after the grand jury has thrown out the cross bills of perjury—"Whatever is once right is always right" (27)—and the narrative goes forward through the re-presentation of both bills, the finding both true, the attempt of Canning's friends to remove her trial into the King's Bench, the trials of Gibbons, Clarke, and Greville, and the attempt to outlaw Canning. All of these are presented with the now familiar, even reassuring, concomitants of references to the judgment of the liverymen—"You will demand, perhaps, Gentlemen, why was this double trouble? . . ." (31)—and to the formal improprieties and moral obliquity of Canning's friends, whose "methods . . . were likely to furnish them with some sort of evidence to encounter any facts, however obviously true" (32).

The next phase of the discussion is, not surprisingly, Gascoyne's own actions in preparation for Canning's trial, in which "it became highly proper for me to act with reserve" (32). He thus recounts the steps he took to "prove more fully" Squires's alibi, sending George Squires back over his route with Mr. Willis and ordering the "whole rout" of alibi witnesses to London. From this point on Gascoyne mingles the narrative of his own actions before Canning's trial with materials drawn from the trial itself. Thus the account of the securing of the alibi witnesses is followed immediately by a comparison of their "clearness, certainty, and consistency" (33) with the deficiencies of the Enfield witnesses brought by Canning's defense, and Gascoyne's second pretrial objective, "shewing the falsity of [Canning's] pretended confinement" (34), mingles Alderman Chitty's misleadingly labeled "Minutes taken upon the examination of Elizabeth Canning on the 31st of January, 1753" (from which the final two sentences of the document read at the trial, which testify to Canning's terrible physical state and to her previous good character, are silently omitted) with Gawen Nash's sometimes contradictory testimony and with observations drawn from Robert Scarrat's and Joseph Adamson's testimony, a description of Wells's hayloft, and the prosecution's own Enfield evidence, the tree-lopping story and Ezra Whiffin's visit to the loft in search of sign irons.

Gascoyne's third avowed pretrial purpose "was to trace, if possible, where or under whose direction Canning was, and the cause of her pretended absence" (40), and since in this purpose he had completely failed (see chapter 3), it becomes somewhat clearer why he employs the strategy in this presumably climactic phase of his narrative not of giving an account of the trial itself but of quarrying it for support for his own pretrial objectives. The trial itself included much material extraneous to Gascoyne's purposes—the whole defense might be so described, as might the disputes over the verdict and sentence—and a focus instead on his own purposes made it possible for the former lord mayor to refer to the trial fairly extensively without directly describing it. This portion of the text thus occupies about a quarter of Gascoyne's total number of pages, giving to readers, liverymen or not, the sensation that they have read a discursive account of the trial without their actually having done so. The text of the trial had not yet appeared, but when it did it would occupy 397 columns of small print, far more than Gascoyne's handsomely printed ten-and-one-half pages.

The trial as a point of reference, however, is vital to Gascoyne's rhetorical strategy in his final appeal to the liverymen. "[N]ot conscious of the least misrepresentation or omission of any thing worthy Your consideration," Gascoyne turns once more to "the reproaches I have sustained" as something he is—personally— "willing to forget, nor should I have taken any notice of the dangers I have been exposed to, was I not prompted to it by the gratitude I owe my Lord-Mayor [Thomas Rawlinson], Sir Charles Asgill, and Mr. Alderman Chitty, for exposing their own persons, for my security, to a numerous and tumultuous assembly of people, who, misled by their own ignorance, and enraged by faction, insolently dared, during the trial, and in the very avenues leading to the court of justice, to threaten my life, in contempt of all law and authority" (44–45).

The association of Gascoyne's own person, against the mob, with "all law and authority" is here carried through from the very opening of his text to its close, where it is associated as well with the unstated but of course well-known outcome of the trial itself. Just as, for Gascoyne, Squires could not be innocent without Canning being guilty, so Canning could not be guilty without Gascoyne's being vindicated. An Address to the Liverymen is tightly structured so as to present these three separate propositions not only as inseparable but as what the liverymen of London have a right to expect.

If A Liveryman's Reply to Sir Crisp Gascoigne's Address, Showing that Gentleman's Real Motives, and his whole Conduct, Concerning Canning and Squires is really the work of a liveryman, then not all of Gascoyne's audience contentedly played the part assigned them. As the writer observed with considerable sarcasm,

You promised us no more than facts, but you have added to the plums of truth the paper and pack thread of reasonings; you promised only to state cases, but you have drawn conclusions.

How much are we obliged to you! . . . we might have mistaken many parts of your conduct, if you had not been pleased to mark out its candour and ingenuity; we might have thought you officious in this place, and rash in another; in this instance too remiss, and in another precipitate.

How obliged are we to you for these assistances to our judgment; it was kind to help a set of poor ignorant mechanicks, such as some of us I am afraid are; and, honourable Sir, we thank you. (Rpt. in *Canning's Farthing Post*, 224–25)

The liveryman proceeds to point out the deficiencies in Gascoyne's argument, proposing among other things that Gascoyne himself may not actually have written it, in a provocative style which led the *Gentleman's Magazine* to dismiss the *Reply* as "nothing more than one of those excrescences [sic], which naturally grow upon every popular book: It is always hoped that some, at least, will take notice of the fungus, among the multitude who examine the tree, to which if it had not adhered, they know it must have been spurned to the dunghill or trodden under foot." This strikes me as both defensive and harsh. The reviewer acknowledges that "Sir Crisp's address is much read" and asserts that the anonymous liveryman "has not alleged a single fact to contradict it" (24 [1754]: 342), but fact is not only not his focus—it is not really Gascoyne's either. Both are preoccupied with motivation and the liveryman additionally with style. Commenting on Gascoyne's speculations on Mrs. Canning and the cunning man he concludes,

> They prove nothing.
> The circumstance was not necessary for you to meddle with: but some infatuation seems to have hung over you, throughout this whole pompous and ridiculous Address.
> Speak candidly; What would you at this moment give, that no officious agent, or foolish friend, had prompted you to make it[?] (260)

For whatever reasons, Gascoyne made no further public pronouncements on the Canning case, ignoring both the jibes of the liveryman and the arguments of Canning's friends, which did not appear until late in November—"far too late to help the girl" (218), as de la Torre dismissed them, but probably not too late to annoy the former lord mayor.

The *Refutation*, however, does not share Gascoyne's single-voiced style or unified structure. It begins, immediately subsequent to its title page, with a typographically isolated prefatory statement dated 27 November 1754:

> That the force of the following REFUTATION may not be evaded, as the anonymous performance of a writer, who conceals his name that he may safely utter falsehood and defy resentment; we have, on the behalf of ourselves, and the rest of THE FRIENDS OF *ELIZABETH CANNING,* prefixed our names: declaring, that tho' we are ready to retract any assertion, with respect to the support of which we may have been misinformed, yet, as no testimony is admitted of which we have any doubt, no fact is related which we do not believe to be true.

This statement is signed by Nicholas Crisp, John Payne (who was also the *Refutation*'s publisher), James Harriott, Edward Rossiter, Thomas Cox, and John Carter, in effect an authorial committee whose prominence at the opening of the document suggests both that the material to follow has been subjected to group review and that the voice presenting it, whatever it may at some moments seem, is as sharply distinguished as possible from the distanced individual perspective of Sir Crisp Gascoyne, a collective, even a community, utterance, appropriate to the demotic stance of Canning's friends and their acceptance—so different from Gascoyne's rejection—of popular support in any assessment of the merits of Canning's case.

The *Refutation* is divided into three principal parts. The first, essentially a narrative account of the events of Canning's case from the time of the death of her father in July 1751, through the harassment of Canning in Newgate, runs for thirty folio pages, and the print, though smaller than that used in the presentation of Gascoyne's *Address,* is still large and legible. Capitalization of entire words is used very liberally for emphasis, and the text is further diversified by extensive footnotes on twenty-three of the thirty pages, including a four-page chart—itself a very extended footnote—labeled "Abstract of the PROOFS of Mary Squires's being in Enfield parish before and during Canning's confinement in Wells's house." Additionally, nineteen of these thirty pages have marginal glosses, usually more than one, referring readers to a set of sixty-five numbered appendices, the final section of the text, which itself runs for fifty-one pages—the page numbering beginning again, rather confusingly, with "1." These appendices are printed in a smaller typeface and without typographical emphasis apart from the use of full capitals to represent signatures and are arranged in an order roughly chronological with Canning's story. They consist of depositions from witnesses (while the trial had yet to be published, the writers were confident that no discrepancies between their appendices and the same witnesses' testimony in court would be found when it was (1)); the reprinted texts of newspaper advertisements, paragraphs, and essays; parallel column presentations of Canning's and Virtue Hall's informations before Fielding and of their testimony in court, with subsequent analysis; a review of the discrepancies in Mary Squires's alibi as given in her own trial as well as a schematic presentation of the alibi as given at Canning's trial by George Squires; and the testimony given by Susannah Wells in 1736 that later led to her conviction for perjury.

Between the main body of the text and the numbered body of appendices, there appears a further appendix of eight pages numbered in lower-case Roman numerals headed "A Refutation of Sir Crisp Gascoyne's Address, supported by the Facts in the foregoing Narrative." This portion of the text consists of sequential assertions quoted from Gascoyne's text and each followed by a contradiction from the point of view of Canning's defenders. The first of these reads as follows:

> I delayed my *justification* while her *trial* was depending, because I would not pursue a *remedy* at her *expense*. ADDRESS, p. 2.
>
> *At this very trial, he was busy in the court against her; and when he published this* profession of pity, *was opposing the* last act of lenity that was possible, *the permission of her friends to transport her themselves.* (1; italics as in original)

There are fifty-one of these quotation and response pairs, all of about the same length and character as the first.

The text of the *Refutation* ends with something not strictly a part of it but probably not without rhetorical impact, that is, a list of other books published by John Payne, which has the salutary effect of placing the *Refutation* in the company of Johnson's *Rambler* and *Adventurer,* letters from Sir Isaac Newton on the Greek text of the Bible, and various other orthodox religious texts including a forthcoming refutation of Lord Bolingbroke's "Objections to Scripture" (52). Overall, the *Refutation* is undeniably a complex and highly meditated production, intent upon making a case both for Canning's innocence and for Gascoyne's guilt—linked by Gascoyne himself, the two now seem indissolubly united—that would transcend rhetoric and rest primarily on a documentary basis, eschewing "probability" in favor of "evidence," to recur once more to the argumentative poles that have framed the case from that time to this.

Like Gascoyne's *Address*, the *Refutation* begins self-referentially, by explaining who the friends of Elizabeth Canning are and are not—not "a certain set of men known to each other; who having assisted her to prosecute the Gipsey, still adhered to the cause when no body else would have espoused it. [Instead s]he was supported at different times by different persons, many of them utter strangers to each other and to Sir Crisp Gascoyne; and those who principally assisted her to defend herself at the Old Bailey, had no concern in the prosecution of the Gipsey." Additionally, they were "neither eminent nor wealthy; but as they were not destitute of human passions, they were moved with indignation and pity at the sight of a poor wretch, whose life, however mean and obscure, they knew to have been irreproachable, and whose appearance was an incontestible proof of her misery" (1). In every respect, and not least in being many and obscure instead of single and prominent, they were the natural opposites of Sir Crisp Gascoyne. The *Refutation* proposes to give "a faithful and succinct relation of facts," referring the reader to the appendices for their documentation and to the notes "for such observations as confirm the girl's testimony or invalidate the objections against it; as well as for the particular passages in the address which are contradicted in the course of the narrative." The friends' narrative will use "no arts of persuasion" and "contain neither panegyric nor invective." Supremely unlike Gascoyne's *Address*, it will not be "interrupted by the querulous petulence [sic] of the relator" (2).

On this basis, the *Refutation* launches into what is at least at the outset a very straightforward narrative account, beginning with an almost fairy-tale simplicity: "William Canning, a poor sawyer in Aldermanbury postern, died about three years ago, and left in great distress four children, and his wife pregnant of a fifth. The woman, however, who had but two rooms for her whole family, continued the business with the assistance of an apprentice." After the word "rooms," however, an asterisk appears, and the reader finds at the bottom of the page the note, "Here, therefore, she had no conveniency to secrete her daughter, if it were possible to conceive why she should attempt it" (2). In the main text, the story continues, but from this point on it is never unattended by the stage whisper of the notes, reinforcing narrative with argument. Thus Sir Crisp Gascoyne does not appear in the

narrative until page 11, but the *Address* is cited in the notes as
early as page 6, and once Gascoyne does enter the narrative
proper the tone of argument seeps up from the bottom of the
page into the main text as well, and the fairy-tale element fades
(rather as it does in Swift's similarly complex *Tale of a Tub*):

> However neutral the letter may be, which appears in the address
> to be written by Mr. Ford to Mr. Harris the minister of Abbotsbury,
> it is certain, that other applications were made by interested persons.
> One Shirley, whom Sir Crisp allows to be "a very bad man," and one
> Martin, the son-in-law of this Squires who had so BOLDLY declared
> to Sir Crisp that he was determined to save the Gipsey, had been
> down to procure affidavits in her behalf, which they had ready drawn
> up, with blanks that were to be filled up with the names of such
> persons as could be got to swear them: it is not therefore to be much
> wondered that Canning's friends paid no very great regard to Ab-
> botsbury evidence.

Thomas Myles's affidavit is cited in the margin to this paragraph,
and a footnote adds that the story of the blank affidavits was
told "by Mr. Cooper, of Salisbury, to Mr. Rossiter and Mr. John
Myles" (12).

In general, the *Refutation* avoids the incorporation of documents into the main text, but it makes an exception of Gascoyne's
memorial to the king on behalf of a pardon for Mary Squires (see
chapter 3 for a full text). Here the same method as in the appendix on pages i–viii is used, with each now numbered point of
the original memorial followed by a short statement of contradiction, e.g.:

> VI That in none of the examinations he had taken, there was any
> circumstance that could lead him to doubt the innocence of the
> convict.
>
> This may be true of Sir Crisp; but, surely, sufficient reason has
> been given for the doubt of OTHERS. (18)

By this point, Gascoyne has completely eclipsed Canning as
the *Refutation*'s central figure—as indeed its title suggests—and
the trial is presented as the culmination of his vendetta against
her. Despite his earlier statement—reported, another footnote

tells the reader, by the *London Daily Advertiser and Inspector*, in other words by Hill—"that he would not be present at the trial, [he] was not only PRESENT but BUSY; he was sometimes at the bottom of the court among the crowd, and sometimes crying out, 'it is a plain case, gentlemen, it is a plain case,'" while his ally Hill supported his side with "such calumnies . . . that the Court recommended an information against the printer and publisher; and if Canning had not been poor, they had certainly been punished. . . . Under these disadvantages was Canning's trial commenced and carried on" (25).

As the "disadvantages" of Canning's trial, condemnation, and imprisonment provide the remainder of the *Refutation*'s narrative, its tone becomes more heated, its use of emphatic capitals more profuse. The final section is a restatement of Canning's story as a series of twenty-one factual propositions. Fewer than half of these are specific to her, e.g., "The girl disappeared for twenty eight days; and in that time was reduced from a state of health to extreme languor and weakness, so as to be in danger of DEATH," and "While she was in prison, she was falsely represented as an ENTHUSIAST and a DRUNKARD," while most of the remainder refer to Sir Crisp Gascoyne:

> The Court, at least Sir Crisp, was SATISFIED WITH THE VERDICT.
> He afterwards PRETENDED the contrary. . . .
> The witnesses, for whose honesty he VOUCHES, were INFAMOUS in the highest degree. . . .
> Unfair and false pretences were used to prevent the removal of the cause into a SUPERIOR COURT.
> Unfair methods were taken to INJURE the prisoner, when tried at the Old Bailey.

The conclusion of this series of propositions reinforces the fusion that has taken place for virtually all of the eighteenth-century writers on the case of Canning's own situation with the reputation of both her enemies and her friends:

> Such is the STORY and FATE of *ELIZABETH CANNING!* whose friends have been stigmatized as THE SUBORNERS OF PERJURY; A FACTION FORMED AGAINST MAGISTRACY AND LAW, DETERMINED TO PROTECT A KNOWN CRIMINAL IN MERE OPPOSITION TO HER PROSECUTOR; a slander which, with almost every allegation in the address, they do hereby affirm, in direct terms, to be FALSE. (30)

Despite their differences in rhetorical strategy, the *Address* and the *Refutation* are alike in their overt adherence each to one side in the conflict. Neither makes the least pretense, much less any actual effort, to consider the evidence or arguments of the other side, and it seems likely that they drew the bulk of their audiences from partisans of their own positions. Between these two overtly tendentious works, however, there appeared the *Genuine and Impartial Memoirs*, which offered itself as a work of mediating objectivity. While it becomes obvious in the course of reading the *Memoirs* that this, too, is a rhetorical device, its initial assertion may well have made a strong appeal in a situation where "the Sentiments of the Publick, even after two solemn Trials, . . . seem to remain to the full as much undetermined as if no such Trials had been" (iii).

This assessment of public uncertainty comes at the beginning of a three-page Preface signed "The Editors" and introduces what purports to be a sequence of sixteen letters, all addressed to T____ J____n, Esq., and concluding with a date and some variant of "Your Humble Servant, / ***." The "Editors" Preface offers no explanation for the form and no identities for either the author or the recipient of the alleged letters but instead stresses the purpose of "This Undertaking . . . to do equal Justice to the Arguments" of both sides and to present facts without misrepresentation, a tacit, perhaps inadvertent, admission that the *Memoirs'* epistolarity is a contrivance and as such not a completely convincing support for the reliability of the following text. Nevertheless,

> This Performance . . . is not intended for the particular Service of either Party; the Cause of Truth was only designed to be served by it.
>
> As to the unhappy Object that has given rise to these Memoirs, it must be allowed that however *improbable* her Tale at first might seem, yet it was *affecting;* also, that her *Prosecutor* was possessed of both *Power* and *Riches:* Should it at least appear that she is innocent, how comfortably may she say, with Dumont in Jane Shore,
>
>> Yet Heaven that made me honest made me more
>> Than ever King did, when he made a *Knight.*
>
> (iv–vi)

Suspicious readers might find clues of bias even in these professions and more in the anonymity of both the editors and the letter-writer, but the first letter is designed to reassure them. Dated 6 February 1753, it purports to be a response to an enquiry from the letter's recipient about the 31 January newspaper para-

graph relating Canning's homecoming. The recipient is represented as having found the story "ridiculous and contemptible,"
but the letter-writer assures him that "it has met with extensive
Credit," and that in spite of the "highest Improbabilities" in her
story Canning's own personal reputation and that of her family
and supporters were excellent, particularly in certain appropriate negatives: "It is certain her Person has nothing extraordinarily attractive, nor is her Understanding reported to be very
penetrating" (4).

The writer's next letter responds to further skepticism on the
part of T____ J____n:

> Though you, Sir, are pleased to ridicule the Pretensions of my
> Heroine, as you term her, to Virtue, and say, you ought to expect,
> from the Specimen I gave you in my last, a realized Pamela, I have
> yet but little reason to alter my Opinion. I need not tell you, that
> Virtue is not an inseparable Appendage to Learning, Sagacity, or
> Riches: It is, perhaps, as frequent to be met with in the Cottage as
> the Palace; and suppose it granted to you, That a parish-school and
> and Alehouse are not the most promising Seminaries to inculcate
> Modesty, yet if, upon a serious Enquiry into this Affair, it should be
> proved that this Girl has had Fortitude enough to resist the most
> flattering Allurements, as well as to sustain the cruelest Oppressions
> in support of her Innocence, will not her Character appear by so
> much more Praise-Worthy, even for having labored under all these
> Disadvantages in her Education? (5)

Letter II is fourteen pages long and incorporates whole newspaper items, printed as notes. In spite of a postscript referring to
the letter-writer and his recipient as old schoolfellows, it should
surely be clear to even the most gullible readers by now that the
epistolary form is a deliberate narrative device, not a matter of
chance, still less an authentic publication of actual letters. The
choice, despite its transparency, has several strategic advantages:
it gives, in the first place, a sense of immediacy to the various
stages in a story that by now reached backward over a year; in
addition, the story can be told with some suspense—"it is highly
probable Curiosity may lead us to pay a visit to Virtue Hall . . ."
(18)—no matter how long after the fact it may actually have been
composed. Perhaps most important, however, as the allusion to
a "realized Pamela" suggests, the choice of the epistolary mode
allows for the incorporation of a powerful fictional element, the
dramatization of a developing narrator, a writer at first taken in

by, or at least open to, Canning's story and only gradually brought to a realization of her iniquity.

In Letter III, therefore, the writer is still protesting: "It does not belong to me to pretend to Infallibility; I may very possibly have been mistaken, but if I am, remember it is on the charitable Side of the Question, in behalf of a helpless Object, whose Sufferings, if true, certainly deserve Compassion, and whose Story, till it is contradicted by something more than bare Conjecture, demands Credit" (19). The narrator thus relates Squires's and Wells's trial, observing that Gibbons, Clarke, and Greville were prepossessing witnesses and that the activities of the mob outside the courtroom were highly improper but still concluding that although "some other Circumstances that I have heard, but which I do not think sufficiently authenticated to report, make me less sanguine in this Cause than I was before" (33), he will not yet form any conclusion against Canning. The way is prepared for Letter V, when the recantation of Virtue Hall shakes his confidence, and he hopefully informs his correspondent that the forthcoming pamphlets of Fielding—"whose Capacity, as a Writer, we have often jointly admired, whose Knowledge of the human Heart is beyond Contradiction"—and Hill—who "assumes an authentick Acquaintance with what relates to this Matter, and promises very largely" (44)—will perhaps resolve the terrible and increasing suspense over the truth of Canning's story.

For the reader, the enlightenment of the narrator is also a matter of suspense, one the writer plays knowingly with in the beginning of Letter VI:

> The Multitude are certainly with her; but manifold Experience sufficiently evinces, that a Multitude may be, and often are, greatly mistaken.... You will, I presume, be ready to infer, from this Introduction, that I have absolutely changed Sides, and am become a perfect Convert to your Sentiments. But this is not altogether the Case; what I am concerned at; and what I sincerely wish might be avoided, is, that Bitterness and Rage which each Party expresses against the other, for not concurring in the same Way of Thinking about this perplexed Affair. (46–47)

Having thus reasserted his own disinterestedness, the writer makes what can only be called an attack on Fielding's pamphlet, which he says ought to have been called "An Apology for the Author and his Client" (47), and anatomizing it for the following twenty-two pages and confounding Fielding's text with Canning's own story, which is now, primarily on the dubious basis of "what she had sworn [sic] before Alderman Chitty" (62), treated as a mass of contradictions. According to my reading of the *Genuine and Impartial Memoirs*, this is the position which its author occupied from the beginning, but its appearance has been very carefully prepared, and the writer never completely abandons the persona of the public-spirited and fair-minded friend.

Thus, although Fielding's inept advocacy has convinced him unintentionally of Canning's guilt, he remains, though sadder and wiser than before, a man whose sympathies are available to the truly deserving:

> I never was fond of being deemed a Retailer of Scandal, which, from the Time of the Abbotsbury Discoveries and Virtue Hall's Recantation, has been very liberally, and indeed very shamefully, dispersed by the Friends of the Girl against everyone who presumes to entertain the least Doubt of her Veracity and Innocence, or that ventures to shew any Sort of Tenderness or Compassion for the Convicts. The Lord Mayor's Activity and declared Resolution to spare no Pains to come at the Truth of this mysterious Affair, has rendered him the more immediate Object of their Resentment and Invectives. (87–88)

Nevertheless, the writer maintains his fairness, defending Canning's character from the attack made upon it by "those who espouse the Gipsey":

> Their not being able to assign any adequate Motive for the Girl's Concealment, is no Justification of the many wanton and cruel Surmises that have been suggested to the Prejudice of her Reputation, as, that she had been salivated, been brought to Bed, or had miscarried. These Reports have been as currently propagated in Conversation, as if they were well known and established Facts.—Her Character, as I have before observed, has been the principal Foundation of the Credit given to her Tale, and it must be her future Support; consequently it ought not to be attacked from mere Spleen and Resentment; in short, it is greatly to be wished more Moderation had been expressed on both Sides. (Letter VIII, 31 May 1753; 102–3)

A very cynical reader might take this paragraph as a devious means of incorporating the very rumors it denounces within the text, but the writer is still protesting in Letter X, under the date 12 September 1753:

I scarce know how to comprehend Canning's being a perfect Impostor; that a young artless Girl, hitherto not only unpracticed in, but also unsuspected of, any Vice, should at once render herself guilty of the joint Crimes of wilful Perjury, and intended Murder, is inconceivable to me, and, I believe, to any common Apprehension. Those who espouse her are Men of Weight, Fortune, and Reputation; can it be imagined such People would venture the Forfeiture of the Respect now justly paid them, in Support of any Thing they had not full Conviction was right? The whole Story is as truly marvellous as the consequent Proceedings have been really unaccountable. Have you ever, in the Course of your Acquaintance with Men or Books, met with any Thing equal to it? (134–35)

The balance of the text, however, without ever completely abandoning the narrator's pose as a disinterested observer, shifts from this juncture to a consistently anti-Canningite stance. Having once more animadverted on "the Part Mr. Fielding has acted in this Drama" (276), objected to the publication of Sollom Emlyn's replies to the questions put to him by the friends after the trial, and related the Elizabeth Knot story from the anti-Canning point of view, the writer, drawing near the end of his labors, exclaims:

But I am weary of wading through Dirt; let us just take a Review of the Arguments offered in Favour of the Girl's Innocence; which may be reduced to these Particulars: First, That Things as strange have happened heretofore: And, Secondly, The Difference between the moral Characters of Canning, and the Persons she accused.—In Support of the first, History has been consulted, and all the unaccountable Stories that have been reported within the last two Centuries, have been again retailed; . . . But admit the whole of her Tale possible, we cannot be obliged to believe it, merely because it is so, when it stands contradicted by such a Chain of Evidence.—As to the second Particular, I shall only observe, that as Canning's Reputation was not call'd in Question in Court, it would ill become me to say any Thing to it: But only believe what is said of her, no Pagan Heroine, or Papal Saint, was ever more illustriously characterized.—Should you but give yourself the Trouble of running through the Heap of Papers you receive with this, you will find continued Sprinklings of the Lustre of her moral Character, blameless, amiable, exemplary, and the like: Who can help smiling to see such pretty Expressions, and so many persuasive Epithets, employed on a Wench, who, to say the best of her, was never in the whole Course of her Life till now, distinguished for any Thing remarkable good or ill[?] (284–85)

Here, I think, the writer's mask of impartiality slips rather obviously, but he is within a few pages of the end of his novel-length and novelistic representation of Canning's story and his imperative now is to arrive at a conclusion characterized by what fiction often offers more credibly than the sort of factual narrative he is purporting to relate: poetic justice. Thus, "Trace the Story from one End to the Other,"—and the writer has just done so—"Was it not in the Beginning strange, inconsistent, and improbable? What have been its Supports but disguised Facts and false Representations?" (288). Little by little, however, the narrator has stripped these disguises away, and the trial has now confirmed Canning's guilt. If anyone still actually believes her innocent—"There are none so blind as those who *will not see*" (289)—such people act very wrongly in trying to mitigate the circumstances of Canning's transportation. The "Court, who judged from better Evidence than private Men can possibly obtain, have found her *Guilty;* and if private Opinion is to justify Attempts to screen Offenders from the Sentences of those who are by Law appointed our Judges, no Government can possibly long subsist" (290–91)

With these the stakes and not, any longer, the mere oddity of Canning's original story, the writer's transformation from sympathetic bystander to something not far from an avenging angel makes perfect sense: the whole social order is under threat, and a case like Canning's may be the entering wedge of a new world of anarchic self-assertion on the part of such socially subordinate figures as maidservants and even children. The writer thus ends his final letter not with any last twist in Canning's case but with the story—"communicated to me by a Gentleman of unquestionable Veracity . . ., though I am not at Liberty to mention Names"—of a nine-year-old girl (a protégé, apparently, of dubious origins, not a family member) placed by an affluent lady at a London boarding school, who went missing after two months' residence there. A gentleman found the little girl wandering almost naked, and since she told him she had been lured away and stripped by a strange man, he took her, at her request, to her friends rather than back to her school. "The Girl repeated the Tale to her Mistress, . . . but suspecting the Veracity of her Scholar, [she] found Means, in three or four Days Time, to come at the real Truth of the Matter; the Girl confessed that she had herself taken off her Cloaths, and thrown them into a Pond." The truth of such a vaguely attested story, if it is not in fact a complete invention, is, of course, uncheckable, although the child's motivations will scarcely be unimaginable to late twentieth-century readers, but the conclusion the writer draws from his tale is unequivocal: "Is it not high Time that very severe Examples should be made on all who attempted the like Practices, when a Child of this Age should contrive such an Imposition; one who could have no apparent Motive, unless to excite Compassion, and that she knew how remarkably her Patroness had distinguish'd herself by her Benevolence to ELIZABETH CANNING[?] . . (291–92)

The author of the *Genuine and Impartial Memoirs* is unknown, though I am inclined to suspect Dr. John Hill: the writer's animus toward Fielding even more than toward Canning suggests it, as does the comment in Rousseau's chronological table of Hill's output that 1754 was "[a]n unproductive year for reasons not clear. . ." (xxix). The preparation of the lengthy and complex *Memoirs* and their anonymous placement with a publisher hitherto not identified with one side or the other in the case would have cost even the prolific Hill some time and labor.

With these later publications, including the first edition of the trial itself, contemporary written contributions to the Canning case first abruptly declined, then ceased altogether. A retrospective and not completely accurate account of it given by Tobias Smollett in his *Continuation of the Complete History of England* in 1760 suggests what may have become the dominant view, that the Canning case exemplified an irrational tendency innate to the English temperament, "a temporary fermentation from the turbulent ingredients inherent in its own constitution. Tumults are excited, and factions kindled into rage and inveteracy, by incidents of the most frivolous nature." The Canning case was "a dispute in itself of so little consequence to the community, that it could not deserve a place in a general history, if it did not serve to convey a characteristic idea of the English nation." Canning was "an obscure damsel, of low degree," whose "improbable and unsupported" story aroused the "fanatics of all denominations . . . to such a pitch of enthusiasm, that the most palpable truths, which appeared on the other side, had no effect than that of exasperating them to the most dangerous degree of rage and revenge." The cause may have been trifling, but the consequences were not—factional bitterness "divided the greater part of the kingdom, including the rich as well as the poor, the high as well as the humble," and the case "became the general topic of conversation in all assemblies, and people of all ranks espoused one or the other party with as much warmth and animosity as had ever inflamed the Whigs and Tories. . ." (154–57). Such a frenzy must finally end in exhaustion and perhaps in embarrassment. Looking back at the Canning case could give few contemporaries, participants or observers alike, any satisfaction, and the case disappeared for a time from public discourse.

Victorians

I have gone into considerable detail about the *Address, Refutation,* and *Memoirs* not only because, along with the trial record itself, they are the principal sources used by all later writers, but also because their assumptions tend to be taken up along with their narrative content. Three out of four of them treat Canning's guilt as conclusively proven, and most later writers on the case do not so much arrive at that conclusion as start from it.

The first retrospective account of the case, James Caulfield's "Elizabeth Canning, Mary Squires, and Mother Wells," which appeared in 1820, indeed does little more than retell the story without analysis or commentary, although it does conclude with rumors that may have been contemporary, though not necessarily the more reliable for that. Caulfield seems to have believed that the mob was motivated against Sir Crisp Gascoyne "by learning that one of the gipsy's sons had been many years in his service, and, it was reported, was privy to some secret offence his master had been guilty of, the fear of divulging which compelled him to the endeavour of preserving the life of the mother." He also reports that "the unfortunate Canning [was] deserted by her friends" and that she became a schoolmistress and married "an opulent Quaker" (3: 148), the first and last of which assertions, at least, are certainly false and the second quite improbable. It is difficult also to see how the mob could be said to have *learned* something so vague as "some secret offence," though many of them may well have believed that they had.

Caulfield himself was an antiquarian printseller, born in 1764, ten years after Canning's trial, who became a prolific writer as well, with a preference for histories emphasizing "eccentricity, immorality, dishonesty, and so forth," as the *Dictionary of National Biography* put it with some distaste. He was known for his good memory and generosity but also for having taken to drink in the latter part of his life, from which period his essay on Canning dates. The essay itself is at best a muddy minor tributary to the stream of received opinion-and-fact that grows into the second, noncontemporary story of the Canning case, but

Caulfield's contributions are repeated by most later writers, with or without caveats.

The next study to appear, John Paget's "Elizabeth Canning," is more substantial than Caulfield's relation, and Paget (1811–98), as a barrister and police magistrate, was at least better qualified to analyze a legal case than Caulfield. His essay appeared first in *Chambers' Edinburgh Journal* in 1852 and was reprinted in the same year in *The Eclectic Magazine* and in 1860 in *Blackwood's*. Paget himself included it in his own 1874 collection, *Paradoxes and Puzzles Historical, Judicial, and Literary*, as the first of the "judicial" category, a publishing history suggesting both that the subject could still arouse considerable interest and that Paget himself was pleased with his own analysis. Certainly his presentation of the evidence, all drawn from the trial record, is a masterpiece of narrative clarity and, in my opinion, of fairness.

Paget assesses Canning's story as basically credible, giving considerable weight to the testimony of her neighbors as to what she said on the night of 29 January and finding her account of the room remarkably correct in spite of "trifling inaccuracies" (*Paradoxes*, 323). On the other hand, Mary and George Squires's immediate assertion of their alibi "without hesitation, specifying time and place . . ., and thus affording means for testing its truth" (326), deserves equal weight. It was the apparent strength of the evidence on both sides, in fact, which made the case of interest to Paget: "We have turned it over and over, looked at it this way and that way, read it backwards and forwards and upside down, and there it remains, puzzling us like a horrid incubus or incomprehensible nightmare. Is any faith to be placed in human testimony? Read the evidence on one side, and it is impossible to refuse our assent to it. Read that on the other, and it is equally conclusive. The *alibi* and the *ibi* are both supported by a train of evidence which appears irresistible" (335).

Paget found Fielding's performance as a magistrate innocent in intent but so flawed in practice that Virtue Hall's evidence was worthless, but her recantation, similarly obtained, was no better. Likewise, although he characterized Sir Crisp Gascoyne as a "man . . . of sense and humanity," he found testimony Gascoyne weighted heavily, that of Fortune and Judith Natus, equally valueless. The argument based on probability also left him unimpressed—"Those who are familiar with criminal courts know well how slight and insignificant are the motives which often impel men to the most terrible crimes" (332)—and to support his point he gave some cogent recent examples. Canning's trial, between the bias of the Recorder and the divagations of the jury, also gave no satisfactory answer.

Paget's essay ends by describing the case as "eminently fitted to give occasion to the warmest, most eager, and most confident partisanship, inasmuch as it is almost impossible, after the coolest and most deliberate examination, to say to which side the balance of evidence inclines" (336). The word "almost" suggests that Paget himself had, though with difficulty, formed a conclusion, but if he had he did not explicitly reveal it, although he seems to lean toward Canning's side. However, the temptation to "confident partisanship" that the case offered was to overcome most of his followers. Few would dissect the trial record with as much finesse and detachment. Most, on the contrary, feeling themselves presented with a mystery, would undertake to solve it. From the middle of the nineteenth century the Canning case thus becomes something of an intellectual tar baby—to touch it is to become caught up in a resurgence of the same attraction that drew many of the original writers on the case to it, the hope of finding a solution which was evading everyone else, and as later writers found earlier arguments unconvincing, the solutions would become increasingly complex, not to say bizarre.

Austin Dobson, writing in the *Dictionary of National Biography* in a volume first published in 1886, may be taken to represent the transition. Dobson took a clear stand from the outset of his sketch by labeling Canning "malefactor" in the capsule description with which it conventionally begins. His version of the case, although it clearly follows Paget's, emphasizes unspecified "discrepancies" in Canning's various tellings of her story, labels Sir Crisp Gascoyne's inquiries "searching," and posits Virtue Hall's recantation as a significant turning point—indeed, the location of a turning point becomes something of an obsession with later writers on the case, perhaps deriving from an assumption that a good narrative ought to have one. Dobson cites Caulfield as a source on Canning's later life but is satisfied to quote the *Gentleman's Magazine* obituary notice as his conclusion, using it to reinforce his own judgment: "how from 1 Jan. 1753 to the 29th of that month she did really spend her time is a secret that has never to this day been divulged." It was an ending that would not satisfy such later writers as Machen and de la Torre, who attempted not merely to describe the case but to settle it, but it is a common refrain among the Victorian writers.

The next to deal with the case, Courtney Kenny, was a prominent legal figure, a former member of Parliament and, at the time of his essay on Canning, 1897, university reader in English law at Cambridge. The *Dictionary of National Biography* describes him as distinguished by "sound scholarship, lucid expression, and charm of style," qualities which to my different perceptions come across rather as an establishment bias, great self-confidence, and a resulting tone of complicity with the reader somewhat at the expense of the subjects of the essay. An early sentence establishes the key: "No less experienced a judge and legal historian than Lord Campbell calls [the Canning case] 'one of the most extraordinary cases of popular delusion on record'; and points out that more than half the nation stood up for the innocence of the person who was ultimately adjudged to be guilty" (368). An authority who is or ought to be so familiar and respected that no further designation than "Lord Campbell" is necessary to identify him is produced to tell us from the outset that the Canning case is chiefly remarkable as an instance of "popular delusion." Differences of opinion over the case are reduced to wrong-headedness on the part of the vulgar, who chose to ignore a legal verdict here presented as unexceptionable.

Kenny makes fun of Voltaire's inaccurate representation of the case—"he gaily multiplies ... the two capital sentences that were passed in the course of it into the statement that 'nine' persons were condemned to death" (368)—and disagrees with Paget's judgment that Virtue Hall's recantation was as worthless as her original information—"it is difficult to see any motives likely to lead her to retract it untruthfully" (376). Despite Kenny's confidence, however, there are some problems here: only one capital sentence was passed in the case, and the subjection of Virtue Hall to persuasion by powerful men is documented with about equal naivete by both the men in question, Henry Fielding and Sir Crisp Gascoyne. The latter, however, is clearly Kenny's principal source, and the legal writer takes the former Lord Mayor very much at his own valuation—"Sir Crispe Gascoyne [sic] threw himself earnestly into the case" (371). Political opposition to Gascoyne thus seemed to Kenny a persuasive motivation for much of Canning's support—"unscrupulous city politicians [were] anxious to checkmate Gascoyne in his civic career by holding him up to public indignation as the unscrupulous oppressor of an innocent and injured girl," giving the pamphlets written in her defense—it is unclear whether Kenny really means all of them, but it seems unlikely that his research had extended so far—"the air of insincerity" (380). This opposition had considerable social and moral resonance for Kenny, not only in its historical dimension but with reference to his own time:

> One lesson of this strange case—a lesson increasingly necessary in our days of sensational newspapers, a widespread franchise, and a plastic House of Commons—is the danger of permitting judicial proceedings to be influenced by mob violence or even by party feeling. That crowds such as those who, during the first trial, assailed the Old Bailey and frightened away witnesses of such primary importance as Fortune Natus and his wife, immediately and fatally pervert the course of justice, is too obvious to need mention. But even the more indirect influence of the mob who rioted round the court during the second trial and insulted the humane ex-Lord Mayor, though it apparently did not affect the actual issue of this particular case, could not become habitual in any country except at the expense of practically annihilating the reign of law. Only a few months ago, in so quiet a town as Shrewsbury, a criminal court was disturbed by displays of violence, inside and outside the building, so turbulent as to be officially declared to have embarrassed the counsel and to have made witnesses, especially female ones, chary of giving evidence. (379–80)

I have already questioned whether Natus and other potential witnesses for Squires and Wells were in fact intimidated from testifying, but the question for Kenny is more ideological than factual—not whether intimidation of witnesses did occur, although he assumes that it did, but whether expressions of popular dissatisfaction are appropriate in a legal context, as he argues they are not.

This matter of public order is placed last in the essay's treatment of the "lessons" of the case, after "the importance of a priori considerations of credibility as guides in forensic inquiries," and the latter, according to Kenny himself, "is the principal lesson of this famous trial," but the placement of the two suggests that their importance is not merely equal but linked. Thus, "[i]n Elizabeth Canning's case it is perhaps not unfair to say that, after the two vast masses of evidence for and against the alibi had similarly neutralized one another, the issue was decided, neither by direct nor by circumstantial evidence, but by the inherent incredibility of Canning's story" (377), although both the protests of the crowd and the struggles of the jury, even the split verdict over the sentence by the judges, suggest that "the issue was decided" only formally, not persuasively. For Kenny, however, the fact that the nine members of the court voting for the harsher sentence "included every one of the six legal members of the Court" (374) added weight to the otherwise merely numerical conclusion that Canning was guilty, and the unstated corollary is that probability is a matter for the judgment of lawyers, although the concluding paragraphs of his essay seem to me to embody an extremely tenuous argument.

In them, Kenny hypothesizes that "theological partisanship came into play in Canning's case. . . . The very eagerness which her friends showed to deny this is the best proof of the truth of it," although he omits any reference to the accusations to which the friends were responding when they produced Canning's reading of Thomas à Kempis and Reverend Reyner's affidavit. Similarly, Fielding's "dozen years' experience at the Bar and five years' experience as a Bow Street Magistrate, all his novels written and all the knowledge of mankind which they embody already acquired," like Canning's earlier and later record of good character, are held not to weigh against "the most generally useful lesson to be drawn from the Canning mystery, useful enough in forensic difficulties but far indeed from being limited to them, . . . the wisdom of a modest agnosticism in all questions that hinge upon the incalculable and insoluble mysteries of the feminine mind" (381–82). Despite Kenny's claims to modesty, however, his argument here seems to be that probability favors the conclusion that a young woman of unblemished good character may nevertheless be reasonably presumed to be lying if her statements, whatever they are, fail to win the belief of a lord mayor and a team of attorneys, particularly if their disbelief is both actively pursued and actively challenged. For Kenny, therefore, Voltaire's presentation of Canning, in spite of Kenny's own exposure of his lack of specific knowledge of the case, as "'une petite friponne qui etait allee a coucher' . . . harmonizes and explains all the undisputed circumstances" (379).

Kenny's desire to harmonize and explain is certainly not his alone, nor is he alone in finding more satisfying harmonies in explanations which condemn Canning and exonerate Gascoyne. His assumptions recur without examination in the later work of his contemporary Hugh Childers,[1] who, unlike Paget or Kenny, makes his position clear from the outset of his essay: Canning was an "apparently well-conducted girl" who certainly told a false story.

[W]hat she did with herself has never been discovered yet, and probably never will be. What she *said* had happened to her furnished a tale which kept the Old Bailey engaged for days and days in no less than three great criminal trials [if we count Gibbons's, Clarke's and Greville's trials as one and apply the term "great" very freely, perhaps], led to the sentence of death (fortunately not carried out) of an innocent woman, and the actual burning in the hand of another, procured her transportation for seven years . . ., divided the town . . ., and caused her portrait to make its appearance in every printshop in London. (3)

Kenny's tone is, in phrases like "modest agnosticism," not without some irony, but it is generally judicious; Childers's is evidently lighter, as his ragbag sequence of consequences of Canning's story ranging from Squires's death sentence to pictures in printshops indicates. His interest is less in lessons to be drawn from the Canning case than in its "many sidelights on the manners and customs of England in the middle of the eighteenth century" (3), embodying what might be characterized as an antiquarian, even a nostalgic approach to the case. Thus Childers reproduces without discussion or provenance five illustrations of very varied authenticity and gives extraneous information on such topics as the construction of the Mansion House and other celebrated law cases in a sequence of footnotes.

Once more, Canning's story is retold. There is no attempt to sort out the sources of its various components and in some places, as for instance Canning's appearance before Alderman Chitty, the version presented clearly interprets as much as it restates:

> The Alderman, after hearng Elizabeth's tale, pressed her to describe minutely the room where she said she had been imprisoned. She did so. It was, she said, a litle square, darkish or dark room, with boards nailed up before the windows, through the cracks of which she could see the Hertfordshire coach pass by upon the road. The contents were an old broken stool, a chair, an iron grate, and a few old pictures. She asserted that she ultimately effected her escape by pulling down, after many futile attempts, one of the boards of the window.

The image of a square dark room here comes from Gawen Nash's later testimony, not from Alderman Chitty's minutes, while the story-followed-by-description sequence and "many futile attempts" to escape prior to success seem to be Childers's own rationalized additions to Chitty's less orderly account. What is perhaps even more important, however, is Childers's note to the name Thomas Chitty: "The ancestor of three generations of famous lawyers" (5). A similar digression occurs, this time in the main body of the text, when Sir Crisp Gascoyne—"a remarkable man"—enters the action:

> He had married the daughter and co-heiress of John Bamber, a wealthy city physician, and thus the Bamber fortune ultimately passed into the Gascoyne family. By the marriage of his great-grand-daughter with the second Marquess of Salisbury the property passed again to the Cecils, who prefixed to their surname that of Gascoyne. Another member of the same family, Isaac Gascoyne, a general with a distinguished active record, was in after years a member of Parliament and was in the Lobby of the House of Commons when Mr. Perceval was shot by Bellingham, whom he at once seized and carried before the speaker. (10)

Pretty obviously, none of this is of immediate relevance to the case of Elizabeth Canning, and while it may be put down in part to Childers's magpielike collecting of "sidelights," I think it carries an additional message as well: Chitty and Gascoyne were men of wealth and family, at least when viewed retrospectively; as such, they were for Childers inherently more believable than a debilitated servant girl and her scarcely solvent neighbors, none of whom apparently left distinguished descendants.

Canning's story was corroborated only by the dubious Virtue Hall, while "some only of the men who went down to make her arrest were impressed with the verisimilitude of it" (12). Male belief, however, was crucial, and thus the turn in the case comes, for Childers, with "the acute mind of Gascoyne" fastening upon "the weakness of the case" against Squires and Wells (14). From this point Childers's account in fact follows Gascoyne's, although when he comes to Canning's trial William Davy shares the honors—"His speech was a masterly one and exposed the inconsistencies and impossibilities of Elizabeth's story in the clearest manner" (22). Childers's summary of the trial follows the closing statements of Davy and Moreton as to its salient points, and although he quotes Paget's judgment that the evidence is "almost impossible" to assess conclusively differs strongly from him in practice: "Everyone is entitled to his own opinion, but where neither time no expense has been spared on either side a strong presumption must and should exist in favour of the verdict of a jury, more especially where that verdict (after long deliberation) reverses a verdict obtained with very little deliberation at all" (36). As I have shown, however, Canning's friends claimed considerable financial difficulty in their presentation of evidence compared to the prosecution, and the jury's deliberations were, on their own showing, incomplete at best. What in fact seems to be at work in Childers's conclusion is a bias in favor of authority similar to Kenny's: Gascoyne's prominence and Davy's professional expertise become evidence for their reliability, while Canning is a nobody.

Childers is not without humanity in this judgment, however, although he expresses his feelings at some expense to the coherence of his argument. He finds Voltaire's suggested solution "uncharitable" although possibly correct, even going so far as to state that it "receives support from some of the evidence [not specified] given at the trial; but even so, witnesses could, in a case where money was no object, have been forthcoming to prove it," a remarkable suggestion in itself if my reading of it—that Gascoyne could have hired witnesses to prove Canning had been lying in at the time in question—is correct (36). Childers's conclusion, if it is not read simply as muddled, perhaps suggests why he chose the epithet "romantic" to describe this and other trials which are likely to strike later readers as almost anything but that. Canning's "crime might even be palliated by the low state of mind and body to which she had, in some way, been reduced, which tempted her, under suggestions from others, to give a plausible explanation of her movements without taking into account the terrible consequences that would follow. And having taken the first fatal step, she was too entangled to retreat. Looked at from this point of view, and bringing her subsequent record from the age of twenty to her death at forty [actually, thirty-eight] into acount, her description as a 'malefactor' seems an oppressively harsh one" (36–37).

Certainly it seemed so to Andrew Lang, probably Canning's most wholehearted defender since the publication of the *Refutation*. Lang was, according to the sympathetic account of him given by the *Dictionary of National Biography*, a man given to "help[ing] . . . lame dogs over stiles," and while he is now better known as a folklorist he was also a historian, one to whom "History . . . meant finding things out, [so that] when he began an inquiry he could not be stopped." It is easy to see these impulses of chivalry and curiosity at work in Lang's treatment of the Canning case. "I am on Elizabeth's side," he states; "the piety, honesty, loyalty, and even the superstition of her people, have made me her partisan" (5–6), but he is not intemperately so, noting that the testimony of Canning's neighbors in April and May 1754 as to what she said on 29 January 1753, must be read with an "allowance for friendly bias and mythopoeic memory" (6).

Nevertheless, Lang is the first writer on the Canning case to apply equal skepticism to Alderman Chitty, who by the time of his testimony at Canning's trial was "a disbeliever," producing what Lang labels an account "not intelligible" and "not satisfactory" (7). Lang reviewed the testimony of the goldsmiths as well as of Canning's neighbors and was inclined to find the latter the more convincing, but the same principle applied to both: "Most accounts of what Elizabeth said on January 29 and on January 31 [i.e., before Alderman Chitty] are fifteen months after date, and are biased on both sides" (11). Unlike other Victorian writers on the case and most later ones as well, Lang makes no exception of Sir Crisp Gascoyne in his analysis of the role of bias in the case, describing him as having "got at" Virtue Hall, whose evidence Lang completely disregards (16).

After reviewing the alibi evidence and that placing Squires at Enfield, Lang concludes cautiously, "It may be prejudice, but I rather prefer the Enfield evidence in some ways, as did Mr. Paget. In others, the Dorset evidence seems better" (24). Lang does not spell out the strengths of the Dorset evidence, but Kenny had:

> all the south-country witnesses identified each of the three gipsies; several of them had been in the same house with them for hours, or even days; and four of them fixed the date by reference to written entries. But of the Enfield witnesses, none could satisfactorily identity either the son or the daughter; none of them had had more than a brief conversation with even the old woman herself; half of them, indeed, had had no conversation but had simply seen her pass by; no two had been together when they saw her. (374)

If the Dorset evidence had these characteristics, however, as it certainly did, they were not necessarily in Lang's analysis strengths at all: "We must remember that the Dorset evidence had been organized by a solicitor, that the route was one which the Squires party habitually used; that by the confession of Mr. Davy, the prosecuting counsel, the Squires family 'stood in' with the smuggling interest, compact and unscrupulous. . . . Again, while George Squires had been taught his lesson like a parrot, the prosecution dared not call his sister, pretty Lucy, as a witness" (20–21).

The Dorset evidence, in short, is coherent in a way that the Enfield evidence, which might better be described as random, is not. Attempts to conclude that one body of evidence on the whereabouts of Mary Squires during December 1752 and January 1753 is superior to the other thus tend to turn not only on which side of the case one favors but on whether coherence or randomness is more in keeping with the writer's view of ordinary human behavior. Lang's conclusion thus places the blame for Canning's conviction on "the common sense of the eighteenth century," which could not accept "a very strange tale" and its breaches of coherence as true. Lang specified the prosecution counsel, Davy and Willes, and the Recorder, Moreton, as the legal embodiment of the worldview whose rationality Canning's story violated but aligned himself with Fielding, "who had some knowledge of human nature" (27), a phenomenon whose manifestations were presumably not fully explained by common sense. In doing so he tacitly aligned himself with the view that fiction, or the fiction-making imagination, might be a better key to the truth of Canning's story than the analytical powers of the law. It was a position that would be taken, even if not explicitly, by most twentieth-century writers on the case, though not necessarily to the advantage of Canning.

The Twentieth Century—I

The first writer to produce a full-length book on the Canning case was Arthur Machen (1864–1947), better known for fiction with a supernatural dimension and for the fictitious but widely believed story of the apparition of the angels of Mons. It was as a rationalist, however, that he approached Elizabeth Canning and as the producer of a convincing argument that he expected his readers to believe his solution of the questions raised by her story. Although it includes period illustrations (mostly the same as Childers's), *The Canning Wonder* (1925) is a popular rather than a scholarly work, citing no sources but drawing heavily if not exclusively on the trial record both for its representations of dialogue and its overall structure. It begins with a preface in which Machen initially describes the case as "beyond all certitude" but then proceeds to provide his own interpretation without qualification: "There is one palmary clue which we must seize firmly at the beginning, and never allow to escape us, and this clue is the sure and undoubted fact that Elizabeth Canning was an infernal liar" (v). This conclusion rests upon "two incidents": the mention in Alderman Chitty's minutes of a penthouse or shed of boards over which Canning made her escape and the fact that on 1 February Canning did not "identif[y] kitchen, stairs, loft at the moment of her entrance" into Wells's house (vi–vii).

Clearly, Machen places more reliance on Alderman Chitty's minutes than Lang or I do. There was indeed no shed of boards under the window through which Canning said she escaped from Wells's house. There was, however, as a contemporary view of the house shows, a cellar door flush with the house wall directly below the window—Canning would have jumped over this in her descent from the loft. No other version of her story includes any reference to this "penthouse," and my own view is that it appears in Alderman Chitty's recollected account as an interpretation made by him of some element in his original notes, which might well have been a reference to the cellar door. There is no evidence that Canning ever even knew what Chitty's minutes said prior to her own trial, fifteen months after her friends carried her before him to secure a warrant against Wells. It is also significant, I think, that they were, then and on the following day, literally carrying her, in a state that even a later hostile witness such as Gawen Nash (who also recollected no mention of a penthouse during Canning's appearance before Chitty) described as convincingly enfeebled. But Canning's physical condition was for Machen no excuse or explanation for her failure to identify Wells's kitchen, stairs, and loft at first sight.

In common with other anti-Canningite writers in what may be seen as a line of descent from John Hill, Machen, in fact, seems skeptical that there was anything much amiss with Canning's health. He hypothesizes

> that someone, perhaps known to her, perhaps a stranger, took possession of her as she was going home on the night of New Year's Day, 1753. I think this someone hustled her into a coach, and got in after her and proceeded to press his suit with a certain vigour and alacrity, whereupon Elizabeth squealed, but was not seriously annoyed. Somebody heard a woman shriek in a coach in Bishopsgate that night. And then, let us conjecture, the unknown took Elizabeth to a brothel and left her there the next morning, and that Elizabeth fell into the ways of the house. . . .
>
> But here arises a difficulty. Elizabeth Canning returned to her mother in a very sad state. There seems no doubt of it. The apothecary said she was very ill: starved, emaciated, in grave danger. How had this happened?
>
> Again, it is mere conjecture; but I surmise that she had fallen out with the Mrs. Harridan who kept the establishment to which she

had been taken; that Mrs. Harridan had endeavoured to starve her into submission, perhaps for four or five days or a week, that Mrs. Harridan had taken away her clothes, and that she had finally escaped at the cost of some slight violence; the famous wound in the ear having been inflicted by Mrs. Harridan's finger nails.

But if all this really happened so, it was not a story Elizabeth would like to tell. (ix–x)

The story which Machen tells begins with the trial of Squires and Wells and maintains for the most part a rather ferociously jocular tone throughout its course. Squires and Wells are "the bad old widows," and when the former is said to have slapped Canning's face and called her a bitch, Machen observes jauntily, "The vocabulary of villainy seems to have been strictly limited, then as now" (3). Probability (helped out by irony) is still the principal argument against believing Canning's own account of what had happened to her: "It is generally believed that a prisoner obtains an almost painfully minute knowledge of every niche of his dungeon, learns by heart every dent and dint and scar on the tragic walls and the unhappy floor and ceiling. It may be that Elizabeth, having had so frightful and prolonged an experience, was a little vague" (8). Machen attributes the verdict against Squires and Wells to the jury's being in no "condition to think at all" because of a mass delusion by which "in the very dead middle of the sober, skeptical eighteenth century we have our stolid, wigged Londoners foaming at the mouth as they contemplate the hideous vice of Mary Squires, the mirific and superhuman virtue of Elizabeth Canning. Common sense, common justice, fair dealing were abolished" (13).

Canning's claim to sexual purity, or at least integrity, though never explicitly made by her or particularly stressed by her friends except in response to Hill's and others' suggestions to the contrary, seems to have struck Machen as particularly provocative: "Elizabeth was a saint and a martyr" (18) whose "glorious chastity . . . raised the faithful imbeciles to a white-hot enthusiasm" (23), the effect of which was to turn at least those of them who ultimately testified on Canning's behalf—James Lord, Mary Myers, Mary Woodward, and Robert Scarrat all come in for this specific accusation, which is then extended more generally—into "deliberate—and infernal—liars" (161).

Machen's book is sloppily and probably hastily put together, a pastiche of the *State Trials* text punctuated with Machen's luridly stated judgments. It is not typical of his work nor prominent in critical studies on it, but it is nevertheless worth noting that its misogyny especially struck a responsive chord with the book's first reviewers. Thus Charles Biron in the London Mercury dismissed Canning herself as a "very ordinary impostor" who after disappearing for four weeks "return[ed], as is usual in such cases, with a cock-and-bull story of being kidnapped. . . . The real lesson remains: learn how dangerous it is to substitute sentiment for evidence, especially when a young woman is concerned" (105). R. Ellis Roberts in the Bookman responded to Machen's emphasis on mass delusion with a rather sinister analogy—"the violent defense of Elizabeth Canning by hundreds of people who knew nothing about the case is as odd a phenomenon as . . . the rage of the Jews shown in France at the time of the Dreyfus scandal"—and described Canning as "a hysterical liar, a neurasthenic, blood-poisoned girl . . ., one of those strange persons who lie from what we now call an 'inferiority complex'" (218–19).

Machen and his reviewers, in fact, are all writing in a world in which the popularization of Freudian psychological theory was in the process of giving a new dimension to an old distrust of female sexuality. Dr. John Hill had certainly expected to be agreed with when he asserted that "Eighteen . . . is a critical Age" (Story . . . Considered, 24), and the belief that Canning had been engaged in some sort of concealment of a sexual dilemma was widespread among both eighteenth-century anti-Canningites and their Victorian successors. It remained for twentieth-century writers to state or imply, however, that Canning's avowal that she had answered no to Mary Squires's invitation to "go their way," whether it had occurred in fact or in fantasy, was in itself a sign of pathology. Female sexual virtue for the eighteenth century was real enough, although its attribution to Canning might constitute a claim above her social station; in the post-Freudian world of Machen and his successors, Canning's self-reported refusal became evidence of her neurosis.

The first American to write on the case, Edmund Pearson (1880–1937), shared Machen's view that Canning was "a minx who had tried to cover up her scandalous escapade with lies" (187) and the perhaps even stranger view of Biron and Ellis that such episodes were a well-recognized part of everyday life:

> All of us have heard, and we still hear, of girls who unexpectedly vanish from home for a few days or a few weeks. The girl is usually seized by two men (sometimes they wear masks) and hustled into a

"big, gray motor-car." She is taken away and kept in a cellar or an attic, and is often abused or starved.

There is no talk of ransom in these yarns, and the cause for the abduction is very mysterious, although the girl often hints that these wicked men were trying—unsuccessfully, of course—to induce her to stray from the paths of virtue.

The truth of these tales, as we frequently conclude, is that the girl has been on a wild party, and that she did not have to be dragged into the car. Or, perhaps, there had been a wild party, some time before, and she has been absent to hide the embarrassing result. (188)

Bold assertions of sexual freedom, of course, would not have made Canning more acceptable—both Machen and Pearson are amused by Virtue Hall's "exquisitely inappropriate name" (Pearson, 197)—but the claim to chastity consistently evokes their irony: "not to hang the gypsy was an insult to the virtuous maid to whose cause [the Canningites] were subscribing money" (200). Pearson's essay on the case is in fact a shorter version of Machen's book, particularly in its proposed solution:

I think the most reasonable suggestion is that she was carried away by someone, perhaps by force. Perhaps no great amount of force was necessary. . . . Having been carried away, it would not be surprising if, for two or three weeks, she led a life which she did not care to tell about. At the end of this time she may have fallen out with the people with whom she was living, or have been deserted, robbed, and betrayed by them. It is unlikely that she was suffering and starving all the time for four weeks, although she did have a bad time for a few days. (202–3)

Both Machen and Pearson ignore the uncontradicted and well-corroborated medical evidence indicating that Canning had undergone considerably more than "a bad time for a few days." They also ignore Hill's brutally stated proposition that Canning was not sufficiently attractive to be sought out for prostitution: "The Cant of the Subscription was her Virtue, but there must have been a Face to stamp the Price on That: without it the Commodity's not marketable" (21–22). For Machen she was "a young girl of the rosy and chubby kind" (2), while Pearson called her "one of those pretty little liars, who are so often found among girls between the ages of twelve and twenty. Many a man has gone to prison, or even swung in a noose, because of the tales told by girls, like Elizabeth Canning" (204). In the presence of Pearson's blandly authoritative voice, it is almost possible to forget that only women went to prison in the Canning case.

Contemporary with Pearson (1936) but focusing more on Squires's alibi than on Canning's story is F. J. Harvey Darton's *Alibi Pilgrimage*, a work whose semi-Victorian flavor arises in part from the fact that its original research was performed before the war and in part from a pervasive nostalgia for a rural way of life that Darton presents as both unchanging and threatened. While he certainly shared the common assumptions that Canning was guilty, and that what she had done was in some sense a status offense—her case had "thrust a London servant girl into the *Dictionary of National Biography*" (11)—Darton's real interest was in the countryside allegedly traversed by the Squires family between 29 December 1752 and 17 January 1753, which he sees in a strongly literary framework—"the conduct of the case reminded me of the trial in *Pickwick*, while some of the scenes appeared to come straight out of *Tom Jones*."

Darton's retracing of the stages of the Squires family's alibi, which he proposes as "a journey to be done by healthy walkers" (12), is both digressive and allusive. There is much information on the regions through which it passes which is not even alleged to be pertinent to the alibi evidence—at Yeovil, walkers should note that "Real Cheddar, of the proper barrel size and shape, originated not far away, and can still be obtained by the judicious. It is also served at the two good inns" (29)—and a plethora of literary references—Crewkerne, for instance,

> some fifty years after our gipsies were in these parts, was known to people who are perhaps more real to us today than many genuine persons of the past. It was a place of call for the Elliots [sic] of Miss Austen's *Persuasion*. "Uppercross" cannot have been far away, for when Charles Musgrove went back thence to Lyme Regis with the old family nurse for the lifeless Louisa, "a chaise was sent for from Crewkerne"; through which, indeed, Mr. William Walter Elliott [sic] heir to Kellynch, had passed a day or two before, "on his way to Bath and London" in a curricle. (27)

It is not surprising that the *London Mercury*'s anonymous reviewer assessed *Alibi Pilgrimage* as "a pleasant book" for readers with "the time and disposition for leisurely perusal" (470), but in fact Austen, William Barnes, Thomas Hardy, and their literary authority do bear on Darton's argument. Ultimately, he believes the alibi witnesses because he accepts their literarily constructed authenticity. Again citing the trial in *Pickwick Papers* as a standard by which Canning's may be measured, he observes,

No man had a better eye than Dickens for the absurdities of truth. Those preposterous trimmings are just the points which make the evidence lifelike and convincing.

The Abbotsbury revellers, when they came into court on behalf of Mary Squires, nearly all provided exactly those extraneous natural touches which a great novelist might invent for purposes of fiction, but which a pack of suborned perjurors could hardly produce with such ease and certainty. . . . [T]he Dorset and Wiltshire witnesses are too spontaneous and also too varied in their evidence to be liars. . . . The talk simply bubbled out of them haphazard, as it does in any cheerful inn fellowship today. It is impossible not to believe it. (101–2)

It is a point Darton recurs to: the rural evidence "is too intimate, too natural in its humanity and its random unconscious humour, to be a concoction" (235). He even finds it appropriate to end his book by borrowing the conclusion of Thackeray's *Vanity Fair*: "Come, children, let us shut up the box and the puppets, for our play is played out" (243). The effect is to place the Squires family on a footing with fictional characters, a footing which paradoxically both enhances their reality by making their story credible and at the same time distances it: "'Into the night go one and all.' Like the sparrow in Bede's *History* they have passed in a flash across a bright room; even if it be only through the murk of eighteenth-century rushlights" (236).

Darton's contribution to the fund of argument directly relating to the Canning case is his relation of the Squires's alibi to their acknowledged connection with smuggling, to which he attributes both the major anomalies in George Squires's testimony, the mystery of how he could have received a letter from his sister Mary summoning the family back to London, and the whereabouts of the whole party between 14 and 17 January, between Coombe and Basingstoke. In both cases "the gipsies were concealing something, or were afraid of some hidden risk if they told the truth" (103), and while Darton in neither case attempts to specify exactly what was being concealed, he does make the argument that smuggling was rife in the area in the eighteenth century—"I would recall, in particular, for detail, the seizure at Crewkerne and the activities of Mr. Gulliver at Eggardon; and, for enormity, the Chater case" (241).

Isaac Gulliver was indeed a colossus among smugglers, but he was a child at the time of the Canning case, and the Crewkerne seizure cited by Darton took place in 1729, but more pertinent evidence is available. Roger Guttridge's analysis of Dorset prison registers from 1782 to 1852 supports the belief of the Canningites that "the smuggling trade was a well-organized network whose tentacles left few corners of the kingdom untouched. . . . [S]mugglers came from far and wide, by land and sea, to carry contraband into Dorset and out of it" (97). Furthermore, most smugglers, unlike Gulliver, were "labouring men, often with large families and modest incomes, which they sought to supplement by carrying or storing contraband for smuggling merchants" (Guttridge, 60), while the trade "almost always relied on middle-class acceptance if not active participation" (104). If the Canningites' suspicions were correct, it was far from impossible not only that the Squires family, the Abbotsbury artisans, and the innkeepers along the alibi route had a more than fortuitous connection but that such respectable figures as the Reverend Mr. Harris and under-sheriff Willis were in at least tacit support of their activities as well. The notorious raid on the Poole, Dorset, Custom House had taken place in September 1747, and the subsequent torture murders of the informers Daniel Chater, a shoemaker who unfortunately happened to know one of the raiders and was obliged to report his identity, and William Galley, a tidewaiter, took place the following February, evidence for all to see that interference with smugglers could be highly dangerous.

Smuggling was a widespread and profitable business, and little progress was made against it before the nineteenth century—Abbotsbury was the site of major incidents even late in its history, in 1818 and 1832, and coastguard cottages were built there in 1822 to facilitate surveillance (Guttridge, 90–96); even so, what was probably the "last run . . . of good French brandy into Dorset" was landed at Abbotsbury in 1882 (105). Seizures were throughout the eighteenth century an inestimable but certainly small proportion of overall goods traded. In 1753 the Custom House at Weymouth, the nearest such establishment to Abbotsbury, listed 63 seizures, which included 2,258 gallons of brandy, 1,808 gallons of rum, 5,809 pounds of tobacco and 1,939 pounds of tea (51), and these were certainly a small proportion of the actual goods run in the vicinity that year. If smuggling was a part of the explanation for the Squires family's activities, it is not surprising that Canning's defense alluded to it only with caution—smuggling was not only difficult to prove but bolder in its own defense than Canning's supporters ever were.

Darton does not seem to have considered the possibility that all of the Squires alibi was reported correctly except for the dates, but that would be one way of accounting for both its consistency and its particularity, the characteristics generally cited in favor of believing it.[2] Reverend Harris's parishioners for whom money was more than ordinary scarce might not, in spite of his assertions to the contrary, have made much of a scruple of misstating a few dates in order to protect their most reliable source of income and a vital link in the chain which supplied it, the itinerant activities of the Squires family.

The Twentieth Century—II

Both Barrett R. Wellington's *The Mystery of Elizabeth Canning* . . . (1940) and Lillian de la Torre's *'Elizabeth is Missing': Or, Truth Triumphant, An Eighteenth Century Mystery* (1947) are by American writers, and each is a substantial and detailed attempt to reconcile all the evidence in the Canning case into a coherent and plausible whole.

Wellington, born in 1885, was a member of the New York State bar who seems to have published nothing besides this book on the Canning case—seemingly a labor of love, including the writer's own very amateurish illustrations—and, much earlier, a legal manual. He does not provide either a bibliography or source notes, but his research seems to have been fairly thorough and his presentation of the evidence is careful, with an emphasis on the legal aspects of the case, particularly on the conduct of the trials. Once more Canning's original story is retold, primarily in chronological sequence but occasionally with the aid of footnotes, e.g., "Mention of the last two articles"—a saddle and a pewter basin—"was on the word of the one witness alone, Mary Myers, and may have been made by E. C. a day or two later as far as Mrs. Myers' evidence shows" (8), to explain the provenance of some details. The bulk of the text, however, over 120 of 209 pages, follows the text of the *State Trials*, for the most part quoting directly but occasionally commenting, as notably in Wellington's summary statement at the end of his presentation of the evidence: "The Crown's witnesses numbered in all seventy-four, the defendant's fifty-five, making together one hundred and twenty-nine. If we count in those testifying at the trial of Mary Squires, the grand total of all witnesses, exclusive of duplications, reaches the remarkable figure of one hundred and thirty-four. Playing on the dark mystery were no less than eleven dozen searchlights. And the truth was not found" (137–38).

Wellington's opinion of Canning's counsel could scarcely be

lower. When he reports Davy's dismissal of Lucy Squires as "rather more stupid than her brother," his comment is that this "put her rather on a par with the counsel [John Morton] who had cross-examined" George (63). He is appalled by Morton's failure to provide a closing statement for the defense, leaving Davy, with "much to magnify, twist, elaborate, glorify, evade, belittle, and gloss over" (139), and Recorder William Moreton, whom he assesses as "unable wholly to conceal his belief in the defendant's guilt and the small credit he thought due to her witnesses" (144), to complete the case before the jury.

Wellington's own reading of the case is sympathetic both to Canning and to her witnesses. Noting Davy's silence on the defense's evidence, he concludes that the testimony of Mrs. Canning, James Lord, Mary Myers, Mary Woodward, John Wintlebury, and Robert Scarrat is not only "just what we should expect to find," but also "radically different from what we should naturally look for" if it were the result of a conspiracy: "One heard one thing, and one another; some recollected her speaking of certain details, which others either did not hear or did not remember. . . . That she told the story which these people swore she did—leaving aside whether or not it was a true one—that her first account of her experiences was substantially as they related it, cannot be seriously questioned. It must be taken as established beyond a reasonable doubt" (149–51).

In response to Machen's conclusion that Canning's entire story was false, Wellington argues, as I have done, both that Alderman Chitty's minutes are a dubious source for Canning's actual narrative and that her "physical and psychical state, never credited in her favor by those arguing against her," sufficiently explains the apparent tardiness of her identification of Wells's kitchen, stairs, and loft (154). Going further than earlier writers, he proposes that "she experienced periods of stupor deeper and longer than she herself realized" and that Virtue Hall and Sarah Howit were indeed in the loft when they engaged in back-chat with the tree-lopping Edward Allen—on purpose, "lest the sight of a wierd human object within . . . should meet his startled gaze" (156). It seems likely that Wellington had not seen the *Refutation*, with its depositions avowing that the story was in fact a lie, but his estimate of Canning's physical state is not only sympathetic but reinforced by more recent scientific evidence than Dodd or Cox could muster, Francis Gano Benedict's 1915 *A Study of Prolonged Fasting*.

The great difficulty in the case, however, as Wellington analyzes it, is Squires's alibi, and he resolves it by positing the existence of, in effect, a second Mary Squires, a twin sister, a person whose chances of existing he estimates at one in 150 (176), high enough but "ten times smaller . . . than the likelihood of joint falsehood's and community befuddling's being the mainspring of all [the Enfield] testimony" (178). Wellington's analysis of the evidence for his supposition yields in summary two distinct personalities—from the alibi evidence he derives the picture of "an elderly woman who was quiet, clean, orderly, unobtrusive, inoffensive, good-hearted, non-china-mending, disinclined to tell fortunes, giving trouble to none" (180), while the Enfield witnesses' testimony reports "a dirty, slovenly, crouching, cringing, china-mending, fortune-telling, beggarly, importunate, spiteful, malicious and potentially stays-ripping old gipsy hag" (181). Wellington is clearly amusing himself by stating these alternatives as extremely as possible, but he provides the evidence for them with distinct lucidity, and they may be read less extremely as the natural product of evidence on the one hand consciously aimed at producing an alibi, on the other as the suspicious perceptions of a transient by a conservative rural neighborhood.

Wellington's emphasis on the "oriental subtlety which is the heritage of Romany minds" (183) as the source of the elaborate deception he posits colors his argument with what might be called romantic racism, but it is also in keeping with the perceptions of the Enfield witnesses of Mary Squires as a person of suspicious origin and questionable character. The confusion of names in Virtue Hall's information (which Wellington accepts as the truth insofar as Hall knew it) thus produces not merely two distinct gypsies but two whole families—Mary, George, and Lucy Squires who were really at Abbotsbury on 1 January 1753, and Sarah (perhaps—the name is a hypothesis of Davy's borrowed by Wellington) Squires and her children John, Katharine, and Mary, all lodging at Susannah Wells's house in Enfield on the same date (191).

On this theory, the alibi was arranged by John Squires, who summoned the other branch of the family, who were, "save possibly for a bit of smuggling, . . . comparatively respectable," from Dorset by "the call of 'the gypsy blood to the gypsy blood'" (195). He met them in Salisbury, in the unsubstantiated part of the alibi journey, and concerted the switch that would discredit Elizabeth Canning, should her story come to be told. George Squires's performance on the witness stand now becomes a cunning misleading of Morton away from the crucial gap in the evidence, and George himself, whom Machen had described as "pathetic," was "not one-thousandth part so pathetic as were the Honourable Sir Crisp Gascoyne, ex-Lord Mayor of London; the Right Honourable Thomas Rawlinson, Lord Mayor of London; the Justices of his Majesty's Court of Common Pleas; the Barons of his Majesty's Court of Exchequer; the twelve jurors, good men and true; the Mortons, the Nareses and the rest of them, all fuddled, deceived, gulled, hoodwinked and lamentably humbugged by a pack of clever gipsies" (202).

According to Wellington, "almost all" of his information on Canning's American life is drawn from Henry R. Stiles's 1904 *The History of Ancient Wethersfield, Connecticut*. From that source he draws the information that one Mrs. Cooke of Stoke Newington established a hundred pound trust fund for Canning, "to be administered by four trustees. The principal with accumulated interest was to be given the beneficiary after seven years if she behaved herself well and returned to England at the end of that time" (205). He hypothesizes that the 1761 *Annual Register* report that Canning had returned to England to claim a legacy was "an inexact reference" to Cooke's trust fund, although, as Lillian de la Torre, referring to the same source, points out, the *Annual Register* was unaware even of Canning's marriage, let alone of the fact that she had given birth to a daughter on 19 September 1761, an event that probably would not have been combined with a long and difficult journey.

What is more interesting than whether Canning collected an uncertain sum of money in person, however, is a letter both Wellington and Stiles give as having been written on 29 April 1755, less than a year after her transportation, by Elizabeth Canning to the same Mrs. Cooke:

> Hon. Madam—I am so unfit to write to such a lady as yourself as has made me offend in not writing so long, and now I do not know how to do it, but I hope you will excuse what is amiss. I am greatly thankful to you for all your abundant favors to me, and hope God will reward you tho' I can never do it, but I will pray for you and hope I shall never forget to do that, and I thank you for them from my heart. I thank God I have had good health ever since I came here, only once broke my leg which has been long well, only a little painful at times. I have lost my master the Colonel, who was a good friend indeed. My poor lady is greatly sorrowful: hope God will comfort her. She is very kind to me. I hope my friends will not have me from her as she is willing to keep me. I do not know where to find such another. I hope, Madam, I shall forever have cause to bless God I ever

came to this House, and for all affliction which was the cause of it, as I always have occasion to bless God for such friends as yourself. Pray, Madam, accept my humble Duty, who am your grateful servant.

ELIZ. CANNING (Wellington 205)

While the survival and publication of such a private letter are obviously unusual, I am nevertheless prepared to treat it as authentic. At the very least, it is a convincing representation of the young woman Canning's mother, employers, and friends all said that she was—modest, religious, and dutiful—and it suggests as well what all the voluminous case otherwise scarcely gives room to, that Canning herself, while far from possessing the literary skills of a Pamela, was not without preferences, at least, if not a decisive voice, in what happened to her. The verb which recurs throughout her letter is "hope," and among the writer's various hopes one at least is clearly personal: "I hope my friends will not have me from her. . . ." The *Refutation* had been published less than five months before, evidence that Canning's friends had not yet completely given up her vindication. Canning herself, however, had apparently had enough, and if the operations of Providence could be seen as having brought her finally from "affliction" to a kind home, she was ready to "bless God" and abandon the chimerical redress it is unclear she herself ever sought.

Elizabeth de la Torre does not give Canning's letter a place in her reconstruction of the case, but she does include another American text, "Extract of a Letter from a Merchant in Boston, to his Correspondent in London, dated Nov. 5, 1764." The Boston merchant claims to be reporting a dream vision experienced by Canning on 30 October in which Mother Shipton appeared to her and exhorted her "to imitate the Maid of Orleans. Canning replied, she knew not who the Maid of Orleans was: to whom the other answered, my pious dear Child, as your Situation has always been that of Servitude, which may have hindered your Study of history, I will in brief relate to you her story." Shipton accordingly informed Canning about the career of Joan of Arc and went on to advocate a similar role for her against the French in America. This is obviously a nonsensical story, the anonymous Boston merchant being probably as completely unknown to Canning as Joan of Arc and for that matter Mother Shipton almost certainly were, but de la Torre's tongue-in-cheek use of it—"Bet Canning never donned the Khevenhuller hat and the scarlet coat of her dream, perhaps because not long after she had

the misfortune to break her leg" (226)—suggests something of
her authorial stance in relation to her subject matter. Her examination of the documentation of the case is evidently far more
thorough than Darton's (who indeed had no such aspiration),
but her attitude to the personae of her narrative is similar—they
are puppets; she is the puppeteer.

This may seem a harsh judgment to pass on the writer whose
knowledge of the case is undoubtedly the most detailed on record, the compiler of the standard bibliography on it, even the
only writer on the subject to that point to oblige later readers
with an index (though not with footnotes), but it is, I think, not
difficult to support. In spite of her insistence that the story is "all
true" as it is told in the participants' own words ("Foreword"),
de la Torre maintains a constant thread of commentary from
beginning to end of her narrative, as in this passage from the
beginning of chapter 1:

> Elizabeth Canning was eighteen years old, and she had never had
> much fun. In the eighteenth century girls like Elizabeth had a pretty
> thin time.
>
> In the first place, half the population was constantly scheming to
> seduce them; and the other half (the female half) was just waiting
> finally to kick them into the gutter if they succumbed. To this obses-
> sion of both sexes everything they said and wrote bears witness.
> The most popular book of Elizabeth Canning's day was Richardson's
> *Pamela*. A best-seller received with moral ecstasies, it is no more
> than the monotonous record of the attempts of a man of fashion to
> seduce his fourteen-year-old servant-maid. . . . Nobody thought this
> behaviour at all odd of him. . . . What reduced the public to a pulp
> of sentimental admiration was the virtuous resistance of the serving-
> wench, and all rejoiced to see it suitably rewarded with the unsuc-
> cessful seducer's hand in marriage. (1–2)

De la Torre retells Canning's story for the most part in chronological order, with considerable space given, as is common, to
the trial, but she also includes two sorts of interpolated chapter.
The first, which she labels conversation pieces, present the observations of a fictional "old gentleman under the clock . . . in
Batson's coffee-house" (9) who functions as a sort of chorus,
presenting a community consciousness and community opinion
that are, of course, de la Torre's own creation, qualified by her
choice of background information and used primarily to frame
her presentation of the pamphlets which were a part of the case.
The old gentleman's view of the world is "exclusively moralistic.

He laid it all to the Devil. In his view there were good people and bad people. The good people worked hard and told the truth. The bad people stole from the good people and then lied about it. The bad people, in his opinion, ought to be hanged. And hanged they were" (11). There are three of these passages in de la Torre's narrative. There are also two specimens of straightforward twentieth-century analysis, an "Interlude" and a "Conclusion" both labeled "for Connoisseurs in Mystery," persons for whom presumably a tale which might be perceived as fraught with suffering and injustice is primarily of interest for the intellectual challenge involved in sorting out a satisfactory explanation of how these phenomena had come about and who had the best claim to the status of victim.

In the "Interlude" de la Torre sets up three possible positions—that Canning told the whole truth, that Canning's entire story was a lie, and—the position that she herself favors—that Canning's story was a mixture of lies and truth. In the "Interlude" she offers three possible formulas by which the third position might be realized: that Canning was really robbed and abducted but mistook the place and had to stick to her story; that she was actually at Wells's house but "engaged in dalliance"; and that she had been "stripped, starved, and abused by the midwife she chose" for an illicit childbirth. After reviewing these alternatives, de la Torre at last proposes a final "theory of X" that she announces as having a "curious history. On first acquaintance with the mystery of Elizabeth, I invented it out of thin air as a surprise ending for a frankly fictitious adaptation of the case. That piece of fiction never got written; for the more I investigated the girl from Aldermanbury, the more I came to see that it was not fiction, but sober fact" (160).

The full elaboration of this "theory of X" is withheld until the "Conclusion." De la Torre expresses disbelief of Wellington's two-gypsy solution, primarily on the grounds that "[n]o gypsy would willingly put herself in the hands of the law" (233), and finds the west country evidence "rich in truth" (234). She believes that the Squires family

were only ostensibly dealers in smuggled goods, [while] under [that] guise they were in reality government spies, under-cover agents on no payroll but under backstairs protection. . . . The master mind was the old woman. . . .

Therefore when she got into trouble, her under-cover employer gave her his protection. He paid George's journey-money, and found the fees for one of the best-known trial lawyers in London. When even that did not avail, he sent a message to the court that tried her, through its head, the Lord Mayor of London: the gypsy must be saved.

Since she was innocent, a pardon was easy enough. The malice of the gypsies might or might not have been enough to cause the implacable pursuit of the girl who harmed them; but her friends crossed the ambition of Sir Crisp, and the girl had to suffer. (237–39)

If this seems farfetched, it is on the other hand not really vital to de la Torre's final reconciliation of the mysteries of the Canning case—"The gypsies were never an integral part of it anyhow" (239). De la Torre acknowledges that the witnesses to what Elizabeth Canning said on the night of 29 January must be for the most part telling the truth, although with regard to the later depositions of Wintlebury and Scarrat, she offers convincing grounds for the suspicion that "their wishes are getting mixed up with their memories." She also notes the weaknesses in Alderman Chitty's minutes as a source of evidence on the story Canning actually told. "Nevertheless," she concludes,

> sift as you will to be sure to play fair with the girl, you cannot maintain she never lied. The Lord Mayor could not get over the alibi of the gypsy [or, if you accept de la Torre's own argument, here passed over by its creator, could not get over explicit orders from some shadowy higher-up], the jury could not get over Elizabeth's contradictions as to when she drank her water [although this contradiction only exists if Alderman Chitty's minutes are accepted as authoritative, as de la Torre has just declined to accept them]; and neither can I. (242)

As my interruptions of de la Torre's sentence suggest, I find her reasons for disbelieving in Canning's truthfulness specious— not only on my own account but in the context created by her own previous argument. They do, however, provide her with as much basis as she needs for the launching of her own theory, the one initially devised for an account "frankly fictitious."

De la Torre's ultimate explanation of the anomalies of the Canning case is that Canning "was trying to tell the truth" (243) but was unable to do so because she was subject to hysterical amnesia, "one . . . of many neurotic manifestations" (248). The basis for Canning's neurosis was, of course, sexual: "Hysteria in adolescent girls is often connected with sexual frigidity and anxiety. Think of the 'good character' Elizabeth bore for 'modesty.' . . . The threat of sexual assault was enough to throw the girl 'first into a fainting fit, then into a fever.' The actuality, at Mother Wells's bawdy-house brought on hysterical fasting, and covered itself with the hysterical blocking of memory called amnesia" (249–50). Not that Canning's account of what happened to her in Wells's kitchen was accurate: "'Will you go our way?' . . . is the wishy-washy invention of a green girl who has no idea in the world of the language or behaviour of bawdry," while "twenty-eight days on bread and water . . . is a child's notion of the severest kind of punishment" (244). De la Torre's theory, finally revealed, is that John Wintlebury, Canning's former employer, had had her kidnapped and taken to Wells's house where he quickly, however, became disenchanted by her moping and abandoned her to the "tender mercies" of Wells, who put her, along with "the ninepenny lodgers," in the attic, from which she soon wandered off. When Wells's house was named by Scarrat, Wintlebury paid off the residents to keep his secret, while hysterical amnesia conveniently kept Canning herself from revealing it (256–58). Her story was thus a piecing together of what she half-recollected seeing during her real month in Enfield but an invention nonetheless.

There is, of course, no evidence for any part of this hypothesis. Wintlebury "knew the Hertford road" and "had a horse of his own" (256), but he also had a public house that kept him busy and a host of neighbors all demonstrably very well aware of each other's business. The real basis for de la Torre's hypothesis, in fact, in spite of her thorough knowledge of the documents in the case, is in the twentieth-century perspective provided by Freudian psychology. De la Torre quotes Freud himself to the effect that "hysteric subjects . . . 'unconsciously conceive horrible or fantastic images, which they construct from the most harmless and commonplace things they have experienced'" and refers to her own consultation of four practicing psychiatrists as well as of ten works on abnormal psychology by Freud and others (250–51). Retrospectively, this perspective colors de la Torre's whole retelling of Canning's story, with its constant assumption that the narrator understands the actors better than they can understand themselves. A final allusion to the dream reported by the Boston merchant—"Even in the matter of seeing visions . . ., Elizabeth, what with Mother Shipton . . ., ran true to the hysterical type" (249)—suggests the quality of evidence de la Torre found sufficient for her diagnosis of hysteria, but if the story of Canning's assault can be read as a "self-glorifying fantasy" (257), then so, obviously, can a call to take on the mantle of Joan of Arc, even if Canning had never, outside of a dream imputed to her anonymously, heard of her before. There is no room here for the worn but cautiously optimistic young woman who seems to have written the letter quoted by Wellington, and de la Torre, who certainly knew Stiles's work and even drew her reference to Canning's broken leg from it, does not mention it.

Despite their widely discrepant interpretations of the evidence, however, both Wellington's and de la Torre's books were well received by reviewers. The *New York Times's* reviewer called Wellington's solution "ingenious and logical" while de la Torre was credited by the *Springfield Republican* with the analysis of the case "probably the closest to the truth" and by M. L. Becker in the *Weekly Book Review* with "reach[ing] the heart of the mystery." Several factors seem to be at play here—one is obviously the common preference for solutions over irresolvable conundrums, another the conventional reviewer's value for what can be labeled "good reading" (*The New Yorker* 21:84) or "a delightful detective story" (North), "colorfully presented" (*Springfield Republican*). There is also implicit a testimonial to the effectiveness of the authors' rhetorical stances—the reviewers take them at their own valuations. Wellington's version of the Canning case is thus a "sympathetic retelling" which the story "may well bear" (*New York Times*) while de la Torre's far from sympathetic account is described as having "a gusty 18th century wit" (North). It is left to rival writers to produce more skeptical readings so that John Treherne, the most recent author of a book on the case, the 1989 *The Canning Enigma*, finds "insuperable difficulties" (140) in de la Torre's theory and labels Wellington's simply "daft" (141).

Treherne, until his death in 1989, was the president of Downing College, Cambridge, where he had been a fellow since 1966 and university reader in invertebrate physiology since 1971. Well-known as an entomologist, he began to publish in other fields in 1983, at first historical studies of odd crimes (*The Galopagos Affair; The Strange History of Bonnie and Clyde*) and then, in 1985, novels as well (*The Trap; Mangrove Chronicle*). *The Canning Enigma* is thus the work of a professional scholar if not of a professional historian. It opens with an "Author's Note" somewhat reminiscent of de la Torre's "Foreword": "This account is based on a wealth of contemporary writings: documents, letters, pamphlets, broadsheets, cartoons, books and court proceedings. The characters are authentic, their names are real. There are about one hundred fifty of them and—irresistibly—they speak with their own words, which I have not altered."

Treherne also resembles de la Torre, however, in his appropriation and deployment of these words. Since neither uses notes, any given utterance may come from any ungiven source; the reader must trust the narrator both for its accuracy and, often, for the manner of its delivery—e.g., "'Child, you must not take it away with you,' Sir Crisp warned her [Canning, about the bed-gown] in a kindly way" (44). He or she must also trust Treherne for states of feeling—"The allusion to Henry Fielding [by Virtue Hall] was music to John Hill's ears" (44) and interpretive pictures of demeanor—"Elizabeth Canning stood, demure and passive, at the centre of the packed courtroom" (86)—neither of which are in his sources. The reader, however, although Treherne does provide a bibliography and index, has no way short of replicating all of Treherne's own reading of determining exactly what parts of his text are from eighteenth-century documents (much less which ones, or what biases or purposes they were originally meant to serve) and which are the result of the play of his own consciousness over his materials.

Not surprisingly, Treherne's reviewers too seem to have taken his version of the story as unmediated event. Both Peter Lewis (31: 75–76) and Roy Porter (1408) refer to Canning as a "scullery maid," a term Treherne uses repeatedly to identify her, but one for which there is not only no documentary evidence but even some presumption *against* its accuracy. A scullery maid occupied the lowest rung on the hierarchical ladder of female service in large households—"[she] kept the kitchen, pantry, and wash-house clean, polished the pots and other cooking utensils, washed and put away the dishes" (Hecht, 68), and it is unlikely that either the Wintlebury or the Lyon household was so large or affluent that it could afford such a proliferation of servants with distinct tasks. The only functions specifically referred to at the time as having been performed by Canning as a servant are laundry and carrying parcels, which suggests that her role was more that of a maid of all work—still inglorious but responsible as well, and the testimony is unanimous, and acknowledged by all later writers, that Canning was a responsible servant.

Treherne gives his version of Canning's story in the familiar chronological form, but he also provides some response to earlier versions as a part of his framing of his own opinion. Thus, "Henry Fielding's immediate and uncritical acceptance of the scullery-maid's rigmarole is one of the most astonishing aspects of the Canning affair." Although "Fielding's basic premise—that Elizabeth Canning was an innocent victim of kidnap—has survived, in one theory or another, well into the present century," this is "surprising, because her testimony was flawed from the outset, in particular by the wildly inaccurate description of the place in which she was imprisoned" (136). Like all writers in the case who make much of anomalies in "the" description of the room, Treherne is relying here at least as uncritically on Alderman Chitty (helped out by Gawen Nash, a distinction clear in the trial record but not noted by Treherne) as Fielding can have been on Canning herself. Treherne, howeover, is inclined to share de la Torre's diagnosis of hysteria—"the hysterical personality tends to be adolescent and female; shy, emotional and incapable of pity. Hysteria can occasionally be accompanied by fits and other disturbances in physical functions, including constipation and cessation of menstruation: all characteristics exhibited by Elizabeth Canning" (139)—but not her assignment of the role of seducer to "poor Mr. Wintlebury" (140).

Treherne's candidate for chief villain instead of Wintlebury is Robert Scarrat, who he hypothesizes had impregnated Canning, arranged for an abortion somewhere in the neighborhood of Wells's house, and named Wells as "a useful decoy" when Canning returned to her mother (145–47). The "crux of the matter" then becomes whether Canning told her lies knowingly or hysterically, but on this point Treherne is silent, though his earlier recapitulation of de la Torre's theory suggests that he leans toward the latter possibility. If Canning did "knowingly threaten the life of an old woman . . . then her subsequent performance was remarkable, not only in calmly standing up to the Lord Mayor of London and convincing most of the skeptics who streamed up to gawp at her in Newgate Gaol, but in persuading one of the greatest writers of the time of her innocence and maintaining it until her dying day" (147–48).

But the whole tenor of Treherne's version of Canning's story has been that "the scullery maid" was not remarkable: "a nonentity—without rank or status and devoid of talent—inflated by chance circumstances, the power of the printed word and the violence of the mob. A figure to test values or release fantasies. . . . A fraud, a virgin, a slut, or the English Maid of Orleans? And to be all of these things the Aldermanbury scullery-maid had to be what she was—an enigma" (159). For Treherne's purposes, a hysteric is a better subject than a young woman so "remarkable" as to know what she was doing, as it seems to him to be inherently self-contradictory that a normally conscious person should be the focus of the sort of attention Canning received. The variety of characters assigned to her is accepted as negating any actual personality of her own, leading to Treherne's constant descriptions of Canning as "unblinking" (122), "calm . . . and resigned" (130), and, repeatedly, "passive" (86, and passim). Rather less mystically, Treherne's view can be read as a psychologized late twentieth-century equivalent of the class outrage felt by such contemporaries as Ramsay and Hill at a servant maid's apparent presumption of entitlement to the compassion of her betters. Treherne reduces Wellington's analysis of the case to its most questionable part, the two gipsy hypothesis, on the grounds that Wellington was "besotted" with Canning (140), but he himself seems actively to dislike her.

The Franchise Affair

The idea of an Elizabeth Canning cold-blooded and deliberate—"the sinister twist that it might be Red Riding Hood who was evil, and her awful captor who was good" (156)—Treherne found best exemplified in Josephine Tey's fictional recasting of the case in a twentieth-century context, The Franchise Affair, published in 1948. Sandra Roy, in her book on Tey, hypothesizes that the source for the background of the novel was either Machen's book or de la Torre's (121). Since the presentation of the novel's version of Canning—Betty Kane—is compatible with Machen's condemnation of her as an "infernal liar," however, while the British edition of 'Elizabeth is Missing,' with its proposed solution by means of hysterical amnesia, did not appear until 1947, the former source seems considerably more likely on grounds of timing as well as of tone. The Franchise Affair makes immense changes in the Canning story, and whatever other judgments may ultimately be made of it, it shows none of the marks of hasty hack-work.

The Franchise Affair is told throughout from the point of view of Robert Blair, a country solicitor at the head of a highly respectable and established family firm in the fictional but archetypically English country town of Milford, where he lives at Number 10, the High Street, usually referred to simply as Number 10 in what seems to be an additional and obvious association of Robert's character with traditional, and genuinely trustworthy, authority. The underlying tension of the novel springs from Robert's faint suspicion that the orderliness of his life, and by extension of the social order in which it occupies an important niche, is sterile—"At 3.50 exactly on every working day Miss Tuff bore into his office a lacquer tray covered with a fair white cloth and bearing a cup of tea in blue-patterned China, and, on a plate to match, two biscuits; petit-beurre Mondays, Wednesdays and Fridays, digestives Tuesdays, Thursdays and Saturdays' (1). Robert is over forty, unmarried, and lives with a devoted aunt. He has a younger cousin, Nevil Bennet, a junior member of the firm who is at the moment playing the role of the arty young man, but who, in the course of the novel, will be converted by means of his innate English sense of justice to sound principles and dark suits.

If all is not entirely well in this rural paradise, it is not too difficult to see from what direction the problems come. A major road links Milford to Larborough, which is "bicycles, small-arms, tin-tacks, Cowan's Cranberry Sauce, and a million human souls living cheek by jowl in dirty red brick" (11). Beside the Milford to Larborough road, in liminal countryside, stands the Franchise, an isolated and ugly Regency house. With a name that might be glossed as "Liberty Hall," the Franchise is ambiguous, capable of bearing both positive and negative meanings not only in relation to the vulgar masses of Larborough and the genteel and upright citizens of Milford but also for all of the central characters of the novel. For Marion Sharpe and her mother, who live there, it is at first, through a family legacy, the means of escape from a London boarding house, then, increasingly, a burdensome white elephant, and finally, after they are accused of kidnapping Betty Kane, a prison assaulted by—literally—howling mobs. For Robert Blair it is first an ugly house with no proper connection to Milford, then a surprisingly vital and attractive home for two women he comes to love. For Betty Kane, who glimpses it from the top of a double-decker bus, it becomes at first the locus for the story she tells to excuse a mysterious month's absence from home and then—because her story is, of course, false—an instrument of her public discrediting. Having served all of these purposes, the house is burnt by vandals on the night before the trial which completely vindicates the Sharpes, and a freedom no longer exemplified by a survival from the past ensues for all of the characters except Betty Kane, who is last seen sitting in court, all of her lies exposed.

Marion Sharpe is a "tall, lean, dark woman of forty or so; much given to bright silk kerchiefs which accentuated her gipsy swarthiness" while her mother, an "uncomfortable old person" who rudely but stylishly says what she thinks on all occasions is "upright and delicate and incongruous" (6). Only the initials and the "gipsy" appearance survive to suggest a resemblance between the Sharpes and Mary Squires—they are "self-sufficient" (12) and know their wines, and Robert is only the first of the novel's characters to recognize at once and instinctively that they cannot, in spite of all appearances, have committed a crime.

According to Betty Kane's story, however, these admirable women have abducted her and confined her to an attic room, beaten her, and made her sew in exchange for bowls of stew—the purpose of the original abduction having been to enlist a domestic servant. Betty Kane's story, in short, is thus considerably stranger than that originally told by Elizabeth Canning, but this is in fact advantageous to Tey since it accords with the plot she has chosen, one in which the false story is completely and satisfactorily exploded by the production of the true story, not one that ends in an irreconcilable conflict of evidence. It is also necessarily adapted to twentieth-century Britain—Betty Kane is a schoolgirl, not a servant, and her disappearance is from a several weeks' holiday with an aunt and uncle in Larborough—but the dénouement is the same: "'She walked into her home near Aylesbury late one night wearing only a dress and shoes, and in a state of complete exhaustion.'" Unlike Canning, Kane does not tell her story at once: "'She said she had been "kidnapped" in a car, but that was all the information anyone got from her for two days. She lapsed into a semi-conscious condition'" (16). Kane is a war-orphan, adopted by the family to whom she had been evacuated earlier, and Robert Blair soon discovers some very pertinent facts about her: her mother, killed in the blitz, was "a bad mother and a bad wife" (82). Kane herself has a "photographic memory," is "greedy" and "bored with school," and has recently been unsettled by the engagement of her adoptive brother, all facts her pleasant foster mother Mrs. Wynn reveals to him without realizing they may qualify Betty's story, as she also reveals the unaccountable presence of a new lipstick in the pocket of Betty's dress.

There is no suspense throughout the novel over whether Betty Kane's story is true—it is certainly not, and all right-thinking persons know that at once. What matters to the plot is whether, or perhaps only how, the innocent Sharpes will be exonerated, and who along the way will reveal him or herself as right-thinking or the reverse. Marion Sharpe establishes her own credentials by diagnosing Betty Kane at their first meeting as "over-sexed," a trait she associates with dark blue eyes—Robert first attributes this judgment to "feminine intuition" but a quick mental review of his acquaintance corroborates it (35)—while Stanley, the garage keeper whose help Robert enlists, has only to look at Betty's photograph in the newspaper to be reminded of "a bint I had in Egypt" and thus to conclude that during her disappearance Betty Kane was "definitely—oh, but definitely—on the tiles" (58–59). More gullible, though not necessarily more wicked, persons, like the proprietors of Milford's Tudor tearoom, are, however, taken in, and the case takes a marked turn for the worse when a scurrilous newspaper, the *Ack-Emma*, constitutes itself the protector of Betty Kane's innocence and gives the story national publicity.

The role of the *Ack-Emma* and, later, a loony lefty art-and-politics journal to which Nevil has contributed unintelligible modern poems, the *Watchman*, clearly parallels the pamphleteering that was such a prominent feature of the Canning case, but while in 1753–54 both sides resorted to the press with perhaps more items published against Canning than for her, here the press is not only entirely pro-Kane (and therefore wrong) but in fact completely indifferent to her or anyone else's well-being, much less that of the body politic. The *Ack-Emma* is a relatively new and wildly successful paper, "run on the principle that two thousand pounds for damages is a cheap price to pay for sales worth half a million," and something of a postwar portent: "The press had always been its own censor, deciding what was and what was not permissible by the principles of its own good sense and good taste. If a 'rogue' publication decided not to conform to those principles then there was no power that could make it conform" (56). In alliance with the highbrow *Watchman*—with a "total circulation of . . . about twenty thousand" (150)—the *Ack-Emma* "had used the Franchise affair as a stunt. Something to be used for its momentary worth and dropped tomorrow" (208) with no concern for the damage done.

Tey frames a general indictment of the British press by associating the two, linking the *Ack-Emma*'s emotional incitement of the masses with the *Watchman*'s fostering of muddled thinking among the intelligentsia—"the *Watchman* had a passion for euphemism: unrest, under-privileged, backward, unfortunate; when the rest of the world talked about violence, the poor, mentally deficient, and prostitutes" (160). Together they constitute what Robert calls with bitter irony "a fine free press" (60)— "catering exclusively for the human failings" (83) and seldom "'carry[ing] a subject longer than three issues'" (151). Not surprisingly, this irresponsible journalism also provokes mob activities—once the *Ack-Emma* breaks the story, first sightseers, then hooligans, assault the Franchise. "FASCISTS!" is painted on the wall of the house. "'They might have written something worse,'" opines a policeman, to which Robert responds, "'They wrote the worst insult they knew'" (123). A few hours later, worse is forthcoming. Rocks are thrown through the windows with notes attached to them: "'Get out!' 'Get out or we'll make you!' 'Foreign bitches!' and 'This is only a sample'" (132). Again, Robert interprets: "'Foreign bitches!' smells of the conservative country, just as 'Fascists!' smells of the progressive town" (136).

Enlightenment, presumably, lies somewhere in between, but it derives more from a mix of tradition and intuition than from the putative virtues of the press, information and argument. Nor, in spite of Marion Sharpe's "gipsy" appearance and the undoubted Englishness of the mobs who attack the Franchise, is "foreignness," or even cosmopolitanism, a positive alternative. Robert Blair is lovingly teased by both Marion and Tey herself for his Englishness, but it is ultimately the repository of the most necessary virtues. Kevin Macdermott, the colorful and successful Irish barrister who defends the Sharpes in court, is brilliant and charming, and, in practical terms, a vital part of the winning of the case, but when Robert says "gloomily" to Marion, "'It's the Irish. . . . [Charm] comes as natural to them as breathing. Us poor Saxons plod along our brutish way and wonder how they do it,'" she responds passionately: "'The Saxons have the two qualities that I value most in the world. Two qualities that explain why they have inherited the earth. Kindness and dependability—or tolerance and responsibility, if you prefer the terms. Two qualities the Celt never had; which is why the Irish have inherited nothing but squabbles'" (190–91).

Nor are the Irish the only people who, despite their other good qualities, fall short because they are not innately English. Ben Carley, a Milford criminal lawyer initially rejected by Marion as "[t]hat awful little man with the striped suits" and not "my own sort" as Robert obviously is (8), is a member of "a race long used to lying low and letting the storm blow past"—a Jew, although Tey does not use the word—and although Carley speaks admiringly of the Sharpes and gives Robert valuable collegial support, he remains an outsider, with a "brash personality" (9) and "too-lively black eyes" (150). Goodness inheres in Englishness, even though Englishness is often encumbered by the defects of its qualities: Robert at one point envies Ben Carley, who "would be in his element; his mind delighting in the problem and in the hope of outwitting established authority. Robert was dimly aware that his own deep-seated respect for established authority was a handicap to him rather than an asset; he needed some of Ben's native belief that authority is there to be circumvented" (168).

In a properly harnessed Ben Carley, this antiestablishment instinct can be a useful corrective when the establishment momentarily errs, as it does when the Sharpes are indicted for abducting Betty Kane. In a Betty Kane, however, it is maniacally out of control and must be not only identified and thwarted but crushed. Betty is at first glance far from threatening: "not very tall, and certainly not pretty. But she had—what was the word?—appeal. Her eyes, a darkish blue, were set wide apart in a face of the type popularly referred to as heart-shaped. Her hair was mouse-coloured, but grew off her forehead in a good line. Below each cheek-bone a slight hollow, a miracle of delicate modelling, gave the face charm and pathos. Her lower lip was full, but the mouth was too small. So were her ears. Too small and too close to her head" (26). Off-guard, however, this bland face can register a revealing "flash of triumph" that is "savage . . ., primitive and cruel" (31).

Behind a surface of ordinariness, in fact, Betty Kane is a monster, but not a unique one—instead, she is associated throughout the novel with a commonly acknowledged tendency for apparently artless young girls to conceal while simultaneously acting upon a strong instinct for depravity. Stanley's "bint in Egypt," Betty Kane's natural mother, the original Elizabeth Canning, invoked by Kevin Macdermott as a girl whose "heart-rending story" led everyone who heard it at first "very thoroughly . . . up the garden . . . [in] Seventeen-something" (88–89), and, most luridly, a "girl who went round shooting taxi-drivers in cold blood for a profit of about seven-and-eleven a time," about whom the bleeding-heart Bishop of Larborough had "sobbed himself practically into a coma" in the Watchman (140), all exemplify the pattern. Robert's ambition to "undress [Kane] in public" (176) is suitable to such a creature, a cuckoo in the nest of the respectable Wynns. It is given to the outsider Carley to note, "[S]he was adopted, wasn't she? An Awful Warning. . . . There was a woman over at Ham Green had a daughter walked out in a pet one day and didn't come back and frantic mother goes hunting to the police and police discover that the girl who had apparently never been away from mother for a night is a married woman with a child and has merely collected child and gone to live with husband" (198–99). The anecdote loses sight of the adoption theme but recurs to the more important one of the untrustworthiness of young women, even—or perhaps especially—by their mothers. Two more of the same general class as Kane, though lacking her demonic power, testify against the Sharpes in court: one motivated by blackmail, the other simply by malice.

According to Sandra Roy, this remarkable onslaught on the credibility of young girls—whose normal behavior, Roy suggests, might be expected to be confined to "sobs, or sulks, or being difficult, or deciding that she was going to renounce the world and go into a convent" (236)—is a reversal of a pattern established by Tey's earlier fiction, in which "clever teen-age girls . . . are witty and, to the author, always right in their character judgments. The ingenues of *A Shilling for Candles, Brat Farrar,* and *Miss Pym Disposes* are some of her most memorable and likable characters" (Roy 17). After *The Franchise Affair,* Tey represented no more female adolescent characters, although Roy sees Marion Sharpe as "the clever ingenue . . . at last grown up," certainly "a type of character not seen at length in Tey's previous books—a bright, outspoken, intuitive woman who, against all odds, is at peace with herself" (114).

Roy also notes that Tey considerably simplified the Canning case, eliminating, most obviously, the conflicting evidence given by the alibi and the Enfield witnesses, but although the truth is revealed only "through a series of 'accidents' . . . [p]erhaps this is more in tune with a modern world of corrupt officials and lying civil servants where the truth can only be guessed at or accidentally revealed" (123). I find this a strange reading of the novel. The press is certainly represented as corrupt, but "officials," most notably the police, are dubious about Kane's story from the start and act on it reluctantly, while Robert's active sleuthing, aided not so much by luck as by his devout aunt's prayers, produces the hard evidence that utterly disproves it. Kane's trial ends not with the herding of the jury into the verdict desired by the court that actually occurred in the Canning case, but with an assertion by the jury that no further evidence is necessary and the judge's agreement, a courtroom scene probably unprecedented in practice but certainly satisfying to readers caught up in Tey's story:

> Kevin moved to call his next witness. But the foreman of the jury was before him.

The jury, the foreman said, would like his lordship to know that they had all the evidence they required.

"What was this witness that you were about to call, Mr. Macdermott?" the judge asked.

"He is the owner of the hotel in Copenhagen, my lord. To speak to their having stayed there over the relevant period."

The judge turned inquiringly to the foreman.

The foreman consulted the jury.

"No, my lord; we don't think it is necessary, subject to your lordship's correction, to hear the witness."

"If you are satisfied that you have heard enough to arrive at a true verdict—and I cannot myself see that any further evidence would greatly clarify the subject—then so be it. Would you like to hear counsel for the defence?"

"No, my lord, thank you. We have reached our verdict already."

"In that case, any summing up by me would be markedly redundant. Do you want to retire?"

"No, my lord. We are unanimous." (264)

Roy notes the "tremendous animosity . . . toward Kane" and the depiction of the "violence, hatred, and destruction" of the mob as unusual in Tey's typically unsensational fiction and relates them to her equally new insistence on the culpability of naive liberals like the Bishop of Larborough who are regularly taken in by "criminals who should be punished since they are morally irreclaimable," unlike the accidental or even well-meaning villains of Tey's earlier novels. She speculates, "It is as if something in her personal life persuaded her to react strongly and emotionally to the facts [sic] of Canning's story" (125–26), but since she also acknowledges that Tey, despite her "reiterative, compulsive, and disturbing major themes of deception, mistaken identity, and isolation" (14) kept her private affairs very much to herself—born Elizabeth Mackintosh in 1897, she published historical dramas and fiction under the pseudonym of Gordon Daviot and the detective stories for which she is better known as Josephine Tey, dying relatively young in 1952—these speculations do not take her far.

I see no reason, however, to confine this analysis to Tey's personal life. The contrast of the whole Milford ambiance—where there seems, for instance, to be no rationing—with the actual postwar condition of Britain (Kane's parents were killed in London by a bomb, and her social displacement is symptomatic, not unique) suggests that a political reading may be at least as appropriate as—and certainly more accessible than—a personal one. In the conclusion of *The Franchise Affair*, Tey thus refrains from providing a complete resolution to the tensions she has depicted, and this is true even after Betty Kane has been completely discredited. Robert proposes to Marion, but she turns him down, partly because Robert's aunt and her own mother constitute real—and for the most part welcome—obligations for both of them and partly because she is too independent a woman to marry. She and her mother are therefore going to Canada to keep house for a cousin who is a professor at McGill. Robert almost settles back into his routine, but at the last moment he too catches the plane to Montreal—he has a sister in Saskatchewan, he tells the astonished Marion, who is "a much better pretext than a cousin at MacGill [sic]" (272). Like much of the dialogue between Marion and Robert, this has neatness and charm, but in fact a resolution is being side-stepped. Is either Marion or Robert really committed to emigration? Will they marry and settle in Canada, leaving Nevil to carry on Englishness in Milford, or will Robert test his love, enjoy it, and then recognize Marion's wisdom about his taste for "good pastry in an uncritical atmosphere" (268) and go home, where he will certainly be welcome and useful? Tey displaces the uncertainties of the Canning case onto the social world in which she relocates it. The dependable untrustworthiness of young girls becomes paradoxically a fixed point in a world of lawless journalists, gullible bishops, and clever Jews and Irishmen who seem to be on the right side but yet not the right sort, and they, in turn, as they circle about Betty Kane, pose new dilemmas of trust and responsibility.

Trends and Themes in Accounts of the Canning Case

A review of the books and articles focusing on the Canning case is more demonstrative of changes of style and of emphasis than of intellectual progress. Certainly the tendency to take a side in the case, beginning in 1753 with Hill and Fielding, has never ceased. Caulfield is perhaps neutral—although his essay might more accurately be labeled merely inconsequential—and while Paget and Darton express themselves with some diffidence, the former is cautiously Canningite while the latter is rather casually Egyptian. Of all the other later writers on the case, Kenny, Dobson, Childers, Machen, de la Torre, Treherne, and Tey all certainly believe that Canning's story was false, although their explanations of its falsity differ, while only Lang and Wellington believe that she told the truth.

According to James Dodd in April 1753, Canning had "more female than male Opponets [sic]. I know not whether the Appellation of Virtue, joined to the Name of a poor Girl, an obscure Servant, is not hateful in the Ears of many, who, perhaps, from the Examination of their own Hearts, think it hath no Existence any where, and that it is a Word alone, and no Reality" (9). If women really did distrust Canning more than men did, Dodd's questioning of their motives was hardly likely to win them over, but I am not sure that they did. Certainly Canning's mistresses, Mrs. Wintlebury and Mrs. Lyon, supported her, as did the female neighbors who had known her from childhood, notably Mary Myers, Mary Lyon, and Mary Woodward. The public management of her case, however, was necessarily left to men, and if this created an impression of a young girl engrossing a suspiciously large share of male attention, it may well have aroused something like jealousy in some female on-lookers. However, no women commented in print on the case before the twentieth century, and the two who did write on it in the 1940s, de la Torre and Tey, separated themselves from its central figure as emphatically as possible.

Roy Porter, although he seems to derive all of his information about the case from the book he is reviewing, John Treherne's *The Canning Enigma*, nevertheless sees Treherne's analysis as one that

> could be pushed further, in feminist directions. For the crucial point is that, whatever the truth of the matter (was Bet Canning a Pamela or a Shamela?) the *affaire* turned into a public trial of women in general, their virtue and veracity. First Squires and Wells, and then Canning, suffered conviction: the thugs who (Canning claimed) abducted her got off scot-free. Moreover, the "victim" was herself victimized, and her character systematically blackened. . . .
>
> The depressing fate of today's sex crime victim is all too familiar, forced, in her search for justice, to submit to media rape, and even then exposed to public disbelief. . . . In the same way, Bet Canning found herself sacrificed to public gossip-mongering and finally criminalized.
>
> In her *Women's Silence, Men's Violence: Sexual Assault in England, 1770–1844* (1987) Anna Clark justly argued that law and opinion served to articulate a patriarchalist ideology, in which female sexuality could never keep above suspicion, and men called all the

shots, enforcing a "justice" whereby certain women had always to be vilified, so that others could be vindicated. (1408)

One of the persistent ironies of discussion of the Canning case, however, is that it is not a case of sexual assault at all. What Canning told her mother and the Aldermanbury neighbors on 29 January, what she reportedly told Alderman Chitty on the 31st, and what she told Fielding on 7 February all agree that Mary Squires's proposition that she should "go their way" was not pursued and that the fear of having her throat cut after being repeatedly struck and robbed was Canning's primary, perhaps her only, sensation on being shoved into Wells's loft. Nevertheless, the public notice inserted in the *Daily Advertiser* on 31 January referred climactically to the "several unhappy young women in the house, whose misfortune [Canning had] providentially escaped" (rpt. in Ramsay, 28), and from that early point female sexuality was treated as a central issue in the case on all sides, even though no sexual crime against Canning was ever alleged or charged against anyone involved.

Overtly, the issue in 1753 and 1754 was whether or not Canning was chaste; covertly, it was whether a plain-faced servant-girl's chastity had any right to be an issue at all—an "issue" being defined as something any substantial segment of the public ought properly to concern itself about. As the writer of the *Genuine and Impartial Memoirs* put it, Canning was "a *Wench* who, to say the best of her, was never in the whole Course of her Life till now, distinguished for any Thing remarkably *good* or *ill*" (285), and so she ought to have remained. If by the twentieth century a more egalitarian spirit has to some extent justified the paying of attention to a person of Canning's low social status—a doubtful proposition in itself, given de la Torre's patronizing tone and Treherne's reiterated "the scullery-maid"—it is more than made up for by the added complication of a widely accepted psychological theory which makes any claim to chastity unwitting evidence of neurosis.

Twentieth-century feminists have indeed been slow to reinvestigate the Canning case, and the reasons for that failure probably include the complex role of female sexuality in feminist thinking. Women may be admired for throwing off sexual constraints and prescribed roles but chastity is generally not held to be a feminist virtue unless it is conceptualized as a form of independence, which was certainly not the case with Canning. The virtues for which her friends praised her—dutifulness, responsibility, and religious devotion—may now be read as the indices of a mystified consciousness, while even her status as a victim may create problems when for many feminists the victim's role or label is to be eschewed in favor of the term "survivor"—though this too might be applied to Canning. Canning can only be taken as a feminist heroine by feminists whose conception of the Other incorporates a historical as well as a gender dimension—Elizabeth Canning is nothing so familiar as a sister.

I believe Canning's servitude, however, rather than her sexuality, is what most sets her apart from everyone who has ever written about her, rendering her a member of an omnipresent but by no means trusted underclass in the eighteenth and nineteenth centuries and increasingly in the twentieth a figure almost exotic. It was, to begin with, not a class that wrote. Canning's bare literacy was for Sir Crisp Gascoyne in itself a suggestion of villainy, although the two specimens we have of her signature suggest that it was marginal. She signed her information before Fielding not with her name but with her initials, perhaps because of weakness but perhaps simply because she was told, on the assumption that she could not write, to "make her mark." Thus Canning's story is always told for her, and the version of it most heavily used to discredit her is the one she herself never signed, the one composed by Alderman Chitty, a member of the class to whom literacy properly appertained.

Bruce Robbins has analyzed the ways in which servants in British fiction are treated both in the narratives in which they appear and by later critics, noting in particular the frequency with which suspicion of their characters follows any prominent role in the narration. He cites readings of *Wuthering Heights* and *The Turn of the Screw* in which Nelly Dean, Mrs. Grose, and the unnamed governess become the principal villains of the texts in which they appear and comments:

> The point to insist on in these readings is that, unconvincing as they may be, they respond to real textual impulses that are part of the way we read the words of servants. Fielding's hostile interpretation of *Pamela* . . . clearly detects a real current of the novel: Pamela's use of the narrative privilege, among other weapons, to hold her own in an unequal class and sexual struggle. It is in large part her letters— which "outshine her virtue," as Ellen Moers comments, and are equally indispensable—that win her master's heart. Her power is in her pen. (99)

There is thus considerable symmetry, to say no more, in Fielding's espousal of the cause of Elizabeth Canning, a "poor little Girl" (6) who possessed no such power when she appeared before him, although she vicariously and paradoxically acquired some of this by the fact of his writing of her story. The title of Dr. John Hill's response to Fielding immures Canning herself within narrative presentation by others, his own as well as Fielding's—*The Story of Elizabeth Canning Considered by Dr. Hill, with Remarks on what has been called, A Clear State of the Case, by Mr. Fielding; and Answers to the several Arguments and Suppositions of that Writer*—and I think it is no exaggeration to say that from *this* prison she has never since escaped.

There is no writer on the case for whom Canning's status as a servant is a matter of indifference, although it is noteworthy that no one makes less of it than the sympathetic (or, as Treherne has it, "besotted") Wellington. In most it is a factor in their arrival at a usually harsh verdict not only on Canning's story but on her character. As Robbins says with reference to fictional characters, drawing upon the practice of providing actual servants with testimonials which might help them to find future employment or prevent them from doing so: "If the awarding of certificates of character to servants is a measure of social control, then the critical gesture of discovering the hidden villainy of a servant narrator is an extreme and paradigmatic example. . . . To opt for 'good' character is to exaggerate it to the point where it can be condemned or dismissed" (102–3).

All of the writers on the Canning case belong to the class that "gives" a character to a servant—probably most of them at least prior to the 1930s had even had occasion to do so in everyday life—and most of them dismiss Canning without one. They find their peers in the case naturally enough in the character-giving classes, wondering at Fielding's naivete without (at least after Hill) condemning him for it but reserving their praise for Sir Crisp Gascoyne, whose own praise of his peers—Reverend Harris, under-sheriff Willis, Alderman Chitty, the three goldsmiths, the liverymen—is notably lavish, the balancing opposite of his determined hostility to Canning herself. Gascoyne, as the text of the *Address* stresses, is not only a proper narrator but a necessary one—he owes his story to the liverymen as employers of servants owed it to each other to report the "characters" of their former employees, and most of his successors take the same stance of warning in their retellings of Canning's story.

Even twentieth-century writers who dislike Canning, however, finding her, as de la Torre and Treherne do, repellently passive and probably disturbed, express some degree of compassion for her, and it is here that they differ perhaps most from their eighteenth-century predecessors. Certainly Davy, Willes, and Recorder William Moreton denounced Canning at her trial as an instance of incredible depravity, regretting aloud and often that prejury was not a capital offense, but their attitude was more widespread than might be explained by the rather calculatedly heated atmosphere of a jury trial. According to Sir Crisp Gascoyne, the whole case had improperly arisen because "credulous . . . men had . . . pitied" (3) the perpetrator of "a contrivance, a most wretched and cruel falsity" (18). One reason initially alleged by Hill against Canning's credibility was that her story was "A Relation . . . that would have taken no hold on any, but as it pleaded to their Compassion" (*Story*, 17), and the writer of *Genuine and Impartial Memoirs*, when he tells his concluding cautionary tale of the child who pretended to have been abused but who had really thrown her own clothing into a pond, claims with horror that the only apparent motive for such an action was "to excite Compassion" (292), a self-evidently dangerous end.

Clearly, compassion here is not the admirable trait we may take it to be today but a human weakness, one likely to have dangerous consequences for the stability of the social order as it may, as William Davy put it in his final statement for the prosecution, "silence the calls of reason and justice [and] prostitute the brightest ornament of human nature; . . . the most deserving object of our tenderest concern is the commonwealth; . . . whenever we extend compassion to anyone, at the expense of the public, we are guilty of the highest injustice and answerable for it to society" (*State Trials*, 19: 607). Compassion to an undeserving and socially inferior object is equivalent to providing an unsatisfactory servant with a written character concealing his or her defects—it defrauds one's fellow employers of servants and, as an intraclass deception, frays the social fabric.

Thus the only twentieth-century writer to attack Canning with the ferocity of Hill or Davy or to share their distrust of compassion is Josephine Tey, the writer whose text most extensively places Canning's (updated) story in the context of a society damaged and perhaps fatally destabilized not only by the mindless mobs of Larborough, from whom probably not much in the way of reason and justice could ever be expected, but also by its self-deluded Bishop, who ought both to know better because of his class and education and also to act better in order to fulfill the responsibilities of his position. Tey represents the witty and sophisticated Marion as saying, "'I could kill that girl; I could kill her. My God, I could torture her twice a day for a year and then begin again on New Year's Day" (174) without any suggestion that this might be excessive, while Robert reminds her of the Bishop's perverse defense of "'Mahoney . . . the Irish "patriot" who put a bomb in a woman's bicycle basket in a busy English street and blew four people to pieces, including the woman, who was later identified by her wedding ring. The Bishop held that Mahoney was merely misguided, not a murderer; that he was fighting on behalf of a repressed minority—the Irish, believe it or not—and that we should not make him into a martyr'" (162–63).

Right-thinking people, "our sort," the character-giving sort, know where to give compassion—to the insulted body politic and the murdered dead—and where to withhold it—from political partisans and girls like Canning/Kane with a "story" that disrupts order, whether actually or potentially. Like the Irish who have, according to Robert Blair, no credible grievances, Betty Kane, by claiming to have been captured for domestic service while in fact indulging her sexual appetites, only reveals a true nature that stirs her to illegitimate rebellion against her proper place in life. The volatile Irish—inheritors of "squabbles" as Marion described them—and the "greedy" Kane reject a subordination essential to the survival of the larger society, including, of course, their rightful masters, whose dangerous compassion for them is thus ultimately suicidal, to be averted by hard-nosed realists from Hill and Davy to Josephine Tey and her hero, Robert Blair. Anyone who has read the various—or not so various— versions of the story of Elizabeth Canning may well be moved to echo Roy Porter who, on the basis of having read apparently only Treherne's, asked rhetorically but pertinently, "From Bet Canning to Patti Hearst, has anything changed?" (1408).

5

Telling the Truth and Telling a Story: The Canning Case and Eighteenth-Century Narrative in Context

What has changed since the time of the Canning case is perhaps not so much the social dynamics by which a manifestly abused young woman, however she came by her injuries, could come to be seen exclusively as the focal point of a conspiracy against not only her alleged attackers but by implication the entire social order as well, but the way in which texts describing sequences of events by at least partially fictional means have come to be distinguished and compartmentalized as nonfiction, presumed to be outside of the proper purview of literary/textual study. Although Josephine Tey was the first writer to use the Canning case as a source for a work labeled a novel, *The Franchise Affair*, after all, was far from the first novelistic treatment of it. The *Monthly Review*'s contemporary comment on *Genuine and Impartial Memoirs* reveals the readerly expectation that a text might satisfy simultaneously demands that are now more commonly assigned separately either to history or fiction:

> This is the long-expected history, for which the public were so often desired to wait, by advertisements in the news-papers. It is compiled with seeming accuracy and candour, and delivered in the form of letters to a friend. The air of moderation which the writer assumes, and the agreeable and familiar manner in which he has thrown together the particulars of a worn-out story, render his history, upon the whole, a more entertaining performance than we might have expected, after having been so often disappointed by the catch-penny things that appeared before it. (237)

A "history" of "particulars" "complied with seeming accuracy and candour" sounds unequivocally factual, at least if "seeming" is given the positive sense of "evident," but the effect wavers for modern readers when we are told that "the writer *assumes* [an] air of moderation," delivers his material "in the *form* of letters to a friend," and achieves thereby an "entertaining *performance*." All of these italicized terms now seem more appropriate to fiction than to "history," but for this reviewer the objectives of information and entertainment are less linked than indistinguishable, with his final assessment, if one can be distinguished, resting on the aesthetic value of the work. The story, after all, is "worn-out," and it is the *Memoirs's* "agreeable and familiar manner" that makes its account more satisfactory than earlier ones. The *Memoirs'* version of the Canning case is not assessed for its truth-value, but it is certainly not disqualified from possessing it by its use of fictional techniques of presentation.

It is a commonplace of literary history that the novel is a form which, at least in the incarnations most familiar to western readers, can be called "essentially an eighteenth-century product" ("Novel"). The fifth edition of C. Hugh Holman's and William Harmon's *A Handbook to Literature* (also labeled the fiftieth anniversary edition and a standard reference in literary studies) goes on to elaborate a complex narrative background for the form but then homes on the familiar statement that Richardson's *Pamela*, published in 1740, is "the first English book that practically all critics and historians are willing to call a fully realized novel." The defining trait of the novel seems finally to be not so much the narrative presentation of character shaped by some overall principle of "plot, theme, or idea" with which the *Handbook's* discussion of the term begins than the later agreement of critics and historians to confer it upon certain works. Fictionality, although it might seem to be the ultimate differentia between, say, *Pamela; or, Virtue Rewarded, in a Series of Letters from a Beautiful Young Damsel to Her Parents: And Afterwards in Her Exalted Condition, between Her, and Persons of Figure and Quality, upon the Most Important and Entertaining Subjects, in Genteel Life* and *Genuine and Impartial Memoirs of Elizabeth Canning, containing a Complete History of that Unfortunate Girl, from Her Birth to the Present Time; also Free and Candid Remarks on Sir Crisp Gascoyne's Address,* is incorporated into the *Handbook's* discussion only in its second paragraph, and then in language which is the opposite of exclusive: "All novels are representations in fictional narrative of life or experience, but the form is as protean as life and experience themselves."

The narrator of *Genuine and Impartial Memoirs,* however, is, as we have seen, a fictional character, assumed to be such without concern by the *Monthly Review's* anonymous critic, and it is at least arguable that his "Elizabeth Canning" is as akin to the fictitious Pamela, whose story Richardson claimed to have based on a real model and to have edited for its instructive value (Richardson, 31), as to the flesh-and-blood figure whose birth was recorded in 1734 in the parish of St. Andrew's by the Wardrobe and her death in 1773 in Wethersfield, Connecticut. The apparently universal agreement that *Pamela* is a novel while *Genuine and Impartial Memoirs* is not forms an artificial gulf between two works which are in fact remarkably similar, a fact that the writer of the *Memoirs* not only knew but made use of in his choice of an epistolary structure for his book and his deliberate allusion to Richardson's work in his statement of the question his letters would—as much narratively as discursively—explore: whether Elizabeth Canning could rightly be judged a "realized Pamela" (5).

Nevertheless, a twentieth-century reader entering a library or bookstore is obliged to make a distinct physical choice between fiction and nonfiction. As members of presumably mutually exclusive categories, these texts are routinely separated, often in ways that ensure that a reader who initially opts for one will experience not even any incidental exposure to the other, and the limitation is reinforced by literary historical studies which picture the novel as "rising" from a mingled fictional/factual matrix that its triumph is to leave behind. This "rise" of the novel, as the common phrase fixed in critical consciousness by Ian Watt's 1967 study, *The Rise of the Novel: Studies in Defoe, Richardson, and Fielding*, has it, is always assigned to the mid-eighteenth century, but the concern of later literary historians has been less the recovery of the literary world of that time than an explanation, by one means or another, of how the "distinctive literary qualities" (Watt, 7) of that now valued form, the novel, freed themselves from it. Thus Watt's classic study concentrates on the canonical figures of Defoe, Richardson, and Fielding and so equally do such varied revisionist views of the field as Lennard Davis's *Factual Fictions: The Origins of the English Novel*, Michael McKeon's 1987 *The Origins of the English Novel, 1600–1740*, and John Bender's *Imagining the Penitentiary: Fiction and the Architecture of Mind in Eighteenth-Century England*. J. Paul Hunter's *Before Novels: The Cultural Contexts of Eighteenth-Century English Fiction* indeed focuses on non-novelistic texts but stresses those aspects of them which he believes must make them unappealing to contemporary readers whose expectations have been shaped by novels. I have learned much from all of these studies and have no intention of denigrating them, but it is also true that I have learned nothing from them that tells me how to read *Genuine and Impartial Memoirs of Elizabeth Canning*. If anything, their tacit advice in most cases is to ignore such works, confine myself to the fiction shelves, and reread *Pamela*.

In spite of the connections demonstrated at length by Davis and McKeon between historical and fictional writing in the Renaissance and seventeenth century and also by William Ray between novel and history at a philosophical level, all of their studies are informed ultimately by the later critical predominance of the novel. Ray notes that his study began with the "observation that the relationship between personal story and public account, between the social act of relating one's perceptions or events to some listener and the collective narrative or history that framed such acts, seemed to form an essential component of the thematic structures and even plots of several novels of the period" (vi), but instead of looking both at personal stories and public accounts as they occurred outside of the novel as well as within it, Ray proceeds to read again the familiar canonical fictional texts, in this case French as well as English, in roughly chronological order from *La Princesse de Cleves* through *Liaisons Dangereuses*. Even in his most general presentation of his chosen subject matter, Ray privileges the novel against its allegedly fettered twin:

> Freed from the limitations of factual fidelity, assured of representing the biases of the culture, the novel can formulate, analyse, and illustrate general paradigms of social interaction explicitly through its plot structure, at the same time that it exemplifies in its gesture of narration the conventions of communication and representation underlying such interactions. In other words, the eighteenth-century novel instantiates or stands for the culture it depicts; in this sense the novel can claim to "be" history: it represents the system it represents. (5)

Given the free hand such writers as Hill allow themselves in their discussion of the Canning case, however (and for that matter the earnest claim to factuality made by the erstwhile fiction writer, Fielding), it is difficult to see how this statement has more application to *Pamela* than to *Genuine and Impartial Memoirs*. Nor is the case improved by Ray's very fair assessment of the reciprocal concerns of what he labels "history" and "fable":

History is a story *produced by* reality, fable a story *productive of* reality, and both are presumed to stand *outside of* reality. Such pure forms are of course reciprocal delusions, limiting cases of theoretical value which, if implemented, would lead to self-cancelling excesses. The historicist delusion is that there can be an account *of* human reality that is not mediated by an act situated in human reality and vitiated by the biases of the situation—that there can be a narrative produced directly by reality that is immune to the processes of change it chronicles. The converse delusion is that there could be a narrative having no origins in reality, but capable of modifying—or, as is generally the charge, corrupting—reality. . . . One of the implicit theses of this book is that the thematic evolution of the eighteenth-century French and English novel can be understood as a gradual coming to terms with the complexities of a genuine historical consciousness, one which conceives of the identities of individuals and societies, and the orders of authority that modulate their behavior, in terms of a continual process of recounting and rearticulation that is regulated by, and derives its authority from, the accumulating context of its own past narratives. Within such a model, (reconfiguring) narration and (grounding) narrative, story and history, are but different faces/phases of the same equation, as are, from the perspective of the social economy underwritten by that equation, individual behavior and collective norm. To that extent, the gradual emergence of historical consciousness entails a concomitant reassessment of personal freedom and collective authority. (8–9; emphasis in original)

This presentation of the mutual imbrication of history and fable seems to me clear and persuasive—but a strange preliminary for an analysis focusing exclusively on fables. Merely to sketch the points at which Ray's language here suggests both the events and the documents of the Canning case—its preoccupations with both social and personal identity, with the repetition and variation of narrative accounts of events, and with the assertion and conflict of individual behavior and collective norms—is to suggest that the exclusion of nonfictional texts from consideration is to conduct one's literary studies at least on the brink of just that delusion Ray proposes which conceives of fiction as free of its origins in reality.

Certainly changes in the ecology of literary forms were occurring in England in the middle of the eighteenth century, even if our later conceptualization of them as progressive oversimplifies the phenomena as they were understood by contemporaries. Samuel Johnson, for one, notoriously expressed considerable misgiving over those "works of fiction . . . which exhibit life in its true state, diversified only by accidents that daily happen in the world, and influenced by passions and qualities which are really to be found in conversing with mankind" (*Rambler* 4, 19). After sympathizing momentarily with any author so liable to correction "from every common reader," however, Johnson turned to the "most important concern that an author of this sort ought to have before him," the fact that his largely young, ignorant, and idle readers would take his writings "as lectures of conduct, and introductions into life" (20–21). Life itself, as Johnson observes, is "often discoloured by passion, or deformed by wickedness," and although the imitation of nature is properly considered "the greatest excellency of art," the selection of what aspects of life to imitate is by implication appropriately guided by moral considerations in order to achieve its artistic ends: "If the world be promiscuously described, I cannot see of what use it can be to read the account, or why it may not be as safe to turn the eye immediately upon mankind, as upon a mirror which shows all that presents itself without discrimination" (22). Although Johnson confines his argument to "narratives, in which historical veracity has no place" (24), implying that historical writings are obliged—or permitted—to represent potentially corrupting examples, he calls for fiction to "inculcate . . . that virtue is the highest proof of understanding, and the only solid basis of greatness; and that vice is the natural consequence of narrow thoughts, that it begins in mistake, and ends in ignominy" (25).

This characteristically resonant call for a morally exemplary literature is now normally taken as a rather prudish and backward-looking reaction to Fielding's *Tom Jones*, published just the year before. Certainly Johnson would not have endorsed Clive Probyn's recent assessment that the eighteenth-century novel brought about a "significant literary revolution [by] . . . the questions it raises about the validity and significance of the individual's experience in oppositional relationships with society" (23). That revolution and opposition should be offered as fictional phenomena at all would seem to him an unwarranted encroachment on the province of history, but that they should be taken as the signs of its value for readers runs counter not simply to his traditional moralism but to his fundamental assumptions about fiction's audience. Like the depiction of "men . . . splendidly wicked, whose endowments [throw] a brightness on their crimes, and whom scarce any villainy [makes] perfectly detestable" (23), these are the subjects of serious historical writing, of truthful narratives, addressed to educated and thoughtful readers. What seems to have taken place in the conceptualization and writing of literary criticism over the past two and a half centuries is, accompanying a certain aggrandizement of the fictional audience, a leaching of perceived significance from historical/ nonfictional/factual writing to fiction, so that we tend now to use the umbrella term literature only to cover the latter category, and to look for our subjects only within its shelter.

This was not the literary world as Johnson knew it, nor is it easy to believe that Fielding himself would have been entirely pleased to find himself—side by side with Defoe, Richardson, and Sterne—seated in the pantheon, "distinguishe[d]," as Probyn puts it, "from their less able contemporaries [by] their imaginative domination" (23) rather than their moral force. Since the less able contemporaries are, for Probyn, the "minor novelist[s]," while nonfictional works and their authors are not even entered for the competition, Fielding and his peers would also find themselves, in their new eminence, divested of much of their own writing—most voluminously in the case of Defoe but perhaps most significantly in that of Fielding. Students of the eighteenth-century novel are of course aware that Fielding wrote a good deal besides his novels. Fielding's journalism, however, tends to be studied in rather archival terms as written for money and hence without aesthetic seriousness, while his late pamphlets, *A Clear State of the Case of Elizabeth Canning* among them, are categorized as off-shoots of his work as a magistrate—paid employment again, which is often represented as something of a blight on Fielding's creative potential.

It is a well-known element of Fielding's biography, however, that the writer took his duties as a magistrate with great seriousness, and neither Martin Battestin, his latest and fullest biographer, nor Malvin R. Zirker, the editor of his social pamphlets for the Wesleyan edition of his works, understates their importance to their author, although Zirker, at least, was not entirely comfortable with what he found:

> A reader unfamiliar with the writings in this volume may well share the shock I experienced when I first read *An Enquiry into the Causes of the Late Increase of Robbers*, and may wish, as I did, to uncover an underlying irony which would harmonize its statement with the apparently more generous values of *Tom Jones*. But no such irony exists.
>
> We must accept, if regretfully, Fielding's failure to escape the assumptions and attitudes of his time and class. The intention of my commentary has been to illuminate the historical context which ren-

ders his views comprehensible and even predictable. Fielding was
. . ., at least as a justice of the peace, . . . very much a man of his age.
(in Fielding, *Enquiry*, ix–x)

I am not persuaded that this is matter for shock, and I suspect
that the cause of Zirker's dismay is not a discrepancy in Fielding's character but in our own conventions of reading. Fielding
seems to have seen himself consistently as a morally instructive
writer, engaged in improving (or attempting to improve) the
world as he also attempted to earn his living, although it is also
true that his ideas both of what instruction the world wanted
and of the best means of offering it altered over time with his
own circumstances and increasingly varied experience. Somewhat inappropriately for later critics, however, his most highly
valued works seem to come almost accidentally in the middle
of his career, as if he himself were unaware of *Tom Jones*'s status
as a consummate artistic achievement. Without even pausing in
his work, Fielding went on to write not only further journalism
but also what even Martin Battestin, who admires the book and
produced the Wesleyan edition of the text, calls in his introduction the "problematic" *Amelia* (xv).

If Fielding could now be seen as attempting to recreate the
success of *Tom Jones* and failing to do so, his failure could be
treated as normal, even tragic, but the differences between *Amelia* and its predecessors are more complex than that. The novel
was, as Fielding himself said, his "favourite child" (quoted by
Battestin, xvi). It was written, however, during the period of his
magistracy and reflects the world that presented itself to him as
a magistrate—a world not merely criminal but both systemically
unjust and alarmingly random. These perceptions did not lend
themselves either to the "festive comed[y]" (xv) of *Joseph An-
drews* and *Tom Jones* or to the moral certainties called for by
Johnson, and it is arguable—though perhaps more often assumed—that *Amelia* suffers from the strain of incorporating the
mixed modes of romance and history within a single narrative.
Roger Sell has characterized *Amelia* as a work of "reluctant naturalism"—"the involuntary naturalism of Fielding's gut reaction
to life, and equally to the dismayed defensiveness of some of his
conscious responses to this" (12). Sell's further analysis shows
a later phase in this reactive process as in turn reached by Fielding's critics (both F. R. Leavis and Frank Kermode figure prominently in the argument), who demonstrate "a preference for a
type of novel more Puritan in seriousness, and perhaps also more

tragic; a novel which confronts its characters with moral choices more momentous, regards sexual relations as more profoundly significant, and advertizes more openly its own penetration into character, the novel, in short, as written by Richardson or Lawrence" (16–17). This argument visibly places the aesthetic demands of modern critics in a line of descent from the moral demands of Johnson, a heritage not often avowed but also evident in Battestin's frustration over the failure of *Amelia*'s irony to "excite . . . our laughter" and to present "scenes and characters . . . which carry us through and beyond the historical moment to the timeless situations and universal truths of the human comedy itself" (xvi), and Zirker's "regretful" acknowledgment that Fielding "fail[s] to escape the assumptions and attitudes of his time and class" (ix).

Fielding, however, stood by *Amelia*, even revising the text at a time when his own death was a nearer and more certain prospect than a second edition, but he did not write another novel. Instead, the last years of his life were devoted to his magistracy and to such literary outgrowths from it as *A Clear State of the Case of Elizabeth Canning* and its immediate predecessor, *Examples of the Interposition of Providence in the Detection and Punishment of Murder*. The latter work is even more free of irony than *An Enquiry into the Causes of the Late Increase of Robbers*. Consisting of thirty-three numbered exemplary tales ranging over time from classical antiquity to such recent causes célèbres as Mary Blandy's 1752 trial and execution for the murder of her father, the pamphlet was aimed at a popular audience and sold at bulk rates—"Ten Shillings a Dozen to those who give them away" (lxxxix)—in order to encourage its dissemination. "Example XVIII" is fairly typical:

> A man was taken up on suspicion of Murder, but when brought to the bar, the evidence appeared not strong enough to convict him. He behaved with great apparent boldness, for he knew there were no witnesses to the fact; and he had also taken all necessary caution to prevent a discovery. But the judge observed in the man's countenance, a terror and confusion, which his pretended boldness could not hide, and therefore kept his eye steadily fixt on him the whole time. As soon as the last witness was dismissed, the man asked, if they had any more evidence against him; when the judge looking sternly at him, asked him if he did not himself know of one more that could appear against him, whose presence would put the matter out of doubt. On which the man started and cried out, "My lord, he is not a legal witness, no man can speak in his own cause, nor was

the wound I gave him half so large, as what he shews against me."
The judge presently perceived by the man's staring, and the wildness
and terror of his look, that he either saw the ghost of the murdered
man, or that his imagination had from his guilty conscience formed
such an appearance; and therefore making the proper answers from
such a supposition, he soon brought the murderer to confess the fact,
for which he was condemned, and hanged in chains, at the place
where he declared the murder was committed. At his death he
averred, that the ghost of the murdered person had appeared before
his eyes at his trial. (203)

With few exceptions, all of Fielding's cautionary tales are as
unlocalized as this one. When the characters are named at all,
they are usually given only one name—such as Laurietta, Po-
ligny, and Belvile in "Example XVII"—and placed without dates
at a remote location, in this same instance at Avignon. Accidental
witnesses and discoveries, disloyal hireling killers, ghosts, even
a faithful dog become the engines of the various murderers' un-
doing, and in most cases their action triggers less a discovery by
others than the murderers' own self-revelation, the workings of
guilty consciences which then lead to community awareness and
punishment.

Such stories are far indeed from *Tom Jones*. Zirker places the
Examples in both a literary and a hortatory tradition whose earlier works Fielding himself quarried for most of his tales but
finds it not so much impossible as irrelevant to place it in Fielding's literary oeuvre, although he ingeniously traces allusions
to "special"—as opposed to "general" or "common"—"providence" in both *Tom Jones* and *Amelia*. He refers to the compilation of *Examples of Providence* instead as a "desperate act,"
evoked by the miserable cases that came before Fielding as a
magistrate, detailing one that seems particularly pathetic and
commenting, "What could Fielding (or what can we) make of
such a story? Perhaps very little, but at least he didn't turn away
from it. . . . *Examples of Providence* seemed to Fielding a way of
doing good and perhaps should be called naive only by those
who could have done better" (lxxxviii–lxxxix). It is not clear to
whom this defensive reaction is addressed, and it is tempting to
read it as an externalization of Zirker's argument with himself
as a literary critic attempting to come to terms with the unironic
texts of a writer previously valorized as a great ironist.

There is no evidence, however, that Fielding himself experienced any such conflict, and in fact if *Tom Jones, Amelia, A
Clear State of the Case of Elizabeth Canning*, and *Examples of*

the Interposition of Providence in the Detection and Punishment of Murder are all treated as instances in the art of persuasion, a good deal of the conflict disappears. As a rhetorician, Fielding both identified and to some extent created various audiences; the sophisticated audience for Tom Jones was appropriately addressed with irony and allusion while the tone assumed in the Examples of Providence summons up an audience of humble if superstitious Christians. In a sense unintended by Battestin, they were also an audience deemed to be in need of "timeless situations and universal truths," while the audience for A Clear State of the Case of Elizabeth Canning was still differently constituted as a body of rightfully suspicious and judgmental citizens, demanding of documents, evidence, and rational argument. We have perhaps over time lost sight of some of Fielding's rhetorical flexibility, as we have certainly lost the ability to participate equally in his different audiences, but without some sense of their diversity we run the risk not only of losing the ability to read "history" but "fable" as well—the distinctions must be felt to be constitutive.

If this assessment is correct, then individual texts must also propose to their specifically constituted audiences both appropriately credible narrative voices and resolutions satisfying not only the expectations they themselves have created but also those that preexist in the culture of their audience. As my extended discussion of the documentary history of the Canning case has already shown, few writers took up the subject, at least above the level of the "catch-penny," without paying careful attention to the matter of narrative authority. Fielding used his public position as a well-known magistrate and writer on questions of social order to reinforce his evaluation of the truth of Canning's story, while Sir Crisp Gascoyne used the dignity of his position as lord mayor. Less obviously qualified writers such as the painter Allan Ramsay and the anonymous author of Genuine and Impartial Memoirs adopted more fully fictitious personae characterized by detachment, fairmindedness, and a concern for public order. Later writers, too, make a point of establishing rhetorical bona fides, evidently with considerable success, as in my survey of reviews of the books of Machen, Pearson, Darton, Wellington, de la Torre, Tey, and Treherne I did not discover a single reviewer who expressed the slightest reservation about either the solution to the case proposed by the writer or the reconstruction of its details—no matter how greatly these narratives and solutions varied from each other. It would seem that while authorial rhetoric may no longer be a com-

mon critical focus, no readerly transcendence of it to a hypothetical objective response to a narrative's subject matter can therefore
be assumed.

It is in their resolutions, however, that we might expect to
find—and often indeed do—substantial differences between fictional and factual narratives. As Smollett's title *Continuation of
the Complete History of England* awkwardly reveals, narrative
resolution is an artifice constantly belied by actuality: no history
is really ever complete because no history can be seen from a
perspective outside of time, although written narratives constantly purport to do so by providing seemingly appropriate clo-
sures. Fielding's use of the traditional structures of folk narrative
in *Examples of Providence* removes every shred of doubt from
the initially concealed criminality of his murderers, while Tey's
courtroom scene at the climax of *The Franchise Affair* demonstrates Betty Kane's guilt so conclusively that the jury has to fend
off the excess evidence in self-defense.

The Canning case itself failed to provide anything so conclusive, and the rhetorical devices used by writers on it to bring it
to a more satisfying end are among the most interestingly varied
features of its subsequent accounts. Thus Canning's failure to
confess is made by many to serve as the final proof of her obdu-
rate depravity, as in Austin Dobson's brief account in the *Dictionary of National Biography*. The writer of *Genuine and Impartial
Memoirs* substitutes for Canning's missing confession both his
narrator's own admission of error in having initially believed her
and the proof of the anonymous child's confession that she had
thrown her clothing into a pond and invented a story of abuse
as an image in effect of what Canning ought to have done. Lillian
de la Torre brings in a panel of experts to support her diagnosis
of Canning's hysteria, while John Paget, one of the few writers
inclined to believe Canning's charges against Squires and Wells,
ends deliberately on a modern note of ambiguity—"Thus ends
the case of Elizabeth Canning—a case evidently fitted to give
occasion to the warmest, most eager, and most confident partisanship, inasmuch as it is almost impossible, after the coolest
and most deliberate examination, to say to which side the balance of evidence inclines" (336)—phrasing which neatly incorporates the doubtful end of the case with a reminder of the
superlative coolness and deliberation of the narrator, the reader's
only and indispensable guide through its mysteries.

Lincoln Faller has written of eighteenth-century criminal bio-
graphies of "familiar murderers" in language descriptive not

only of Fielding's *Examples of Providence* but of the Canning narratives as well:

> Every effort is made to fix such murderers firmly within the context of the "real world," even to the extent of inventing what would otherwise seem to be actual facts. There is a marked concern as well with the criminal as a person (however factitious this may actually be), particularly in his consciousness. . . . Such narratives are tightly structured, too, in the sense that each event they relate is made to seem part of a causal chain. Here, it seems to me, the aim of the mythologizing process is to reconstruct the real along "happier" or at least more tolerable lines. The myth sought to limit the damage that crime—particularly heinous crime—could do not only to people's sense of themselves and their God and to their sense of what it was that held (or might hold) society together. (4)

Much of the intensity of such texts as Gascoyne's *Address* and *Genuine and Impartial Memoirs* springs evidently from the difficulty of achieving just these ends, particularly without the aids to closure provided by a confession and/or execution.

Writing on the case of Mary Edmondson, a young woman convicted in 1759 on reasonably solid evidence of murdering her aunt but who was executed while still maintaining her innocence, Faller notes the frustration of pamphleteers at the absence of a confession:

> The writers . . . appear to have been out to meet the unsatisfied needs of their readers' imaginations. Because Mary would not confess, it was up to them to provide her crime with plausible antecedents—thus this account of her character and motives—and to confirm with convincing details the supposition of her guilt—thus the blow-by-blow description of the murder, what went through her mind as she planned it, the "cooked" trial transcript. All that . . . these accounts lack . . ., of course, is Mary's endorsement.
>   But this, I would suggest, was a gross and troubling deficiency—no happy ending was possible without her confession and repentance. . . . It was only through fictions and quasi-fictions that these pamphlets could make the concreteness of the case add up to a plausible and significant whole. . . . [O]nly two alternatives . . . were, after all, available; she was innocent or she was inexplicable. And to a public wanting the assurance . . . that Mary was guilty, confession or no, and her act comprehensible, neither of these alternatives could have seemed at all preferable. (37–38)

These alternatives were equally unacceptable to the public following the Canning case, which was additionally complicated first by the roles played in it by such prominent figures as Fielding, Hill, and Gascoyne and second by the unprecedented accumulation of contradictory eyewitness testimony presented in the context of a trial equally unprecedented, with an outcome completely satisfactory to no one. Smollett's placement of the case in his *Continuation of the Complete History of England* thus uses paradox as the best means to elicit sense from its contradictions: both the case and the public attention given it arose in an absence of "foreign provocations" and "unpopular measures of domestic administration" because "[t]he genius of the English people is perhaps incompatible with a state of perfect tranquillity" (155).

Faller warns against "the danger that lies in wait for *any* effort grounded in modern patterns of thought (this included) to recreate the psychic realities of the past" (41; emphasis in original), and the arbitrariness and extravagance of, say, de la Torre's application of Freudian theory to a solution of the alleged discrepancies in Canning's story certainly would seem to exemplify that danger. Nevertheless, there is a suggestive similarity not so much in the cases of Elizabeth Canning and Ida Bauer, better known by the alias conferred on her by Freud himself, Dora, but in the ways in which the two cases have reached the public, through the repeated and conflictive written accounts and analyses of contemporary and subsequent narrators. My point, of course, is not about interpretation per se, if the category is indeed quite distinguishable, but about the preeminence and implications of narrative presentation. Steven Marcus has commented illuminatingly on Freud's own concern with the subject:

> Freud proceeds to specify what it is that is wrong with the stories his patients tell him. The difficulties are in the first instance formal shortcomings of *narrative*: the connections, "even the ostensible ones—are for the most part incoherent," obscured and unclear; "and the sequence of different events is uncertain." In short, these narratives are disorganized, and the patients are unable to tell a coherent story of their lives. What is more, he states, "the patients' inability to give an ordered history of their life in so far as it coincides with the history of their illness is not merely characteristic of the neurosis. It also possesses great theoretical significance." What we are led at this juncture to conclude is that Freud is implying that a coherent story is in some manner connected with mental health (at the very least with the absence of hysteria), and this in turn implies assumptions of the broadest and deepest kind about both the nature of coher-

ence and the form and structure of human life. On this reading, human life is, ideally, a connected and coherent story, with all the details in explanatory place, and with everything (or as close to everything as is practically possible) accounted for, in its proper causal or other sequence. Inversely, illness amounts at least in part to suffering from an incoherent story or an inadequate narrative account of oneself. (70–71; emphasis in original)

As Marcus and many other writers have, however, demonstrated, Freud's own narrative is marked by gaps and contradictions, even as it remains our only substantial source for Ida Bauer's experience, and the analogy to the Canning case is quite obvious. All of Canning's own utterances, from her responses to questions at the trial of Squires and Wells to her story as given in Alderman's Chitty's minutes, are framed, and more often recast altogether, by other voices and other pens, while her coherence, therefore her plausibility, therefore her truthfulness (for her age, the moral equivalent of "mental health") are questioned on the basis of those highly mediated accounts of her experience. But if "human life is, ideally, a connected and coherent story," then the failure of coherence is sufficiently threatening to moral and social order to require intervention—if not into intractable and in any case bygone realities then into the narrative accounts by which they make their impact on the world. Dora's story and Canning's had and have to be retold until they in some satisfactory way are made to come right, and the repeated retellings and analyses of both represent just that striving toward mastery through narrative coherence.

According to Marcus, Freud's "Fragment of an Analysis of a Case of Hysteria" formally most resembles "a modern experimental novel. . . . Its continuous innovations . . . seem unavoidably to be dictated by its substance, by the dangerous, audacious, disreputable, and problematical character of the experiences being represented and dealt with" (64). Similar pressures may be seen at work on the various writers who have undertaken to present the Canning case over time, most obviously to contemporaries but also to such later examples as Paget and de la Torre. Like Pamela, Canning as a servant girl making a claim of personal integrity was potentially disruptive of social order, and most narrators of the case have sought to reestablish the order in which such a figure remained conventionally invisible and mute.

Lennard David has noted the rise of "plots of self" (*Resisting*, 202) as a feature of the eighteenth century's developing discrimination between the novel and, on the one hand, history, on the other, romance, epic, and folktale, and has argued that "novelistic plots" differ from "plots in general" (203) because they are teleogenic, shaped toward an end that significantly reorganizes what precedes it in the perceptions of readers—as "in the case of Pamela, her successful marriage to Mr. B. revises and justifies the entire earlier part of the novel and her behavior" (208). The goal of the teleogenic plot is to persuade "readers to believe that there is an order in the world" (212), and it seems obvious that this was equally the goal of—and these are of course merely examplary figures—Sir Crisp Gascoyne in his *Address to the Liverymen* and of the writer of *Genuine and Impartial Memoirs of Elizabeth Canning*. It is likewise true that for all the contemporary writers on the Canning case, both Canningites and Egyptians, the order of the world was in some degree called into question by the events they were narrating: neither a story of poverty, random violence, and irrational cruelty nor one of deceit, concealment, and conspiracy could be rendered as satisfyingly resolved, however, after the excesses of Canning's trial, and the note of suave jocularity struck by such otherwise varied later writers as Kenny, Machen, de la Torre, Tey, and Treherne, with its invocation of an amused later superiority to eighteenth-century anxieties, suggests paradoxically that the issues of justice, gender, class, and credibility, which the case initially raised, remain equally for us among the dilemmas our own narratives, both historical and fictional, still seek to resolve.

I see no grounds for believing that the separation of fictional and nonfictional narrative treatments of the "plot of self" is anything but delusive in this pursuit of order, or that any of the resolutions these narratives offer us is or can be fully satisfactory. The juxtaposition of multiple resolutions, however, with its kaleidoscopic deferral of any final pattern by an endless sequence of temporary ones, is at least striking, at most an expansion of our understanding of what solutions might be possible, providing a standpoint from which teleogeny itself can be usefully held in suspension.

Epilogue: Solving the Canning Case

As I have tried to demonstrate throughout this study, I do not believe that a solution to the Canning case is possible—although that does not mean at all that no one can or should form opinions, or even conclusions, about it. A solution, however, in the full sense of the term, must be an illusion, shored up by the possibilities the solver believes in, dismissing the difficulties presented by elements in the evidence that fail to fit or at least qualify the version of the story for which credence is sought.

When I began exploring the Canning case, my primary interest lay in the fictionalizing propensities of the writers on it. I had read *The Franchise Affair* perhaps twenty-five years ago and remembered it dimly; now I refreshed and complicated that memory by reading first Fielding's *A Clear State of the Case of Elizabeth Canning* and then, because it happened to be available in the special collections of the library I was working in at the time, those of the University of Pennsylvania, *Genuine and Impartial Memoirs of Elizabeth Canning*. In all three works, the tense interplay between the categories and techniques of fiction and the constraints—if that was what they were—of fact fascinated me, and I thought there might be interesting connections between the nonfiction accounts of the Canning case and the much-labored "rise of the novel." I thought as well that I could refer to the documents in the case without feeling any obligation to undertake to sort out their contradictions, but in that I was mistaken—the Canning case seems to call for, if not a solution, then a more common outcome of fiction, a resolution, and I now feel that I need to state my sense of what a satisfying one might be.

I have come to believe, then, that Elizabeth Canning's whole story was true. This does not mean that her memory was either "photographic," like Betty Kane's, or infallible, but that she reported its contents as accurately as she was able to, and that the defects in her recollection were of the sort common to human fallibility, not peculiarly pathological. In my reading of the evidence, the best source for what she actually experienced is the reports of her mother and neighbors of her return home on 29 January 1753. I agree with Barrett Wellington that falsified evidence of that crucial but confused hour would read much more smoothly. The worst source for the same subject I believe is Alderman Chitty's minutes, written down from since-vanished notes at some later date and based on a scene with many more contending voices than that in Mrs. Canning's front room and never signed or witnessed by Canning herself. Even Chitty's principal supporting witness, Gawen Nash, differed with him on important points on what was said on 31 January in the Guildhall justice room.

How serious are the discrepancies, then, in Canning's description of the room in which she was held and what the arrest party found in Wells's loft on 1 February? There were evidently more objects in the room than Canning had previously mentioned, but she had never actually been asked to give an inventory of its contents, and her extreme debility at the time kept her answers to all questions short and fragmentary. Few writers on the case have seriously acknowledged that Dr. Eaton, who first saw her on 6 February, when she had already had a week's bed-rest and treatment, was even then "very apprehensive that she would die" (*State Trials*, 19: 522)—that is, in a state likely to affect both her memory and her ability to provide alert and thoughtful responses to questions. Also, the residents of Wells's house had had a day to make alterations in the room between the time Virtue Hall discovered that Canning had gone and the arrival of the arrest party, and there is some evidence, notably Adamson's discovery of a freshly boarded window in the otherwise dirty room (19: 517), to indicate that they to some extent did so.

What about the gypsies' alibi? Again, the Squires family had had a day to think about it, and several hours of being shut up in Wells's parlor for a final conference on the subject before anyone was formally charged. The alibi witnesses' consistent inclusion of all three Squireses in their testimony may indeed reflect some uncertainty experienced by them as to exactly which of them would ultimately be charged with what offense. I explain the alibi witnesses' testimony overall as springing initially from the economic loyalties of the smuggling trade and later as reinforced by the manifest willingness of Sir Crisp Gascoyne to pay for the best evidence money could buy, though he may have had no overt intention of influencing the witnesses whose expenses he paid.

The simplest explanation for the consistency of the alibi testimony is that it was, as the prosecution at Canning's trial made no bones of admitting, thoroughly polished; I believe it simply combined a real journey with a real time that had originally occurred separately. The absolute congruity between George Squires's memory and the alibi witnesses' testimony—neither remembered anything the other did not—seems to me in itself an extremely unlikely circumstance, while the inconsequence and unrelatedness of the Enfield witnesses are, for me, indicators of reliability, at least to the extent of indicating neither collusion nor malice. Still, the alibi evidence is the factor in the case that must, I think, always stand in the way of a complete solution, since on one side or the other a substantial number of people must have been either lying or in error. My own choice is to believe in the single large lie rather than in the profusion of small but vital mistakes, but both are possible, and on this point, therefore, what the eighteenth century would have called a candid observer must admit that Canning might have been at least badly mistaken. It remains a possibility that the woman who robbed her and pushed her into the loft was someone other than Mary Squires, although who it was then becomes a new problem—it was certainly not Susannah Wells, whom Canning was sure she had never seen before 1 February.

If Canning was telling the truth, how did she get into so much trouble? I do not know why Sir Crisp Gascoyne interested himself in Mary Squires. I am inclined to disbelieve in his motivation by simple altruism, since he ignored Wells, whose guilt or innocence logically depended on Squires's, but whatever else may have moved him to act it left no evidence aside from a few unsubstantiated rumors. It does seem from his own account that obstinacy and self-importance led him to continue once he had begun—the resistance of Canning's friends fuses in it with his conviction of Canning's malice and justifies his pursuit of judicial retribution.

Nothing in the record of the Canning case, in my opinion, amounts to what we now call a "smoking gun," an irrefutable piece of hard evidence proving conclusively that disputed events must have happened in one way and not another. The preponderance of the evidence, however, I believe points toward Canning's innocence. In eighteenth-century court cases, character counted, and Canning's character was never impeached by any other means than innuendo based on sexual generalization—Canning herself was universally reported to be a truthful, obedient, and well-meaning young woman, and no evidence was ever produced even to qualify that reputation, much less to subvert it.

Probability, however, counted too, and in the milieu in which Hill and Ramsay, to name only two, wrote, an honest eighteen-year-old girl was virtually a contradiction in terms—even for Fielding, the emaciated Canning might be credible but not the too-articulate Pamela. Credibility resided normally in the ranks of gentlemen and holders of public office—aldermen, magistrates, clergymen, a lord mayor—who knew and could vouch for each other.

Probability, for me, is a rather different affair. Over the period of my adult life I have witnessed the discrediting of one prominent man after another, from Richard Nixon to Marion Barry, and the repeated unveiling of conspiracy, collusion, and injustice—Watergate, Iran-Contra, and, as I write in England, the reversal of the original convictions of the Guildford Four, the Birmingham Six, and the Maguire Family, are only the most familiar names. It thus seems quite probable to me that respectable figures will lie to the public to serve private ends, and that they will conceptualize their own private advantage as the well-being of the state in justification of their conduct.

On the other hand, in spite of a career that has put me in close proximity with many adolescents, male and female, I have never encountered the phenomenon of a young girl claiming to have been abducted in order to conceal her sexual misconduct. Instead, I have passed through a time in which judgments of "hysteria" have been increasingly understood as obscuring and concealing real instances of abuse, and I am correspondingly suspicious when a girl who tells a story of abuse is condemned for her allegations rather than heeded. Obviously, these are twentieth-century instances, but given the relatively limited degree of change in the representation of Canning's story over the past two hundred and forty years, I think they are not irrelevant—we are in some ways closer to the world of the Canning case than we may like to acknowledge.

Roy Porter asked rhetorically whether anything had changed between Elizabeth Canning and Patty Hearst. Certainly the difference between a dutiful and barely literate eighteenth-century maidservant and an heiress to a fortune attending an American university and living with her fiance seems wide enough, but both were kidnapped (as both were suspected of arranging their kidnappings for personal reasons), and the kidnapping itself put them in a position for which ultimately they were punished.

Shana Alexander, who wrote a long book on the Hearst case and sat through every day of Hearst's eight-week trial for bank robbery, calls her an "unremarkable young woman [who] had become the object of world scrutiny, focused through the media's compound, unblinking eye [while remaining] invisible all the while, a pebble in dark waters" (5). In language similar to Treherne's about Canning, Hearst is described as "an enigma to all the world," not least to Alexander, whose frustration at her own inability to "read" what she saw in Hearst's face (6)—she never met or spoke to her—torments her throughout her report of the trial. Her various attempts at interpretation—Hearst as performer of a "mythic function," acting out many middle-aged Americans' "most secret fantasies," as "a victim," as "an ungrateful child, . . . [or] a modern witch" (156)—lead only to the conclusion that none of these is quite satisfactory. Thus when the prosecutor asks, "'Do you now feel that you had, in fact, been brainwashed at any time, Miss Hearst?'" and Hearst replies, "'I'm not sure what happened to me,'" Alexander observes, "Truer words have not been spoken in this courtroom" (218).

Ultimately, however, and in spite of a good deal of baffled sympathy along the way, Alexander too condemns Hearst, feeling freed from her obsession with the case—and, presumably, from the burden of sympathy as well—when Hearst on television, in an appearance managed by her defense counsel, F. Lee Bailey, condemned her dead comrades of the Symbionese Liberation Army:

> It had been a long time coming, but Patty's statement that the SLA members who were burned up in Los Angeles "got exactly what they deserved" released me from this girl at last. A person in her position has scant business making moral judgments. . . . Out of the courtroom setting I found it offensive to hear Patty say that she believed the SLA when they told her her parents had abandoned her, that the FBI was out to kill her, that the police didn't care about her, that she had nowhere to go, that the sight of the televised incineration of her quondam friends made her think that "if I tried to get away, the same thing would happen to me." It was unpleasant in particular when she showed no awareness that had she not opted to join the SLA, had she not decided to play "girl guerilla," the TV barbecue would never have happened. . . . The Hearst/Bailey insensitivity to these matters was shocking. (535–36)

Alexander here seems to have forgotten both her own conclusion that Hearst was indeed a victim of "coercive persuasion" rather than a free agent who "opted" and "decided" her own actions and the fact that Hearst went to prison at the end of her trial and was not, as Alexander describes herself, "released," but in the end her compassion, like Tey's, goes to the safely dead.

It seems to me that Hearst's case, like Canning's, can breed in the onlooker a condition sometimes tellingly labeled compassion fatigue. As the liveryman put it in his *Reply to Sir Crisp Gascoyne's Address*, if Canning was innocent, then she was "the most injured subject in Great Britain" (22), and sympathy for her led increasingly only to frustration as her legal purgatory continued, her conviction was upheld, and the sentence of transportation was carried out. It was more comfortable to conclude, as Smollett did, that the case had been a "temporary fermentation" precipitated by an "incident . . . of the most frivolous nature," that the evidence had, after all, been conclusive, and that justice had been done (154). As in a novel, not only was the ending appropriate to the plot but, overwhelmingly, there *was* an ending, not merely an echoing uncertainty.

We have no reason to believe that Canning read fiction—given the circumstances of her life, it seems unlikely—but we do know that in Newgate she had a copy of George Stanhope's popular translation of Thomas à Kempis, *The Christian's Pattern*, and there she may have read and applied much that seems relevant to her situation still, as for instance chapter XII, "The Advantage of Afflictions":

The Injuries and contumelious Usage, the Calumnies and Censures of them who think and speak Ill of us, bring their Profit with them too, even when most wrongful, most undeserved. . . . They cure our Ambition and Vain-glory, and convince us how vain a Thing it is, the Thirst after Reputation and the Praise of Men, when even Innocence and Goodness cannot protect us from Slander and Reproaches. They teach us to set a due Value upon the Testimony of our own Consciences, and the righteous Approbation of God, the Searcher of Hearts; when That, which he will not fail to commend and reward, cannot escape the Contempt and Condemnation of the World, nor prevail for so much as fair Quarter, from our mistaken and injurious Brethren.

. . . such Circumstances as these are more effectual than ten thousand Arguments, to convince [a sufferer], by his own sensible Experience, that perfect Security, and entire Satisfaction are not so much as consistent with the Condition of Man in the present World; and therefore we must be content to wait another and Future State, which alone deserves our Affections, because it alone can make us truly and completely happy. (23–24)

Failing Heaven, credible fictions may sometimes be seen to serve, and if fiction has increasingly over the last two hundred years come to replace the hope of heavenly consolation as our chief provider of comforting conclusions, Canning, at least, would hardly be convinced that we were certainly better off. It is there, perhaps, that our difference from her stands clearest, but it is scarcely grounds for branding her a malefactor. As a victim who persisted in hope, she is, however differently constituted than in our own day, a survivor, and deserving of our attention.

Appendix

According to the Corporation of London Records Office, the justice book for 1753 does not survive, but Lillian de la Torre apparently quotes from it in *'Elizabeth Is Missing'*:

Mr. Alderman Chitty scratched his head with his quill and entered the warrant in the justice-book:

Chitty, 31st. Janry, 1753.

WARRANT against a person unknown by the name of mother Wells at S. Eliz. Canyan for an asst. upon her the 2d. instant in the house of the said Wells and stripping her of a pair of stays va. 20s. & upwards afterwards confining her in a room in the sd. house there threatning her to cutt her throat if she stirred or made a noise where she was confined on bread and water ever since to monday last when she made her escape and she further says that the night before she was robbed in Moorfields by two men who knocked her down and took 10s 6 in gold and 3s in silver from her & a gown and cap and that they stopt her mouth with a handkerchief and forcibly dragged her to the said mother Wells's & used her as aforesaid.

Mr. Chitty looked the entry over. It was brief and to the point. It would do for the official records. (37)

While de la Torre habitually invented such physical details as Alderman Chitty's actions in this passage, I have in no other instance found quoted material in her book for which I have been unable to pinpoint an accurately rendered source. It seems likely then that she did see such a justice book although it does not appear in the bibliography of (printed) materials on the case that she published under the name of McCue. One hypothesis is that the justice book existed during the thirties when de la Torre/McCue was researching the case and disappeared during the destruction and dislocations of wartime London. If accurately represented, Alderman Chitty's warrant supports my own argument that his weak command both of sequences of events in time and of syntax to some immeasurable but significant degree contributes to the invalidation of his evidence at Canning's trial. Simply put, Chitty's story is not Cannings's.

Notes

Chapter 1. Elizabeth Canning's Story

1. For background on Hill's and Fielding's earlier relations, see Martin C. Battestin, *Henry Fielding: A Life* (London: Routledge, 1989) and G. S. Rousseau, ed., *The Letters and Papers of Sir John Hill, 1714–1775* (New York: AMS Press, 1982). For more on their opposition over Canning, see Chapter 2. Rousseau's investigation of Hill's career is minute, but he accepts Hill's version of the Canning case more than uncritically, going even beyond Hill in his paraphrase: "Canning . . . claimed that she had been kidnapped by Mary Squires, a procuress, and subjected to every variety of torture and indecency" (57). Such misrepresentations of Canning's story are commonplace in writers for whom it forms a minor incident in some other, more important figure's career: Battestin labels Canning's mother "a devout Methodist" (570) in an equally unsupported fashion.

2. Although writers on the Canning case conceive of probability as a psychological rather than a mathematical phenomenon, some application of the insights of mathematical probability can interestingly qualify their conclusions. For instance, the principle that "rarity by itself shouldn't necessarily be evidence of anything" counters the widespread assertion that Canning's experience could not be true because it was claimed to be extraordinary—"Every bridge hand is quite improbable" (Paulos, 40)—while coincidence, on the other hand, is considerably more common than it is believed to be. The chance that any two Americans will be linked by a chain of only two intermediaries is ninety-nine in one hundred, and eighteenth-century England was a much smaller community (Paulos, 29).

Chapter 2. The Crime, First Version: Assault and Theft

1. As *A Refutation of Sir Crisp Gascoyne's Address to the Liverymen of London* makes clear, Wintlebury spelled his own last name Wendleborough, and he is not the only figure in the case whose self-identification differs from the one conferred upon him by, most notably, the text of *A Complete Collection of State Trials*. Because later writers have consistently used the *State Trials* spellings I have reluctantly done the same as a gesture of clarity toward readers who already have some familiarity with the case or who wish to check my account against others, but the spelling problem acts for me as a constant reminder of the difference between these eighteenth-century Londoners as they lived and their literary and historical after-lives. In crucial ways, they did not see themselves as others have seen them.

2. Bennett, Dyer, and Cobb were all illiterate, signing their depositions with their marks.

3. Where possible, I have quoted newspaper sources from original publications, but the survival of eighteenth-century newspapers is by no means consistent. Here and elsewhere, I have sometimes been obliged to cite newspapers as they were reprinted by pamphleteers.

4. Conjecturally, Fortune Natus may originally have been named Fortunatus _____, the blank representing "the name of the place of his illegitimate or foundling birth. . . . Such a combination of Christian name and surname might in after life be a slight stigma: the place-name would be gradually dropped and the 'Christian' name split in two." This explanation of an obviously very odd name was suggested to F. J. Harvey Darton by "Mr. Bartelot, the learned rector of Fordington, Dorset . . ., who has found such baptisms in his registers." F. J. Harvey Darton, *Alibi Pilgrimage* (London: Newnes, 1936), 229.

5. See chapter 3 for a discussion of Myles's entrance into the case.

Chapter 3. The Crime, Second Version: Perjury

1. This is almost certainly the same William White who described himself as "an officer under my lord mayor" and testified at Canning's trial about his role in the arrest of Squires and Wells and the search of Wells's house (19: 394–97 and see also chapter 2).

2. Aldridge was in fact a working silversmith, but the three were all members of the Goldsmiths' Company, liverymen of the City of London.

3. Rousseau dates this letter from September or October, but I would place it earlier, since the "publick address" it refers to must be *The Story of Elizabeth Canning Considered*, which had appeared at the end of March, and since Hill was writing the Inspector essays on the Museum in late March and early April—his last essay on Canning having appeared on 26 March. Rousseau believes that Hill had given "public testimony in court" on the Canning case, but Hill did not appear in any of the trials that were part of the case or participate in any medical examination of Canning, as his own pamphlet makes clear. He seems to have seen her on the occasion of Virtue Hall's public recantation on 7 March 1753, but there is no evidence that he ever spoke to her or testified in any legal proceeding involving her.

4. The *DNB* gives Cox's date of death as 1750, but his pamphlet, the responses to it, and his signature on a petition in 1754 sufficiently prove this an error.

5. The queries and Emlyn's replies were published as a broadsheet immediately after the trial; the entire text is reprinted in *State Trials*.

6. Despite the assurance of Stephen's judgment, he does not seem to have known the case well. He reports George Squires's name as John and says erroneously of the first trial, "The prisoners were convicted and both were sentenced to death," implying, since Wells is not mentioned in his account, that the second defendant was Squires's son. James Fitzjames Stephen, *A History of the Criminal Law of England* (London: Macmillan, 1883), I:423.

7. The bibliography appeared under de la Torre's legal name, Lillian Bueno McCue.

8. The use of the term "Mob" here for a large number of reasonably well-behaved although dissatisfied people should at least alert twentieth-century readers to some ambiguity in its meaning in eighteenth-century contexts.

9. It has been estimated from a study of marriage registers that ca. 1754,

65 percent of British women remained too illiterate even to sign their names. David Cressy, *Literacy and the Social Order: Reading and Writing in Tudor and Stuart England* (Cambridge: Cambridge University Press 1980), 176.

10. The second stipulation about Canning's stay in Newgate is from another source, Appendix 54, *A Refutation*, 47.

11. Hill's assertion that the book "would not be known" if he named it is absurd. Initially published in 1698, Stanhope's translation of the *Imitation of Christ* had passed through at least thirteen numbered editions, exclusive of reprints, before 1754. Its homiletic style is very much that of the *Book of Common Prayer*.

Chapter 4. Writing Canning's Story

1. Childers, born in 1862, died in 1912, while Kenny lived from 1847 to 1930. Childers's working career was spent as an assistant editor of *The Nineteenth Century. Romantic Trials of Three Centuries* (London: John Lane, 1913) was published posthumously.

2. Darton states unequivocally, "There need be no difficulty in accepting that route [as given by George Squires at Canning's trial] as correct in the main, dates (N.S.) and all" (194), so it is difficult to see why de la Torre reports him as "suggest[ing] that it all happened, but at another time" (234), a suggestion she herself rejects on the grounds that the presence of the exciseman Andrew Wake at Abbotsbury and floods along the way are both untransferably specific. Neither, however, is so far as I can see necessarily tied to the actual presence of the Squires family at the same time.

Works Cited

All references to anonymous and untitled items in eighteenth-century periodicals and to such common reference books as the *Dictionary of National Biography* appear only in the text.

Alexander, Shana. *Anyone's Daughter: The Times and Trials of Patty Hearst.* New York: Viking, 1979.

Battestin, Martin C., with Ruthe E. Battestin. *Henry Fielding: A Life.* London: Routledge, 1989.

Beattie, J. M. *Crime and the Courts in England, 1660–1800.* Oxford: Clarendon Press, 1986.

Becker, M. L. Review of '*Elizabeth is Missing,*' by Lillian de la Torre. *Weekly Book Review* 3 June 1945: 2.

Bender, John. *Imagining the Penitentiary: Fielding and the Architecture of Mind in Eighteenth-Century England.* Chicago: University of Chicago Press, 1987.

Biron, Charles. Review of *The Canning Wonder,* by Arthur Machen. *London Mercury* 14 (1926): 103–5.

Boswell, James. *Life of Johnson.* Edited by George Birkbeck Hill. 6 vols. Oxford: Clarendon Press, 1934.

Canning's Farthing Post. Containing the Whole Proceedings Relating to her Sufferings, From the Time of her being Try'd at the Old-Bailey, for Perjury, the Pleadings of the Council at large. London: T. Jones, 1754.

Canning's Magazine, or, A Review of the Whole Evidence that Has Been Hitherto Offered for, or against Elizabeth Canning, and Mary Squires.... London: C. Corbett, 1753.

Caulfield, James. "Elizabeth Canning, Mary Squires, and Mother Wells." *Portraits, Memoirs, and Characters of Remarkable Persons, from the Revolution in 1688 to the End of the Reign of George II. Collected from the Most Authentic Accounts Extant.* 4 vols. London: T. H. Whiteley, 1820, 3: 108–48.

Childers, Hugh. *Romantic Trials of Three Centuries.* London: John Lane, 1913.

The Controverted Hard Case: or, Mary Squires's Magazine of Facts Re-Examin'd. . . . London: W. Reeve, 1753.

Copy of a Letter to a Friend, in *Canning's Farthing Post.*

Cox, Daniel. *An Appeal to the Public, in Behalf of Elizabeth Canning.* London: W. Meadows, 1753.

Cressy, David. *Literacy and the Social Order: Reading and Writing in Tudor and Stuart England.* Cambridge: Cambridge University Press, 1980.

Darton, F. J. Harvey. *Alibi Pilgrimage.* London: Newnes, 1936.

Davis, Lennard J. *Factual Fictions: The Origins of the English Novel*. New York: Columbia University Press, 1983.

———. *Resisting Novels: Ideology and Fiction*. New York: Methuen, 1987.

de la Torre, Lillian. *'Elizabeth is Missing': Or, Truth Triumphant, An Eighteenth Century Mystery*. London: Michael Joseph, 1947.

Disraeli, Isaac. *The Calamities and Quarrels of Authors: With Some Enquiries Respecting Their Moral and Literary Characters, and Memoirs of Our Literary History*. Edited by B. Disraeli. London: Frederick Warne, 1869.

Dodd, James Solas. *The Case of Elizabeth Canning, With an Enquiry into the Probability of her subsisting in the Manner therein asserted, and her Ability to escape after her suppos'd ill Usage*. London: J. Bouquet, 1753.

Faller, Lincoln B. *Turned to Account: The Forms and Functions of Criminal Biography in Late Seventeenth- and Early Eighteenth-Century England*. Cambridge: Cambridge University Press, 1987.

Fielding, Henry. *Amelia*. Edited by Martin C. Battestin. Middletown, Conn.: Wesleyan University Press, 1983. *The Wesleyan Edition of the Works of Henry Fielding*.

———. *A Clear State of the Case of Elizabeth Canning....* London: A. Millar, 1753.

———. *The Covent-Garden Journal and A Plan of the Universal Register-Office*. Edited by Bertrand A. Goldgar. Middletown, Conn.: Wesleyan University Press, 1988. *The Wesleyan Edition of the Works of Henry Fielding*.

———. "Examples of the Interposition of Providence in the Detection and Punishment of Murder." In *An Enquiry into the Late Increase of Robbers and Related Writings*, edited by Malvin R. Zirker, 175–217. Middletown, Conn.: Wesleyan University Press, 1988. *The Wesleyan Edition of the Works of Henry Fielding*.

Foss, Edward. *A Biographical Dictionary of the Judges of England*. London: John Murray, 1870.

Gascoyne, Sir Crisp. *An Address to the Liverymen of the City of London....* London: James Hodges, 1754.

Guttridge, Roger. *Dorset Smugglers*. Sherborne, Dorset: Dorset Publishing Co., 1987.

Hay, Douglas. "Property, Authority and the Criminal Law." In *Albion's Fatal Tree: Crime and Society in Eighteenth-Century England*, edited by Douglas Hay, 17–64. New York: Pantheon, 1975.

Hecht, J. Jean. *The Domestic Servant in Eighteenth-Century England*. London: Routledge and Kegan Paul, 1980.

Hill, John. *The Story of Elizabeth Canning Considered....* London: M. Cooper, 1753.

Hunter, J. Paul. *Before Novels: The Cultural Contexts of Eighteenth-Century English Fiction*. New York: W. W. Norton, 1990.

Johnson, Samuel. *The Rambler*. Edited by W. J. Bate and Albrecht Strauss. New Haven: Yale University Press, 1969. Vols. 3–5 of *The Yale Edition of the Works of Samuel Johnson*.

———. *Preface to Shakespeare, with Proposals for Printing the Dramatic Works of William Shakespeare*. Edited by Sir Walter Raleigh. Oxford: Oxford University Press, 1957.

Kenny, Courtney. "The Mystery of Elizabeth Canning." *Law Quarterly Review* 13 (1897): 368–82.

Lang, Andrew. "The Case of Elizabeth Canning." *Historical Mysteries*. London: Smith, Elder, 1980, 1–31.

Lewis, Peter. "Prose: Past, Present, and Future." [Review of *The Canning Enigma*, by John Treherne, et al.] *Stand Magazine* 31 (Spring 1990): 75–83.

A Liveryman's Reply to Sir Crisp Gascoigne's Address. London: W. Reeve, 1754.

McCue, Lillian Bueno. "Elizabeth Canning in Print." *University of Colorado Studies*. Series B. Studies in the Humanities 2.4 (October 1945): 223–34.

Machen, Arthur. *The Canning Wonder*. London: Chatto and Windus, 1925.

McKeon, Michael. *The Origins of the English Novel, 1600–1740*. Baltimore: The Johns Hopkins University Press, 1987.

McLynn, Frank. *Crime and Punishment in Eighteenth-Century England*. London: Routledge, 1989.

Marcus, Steven. "Freud and Dora: Story, History, Case History." In *Dora's Case: Freud-Hysteria-Feminism*, edited by Charles Bernheimer and Claire Kahane, 56–91. New York: Columbia University Press, 1985.

North, Sterling. Rev. of '*Elizabeth is Missing*,' by Lillian de la Torre. *Book Week* 20 May 1945: 2.

"Novel." *A Handbook to Literature*. 5th ed. 1986.

"P., I." "Fielding the Novelist." *Notes and Queries* 12 (1879): 30.

Paget, John. "Elizabeth Canning." *Paradoxes and Puzzles Historical, Judicial, and Literary*. Edinburgh: Blackwood, 1874; Rpt. AMS, 1977.

Paulos, John Allen. *Innumeracy: Mathematical Illiteracy and Its Consequences*. New York: Hill and Wang, 1988.

Pearson, Edmund. "The First Great Disappearer." *More Studies in Murder*. London: Arco, 1953. Rpt. New York, 1936.

Porter, Roy. Rev. of *The Canning Enigma*, by John Treherne. *Times Literary Supplement* 22 December 1989: 1408.

Probyn, Clive T. *English Fiction of the Eighteenth Century, 1700–1789*. London: Longman, 1987.

[Ramsay, Allan]. *A Letter to the Right Honourable the Earl of _____ Concerning the Affair of Elizabeth Canning*. London: T. Seddon, 1753.

Ray, William. *Story and History: Narrative Authority and Social Identity in the Eighteenth-Century English Novel*. Cambridge, Mass.: Basil Blackwell, 1990.

A Refutation of Sir Crisp Gascoyne's Address to the Liverymen of London. . . . London: J. Payne, 1754.

Review of *Alibi Pilgrimage*, by F. J. Harvey Darton. *London Mercury* 34 (1936): 470.

Review of '*Elizabeth is Missing*,' by Lillian de la Torre. *The New Yorker* 21: 84.

Review of '*Elizabeth is Missing*,' by Lillian de la Torre. *Springfield Republican* 27 May 1945: 4d.

Review of *Genuine and Impartial Memoirs*. *Monthly Review* 11 (Sept. 1754): 237.

Review of *The Mystery of Elizabeth Canning*, by Barrett R. Wellington. *New York Times* 19 January 1941: 8.

Richardson, Samuel. *Pamela; or, Virtue Rewarded.* London: Penguin, 1980.

Robbins, Bruce. *The Servant's Hand: English Fiction from Below.* New York: Columbia University Press, 1986.

Roberts, R. Ellis. Review of *The Canning Wonder,* by Arthur Machen. *Bookman* 69 (1925): 218–19.

Rousseau, G. S., ed. *The Letters and Papers of Sir John Hill, 1714–1775.* AMS Studies in the Eighteenth Century 6. New York: AMS Press, 1982.

Roy, Sandra. *Josephine Tey.* Boston: Twayne, 1980.

Sell, Roger D. *The Reluctant Naturalism of* Amelia: *An Essay on the Modern Reading of Fielding.* Acta Academiae Aboensis, Ser. A, vol. 62, nr. 3. Abo: Abo Akademi, 1983.

Smollett, Tobias. *Continuation of the Complete History of England.* London: Richard Baldwin, 1760.

Stanhope, George, trans. *The Christian's Pattern: Or, A Treatise of the Imitation of Jesus Christ In Four Books.* Written Originally in Latin by Thomas a Kempis. London: W. Innys et al., 1751.

State Papers Domestic, George II, Bundle 127. Public Record Office, London.

Stephen, James Fitzjames. *A History of the Criminal Law of England.* 3 vols. London: Macmillan, 1883.

Stiles, Henry. *The History of Ancient Wethersfield, Connecticut.* 2 vols. New York: Grafton Press, 1904.

Tey, Josephine. *The Franchise Affair.* London: Peter Davies, 1948.

Treherne, John. *The Canning Enigma.* London: Jonathan Cape, 1989.

The Trials of Mary Squires and Susannah Wells; John Gibbons, William Clarke, and Thomas Greville; and Elizabeth Canning. *A Complete Collection of State Trials.* . . . Compiled by T. B. Howell, 21 vols. London: Hansard, 1816. 19: 261–692.

Truth Triumphant: or, the Genuine Account of the Whole Proceedings against Elizabeth Canning. . . . London: C. Sympson, 1754.

Watt, Ian. *The Rise of the Novel: Studies in Defoe, Richardson, and Fielding.* Berkeley: University of California Press, 1967.

Wellington, Barrett R. *The Mystery of Elizabeth Canning as Found in the Testimony of the Old Bailey Trials and Other Records.* New York: J. Ray Peck, 1940.

Index

Date Due